The
Reincarnation
of Edgar Cayce?

D0107642

The Reincarnation of Edgar Cayce?

Interdimensional Communication and Global Transformation

Wynn Free
with
David Wilcock

Frog, Ltd.
Berkeley, California

Published by Frog, Ltd.

Frog, Ltd. books are distributed by
North Atlantic Books
P.O. Box 12327
Berkeley, California 94712

Cover design by Susan Quasha
Book design by Paula Morrison

Printed in Canada

The Reincarnation of Edgar Cayce? Interdimensional Communication and Global Transformation is sponsored by the Society for the Study of Native Arts and Sciences, a nonprofit educational corporation whose goals are to develop an educational and crosscultural perspective linking various scientific, social, and artistic fields; to nurture a holistic view of arts, sciences, humanities, and healing; and to publish and distribute literature on the relationship of mind, body, and nature.

North Atlantic Books' publications are available through most bookstores. For further information, call 800-337-2665 or visit our website at www.northatlanticbooks.com. Substantial discounts on bulk quantities are available to corporations, professional associations, and other organizations. For details and discount information, contact our special sales department.

ISBN-13: 978-1-58394-083-9

Library of Congress Cataloging-in-Publication Data

Free, Wynn, 1946–
    The reincarnation of Edgar Cayce? : interdimensional communication and global transformation / by Wynn Free and David Wilcock.
        p. cm.
Includes bibliographical references.
    ISBN 1-58394-083-9 (pbk.)
    1. Wilcock, David, 1973– 2. Ra (Spirit) 3. Wilcock, David,
1973—Pre-existence. 4. Cayce, Edgar, 1877–1945. 5. Prophecies
(Occultism) I. Wilcock, David, 1973– II. Title.
    BF1815.W49F74 2004
    133.8'092—dc22

                                        2003026170

5 6 7 8 9 10 11 12 TRANS 12 11 10 09 08 07

Mission Statement from the Authors

Millions of people have been influenced and inspired by the work of Edgar Cayce. Most of those who study his material have accepted reincarnation as a modality by which evolution of consciousness occurs. The facts of David Wilcock's life forced him to evaluate if it was possible that he was the reincarnation of Mr. Cayce. In this book, the case will now be presented to you.

If the case should be successfully made herein, it will give credence to an even more important issue. According to the information Wilcock is receiving, which is backed up by his own scientific research, our planet is at the end of a 75,000-year cycle and moving into a dimensional shift that Edgar Cayce, in his own readings, foreshadowed.

In the present time period, there is a rare opportunity for all of us to accelerate our spiritual evolution in ways that are very different from past reincarnational cycles, based on the ability to connect with the qualities of compassion, love, and wisdom.

The authors present this book with the hope that it will help us understand the importance and implications of the choices we make over the next few years, and that it may assist us all (including the authors) in having the conscious realization that we're part of each other and "on our way back home."

—Wynn Free, David Wilcock

Regarding the authorship: This book is written from the perspective and the experience of Wynn Free, the "I" in the majority of the book and, where mentioned as such, "the author." David Wilcock, as support partner, gave many hours of telephone interview time, assisted in some of the editing, contributed a section on his scientific research, and permitted his channeled readings to be included.

Acknowledgments

The author, Wynn Free, wishes to thank the following people for their contributions to this book:

David Wilcock—for his conviction, courage, and dedication to the Law of One; for the service he has provided all sincere spiritual seekers in this and previous lifetimes; and for entrusting me with this important project.

Susan Barber, Editor of *The Spirit of Ma'at*—for giving me my first paid writing assignment after I emailed a couple of poems to her webzine. She actually planted the suggestion that I was the one to write a book about David Wilcock after the publication of my first interview with Wilcock in *The Spirit of Ma'at* (the web magazine founded by Drunvalo Melchizedek). Chapter 19 is based on this article.

Carla L. Rueckert, Jim McCarty, and L/L Research—for their dedication in bringing forth the Ra/Law of One sessions, even at the risk of jeopardizing Carla's health, and for their ongoing contribution to spiritual seekers.

Terry Brown—for her endless volunteer efforts in transcribing tapes, proofreading, editing, and helping me stay alive and motivated.

Mason and Marie Gerhart—for their support and encouragement.

Kathy Glass—for the extremely detailed editing of the manuscript, which has become considerably more readable and precise.

Richard Grossinger—the publisher of North Atlantic Books/Frog, Ltd., who had the vision and awareness to appreciate the value of this book and accept it for publication.

Contents

Part One:
The Connection

Part Two:
The Message

Part Three:
Science of Ascension

Part One

The Connection

Your social structures cannot continue as they are now. You may like them as they are, but you cannot like the idea of a planet that is dead. That is the bottom line. These changes have to happen if any of you are to survive.

—Ra/Wilcock, November 11, 1999

Preface

Here we are in the twenty-first century with a world in upheaval—terrorists, weapons of mass destruction, plagues, financial uncertainty, war and political unrest—a world not so different from the one that Edgar Cayce prophesied many years ago, perhaps less an earthquake or two. Is it possible that Cayce has reincarnated and walks among us today?

We live our mortal lives in this physical universe with our limited conscious awareness, but Edgar Cayce in his readings on reincarnation gave credence to the idea that we live on after death. Anyone who has studied some of the hundreds of books written about Cayce and his readings can't help but give serious consideration to the perpetual existence of our essence and our ultimate return, clothed in a new body somewhere down the road. Each time we reincarnate, once again the memory of all our previous lives is hidden from our waking consciousness as we enter into the new round of earthbound experience. Cayce gave us a multitude of clues as to how this process works, and he addressed the meaning of karma and the importance of service to others, among many other metaphysical topics. Edgar Cayce was born in 1877 and died in 1945. His deep-trance readings predicted that he would reincarnate in our present time period.

Edgar Cayce left a legacy that has impacted the lives of millions. I was one of the people greatly influenced by the Cayce material. I grew up without a very good spiritual foundation but with a thirst

5

for truth. Cayce planted the first seeds of doubt in my agnosticism, and eventually I came to have some sense of my place in the universe and my connection with the Creator. Although I have always given Cayce his due and have great feelings of gratitude for his work, the question always lingered: "Why did Cayce have this special gift of omniscience in his sleep?" I never really expected to get an answer to that question, but here I am thirty years later and it looks like the answer has fallen into my lap. I've come to conclusions that I've never heard anyone reveal, but I don't believe that anyone else has had the same amazing set of clues at their disposal. It involves pieces from dissociated sources that dovetail together and complete a vast cosmic puzzle. One major piece of this puzzle is David Wilcock.

I discovered David Wilcock's website—www.ascension2000.com —late in 2000, with its thousands of pages, somewhat disorganized but extremely fascinating. After overcoming an initial bit of confusion, I plowed through this website and uncovered one gem after another of the wisest material I have ever been exposed to, from a being named Ra whom Wilcock channels. I discovered a section on his website called "Introductory Essay on the Wilcock/Cayce/Ra Connection and the 'Mission'."[1] Beaming from my computer screen was a photo of a young Edgar Cayce next to a photo of David Wilcock. (You can find that picture if you follow the URL on Note 1.) They were the spitting image of each other. Then I discovered that David Wilcock's life circumstances had brought him to 100% certainty that he is Edgar Cayce's reincarnation, thus fulfilling Edgar Cayce's prophecy that he would return in this period of time. I began a voracious study of Wilcock's site, and my intuitions told me it might be real.

I soon learned that Uri Geller, the writer, psychic, and spoonbender, also discovered Wilcock's website and came to the same conclusion, which he posted on his website:[2]

Return of the prophet—January 10, 2000

The greatest psychic of the last century was believed by many to be Edgar Cayce, who dictated medical cures for thousands he had never met.

Already in this new century, one man claims to possess similar powers. His prophetic dreams and visions appear to reveal a remarkable gift. But the weirdest factor of all is this man is Edgar Cayce.

Even in the UFOlogy community, where extreme weirdness is the norm, the claims of David Wilcock are arousing skepticism and wariness. But this 27-year-old vegan, a promising sci-fi writer in the mid-Nineties, predicted the Japanese nuclear meltdown [an accident in early 2000] and the loss of the NASA Mars probes.

His site is packed with warnings such as: "Stock market crash! The Archangel Michael told me, 'The stocks will be devalued so much as to appear to be utter nonsense.'" The Archangel is specific—the Dow will plummet to 2880.30.

It is not just Wilcock's dreams that tell him he is Cayce reborn. It is his mirror: his jaw is slightly less undershot, and his earlobes are bigger, but otherwise Ed and Dave could be twins.

Cayce, who died in 1945, announced he would return in 1998. Wilcock says he first connected his own dreams with Cayce's trances in November 1997.

Luckily, there is enough fascinating, contentious material on the website to ensure you don't have to part with a cent.

I scheduled my own reading from Wilcock, not knowing what to expect. I quickly learned that Wilcock is no ordinary psychic; it is Ra speaking through him. My reading was full of poetic metaphors that seemed to have the ability to penetrate my levels of conscious resistance and to release deep subconscious patterns. The information struck a deep resonance, created a huge impetus for growth, and conveyed a complete understanding of my personal conflicts, with wisdom far beyond the conscious expression of David Wilcock. This reading became the catalyst for me to investigate Wilcock's Cayce claim, and the further the topic was researched, the more unavoidable my conclusion became.

In this book I share with you the steps I went through and the conclusions I arrived at, in my own mission to discover if David Wilcock is, in fact, the reincarnation of Edgar Cayce. Bit by bit, the pieces fit together. I found unexpected agreements from totally independent sources with time-stamped clues spanning 12,500 years. The implications of the intertwining stories are staggering—much more far-reaching than I could have ever imagined. They provide explanations for such previously inexplicable phenomena as changing cycles in the Sun's activity, the ever-increasing pace of world events, unusual weather patterns, Armageddon, and a predicted dimensional shift in the imminent future.

This is a story of epic proportions that has led me to a greater understanding of the meaning of life, the manner in which Creation works, who God is, why we are here, and where we are going.

As I researched, I felt like a detective uncovering each new piece of evidence that gave more credence to the Cayce/Wilcock connection. Furthermore, within the fabric of the storyline, the secret of life itself appears to have been revealed. I don't present any of this as truth. I'll let the facts speak for themselves and let you, the reader, draw your own conclusions. If there is truth here, it will be revealed not only in these pages, but in the unfolding of Wilcock's prophecies for the next ten years. If he's right, perhaps this book will better prepare us for what is to come and help us cope with it, from both a survival and a spiritual perspective.

And thus, you are not only documenting the dreams, which are a rather common human endeavor, but also a much more uncommon one as well, namely this trance contact channeling process. And so, we applaud your efforts, and we shake your hand in the higher realms— or that which you would then conceive of as a hand, but which is more likely an energetic progression from an amoeba-like bodily form of energy. But you understand the point.

—Ra/Wilcock, January 3, 1999, from Wilcock's website, www.ascension2000.com

Chapter

1

The Puzzle

There's a new paradigm on Planet Earth. Could we actually be in the midst of the end times prophesied by Jesus? Who can we trust, if anyone, to guide and help us understand this period? Edgar Cayce is recognized as the premier mystic prognosticator of the Western world and predicted that he would reincarnate in this time. If it can be shown that David Wilcock fulfills Cayce's prophecy of returning, and that all of the threads explored in this book tie together, then the widespread cross-cultural prediction of a spiritual ascension is given added credibility. And regardless of whether or not David is Cayce reincarnated, the combination of the documented prophetic accuracy in his readings and his extremely clear and sophisticated scientific material still makes a very significant case for Ascension.

Part One of this book evaluates the incredible links between Cayce and Wilcock. Part Two presents the message of Wilcock's Source, and Part Three provides scientifically-oriented evidence to back up the suggestions and claims made in earlier sections.

If Wilcock is Cayce's return, he's no longer a sleeping prophet channeling from an unnamed source. Wilcock receives his messages in a waking trance. His Source has identified itself and become his advisor, friend, and confidant. His readings tell of a pending dimensional shift and how to deal with it, as well as address and answer some of life's most profound questions: Who are we? Why are we here? Why does God allow our world and our lives to be so topsy-turvy and unpredictable? Why is love so elusive? Why is there so much injustice? Why do innocent people die? Is a person eternal— and if so, where were we before we were born? Where do we go when we die? And why don't we remember? If we do exist forever, why do we fear death?

We go through our lives so occupied with our day-to-day routines and responsibilities that most of the time we don't pay attention to the deeper questions of life until something jolts us out of our unconsciousness and we are forced to fit another clue into the puzzle of life. Pieces of the puzzle usually arrive in strange, unexpected ways. Something comes along that makes us truly happy for a while: a new job, a new love, or a new child. Someone or something in life needs us, and that need creates a new value for us, a new understanding. Another piece of the puzzle falls into place. Someone crosses our path who seems happier than most. They have a lingering smile that the sorrows of the world just won't wear off. Someone, like a Mother Teresa, lives an exemplary life different from the rest of us, and we wonder what could motivate her. Someone close to us passes on, the World Trade Center collapses, or our children are sent off to war, and we are faced with contemplating our own mortality. We may read something that inspires us, by an author who seems to understand the innate workings of our being and our soul better than we do. Our intuitions are able to recognize truth even when our conscious minds are oblivious to it.

Then we have the anomaly of a life like Edgar Cayce's. As we struggle to find meaning and understanding, as we desperately search for answers, we are suddenly presented with an example of a man who has omniscience, *but only in his sleep!* A man who can know and diagnose what ails someone else while they are thousands of miles away ... a man who can potentially have a correct answer for any possible question ... a man who can see into the past lives of any who ask. Yet, he is also a man who, in his waking state, is not unlike you or me, a man with his own weaknesses, confusions, and challenges.

Hundreds of books have been written about Edgar Cayce, carefully documenting every twist, turn, and coloration of his life and his psychic data. Cayce helped millions of people fit a new piece into their puzzle—or even rethink the entire puzzle. In spite of the blank state of our memory banks, Cayce gave his readers the confidence to believe that they had lived before, and that life would go on after the body's demise. But the question remains: *Why Cayce?* Out of all the billions of people, why was Cayce able to have this awareness, albeit if only in his sleep, as the rest of us walk around in our somnambulistic waking trances? These are questions that I hope to answer in this book.

Obviously, if Edgar Cayce has reincarnated, this is a major event in the world of spiritual seekers everywhere who have been inspired by the Cayce material. In telling this story, I will draw on a number of sources, spanning 12,500 years, in the hope of validating my hypothesis. If it weren't for all the amazing parallels among so many totally disconnected puzzle pieces, I too would have a hard time believing this. So, with the same optimistic spirit that you feel as the lights dim and the crowd gets quiet before a great movie or performance, I ask you to suspend your own judgment and disbelief until you have completed the entire book, and then see if it all fits together for you. The implications of this story go far beyond the issue of whether Edgar Cayce has reincarnated; we shall be discussing the nature of life itself and a course of events that, if true, will affect every life form on our planet over the next decade.

Edgar Cayce's prophecies painted a portrait of some of the calamities of modern times about seventy years ago. As one of many examples, Cayce said, "... in the machinery of nations' activities, so shall ye see those in high places reduced," and that for "those ... teachers among men, the rottenness ... will be brought to light, and turmoils and strifes shall enter." [Cayce reading 3976–15] The bankruptcies of MCI/WorldCom and Enron, the ongoing collapse of the

Bush Administration's war campaign in Iraq, and the sexual scandals of those in high church positions could be examples of the fulfillment of this Cayce prophecy. Simultaneously, we can observe a continuing increase of spiritual awareness, empathetic connection, and reaching out by common people everywhere for peace, tolerance, and love. Indeed, the world is getting smaller every day. The Internet is breaking down barriers, and communication and the dissemination of news occur globally. In some sense we, humankind, are writing our own story. With this acceleration of world events and communication, perhaps we can begin to grasp for the first time how our minds interact and how we are all connected in what Ra calls "the Law of One." Even science, with the Global Consciousness Project[1] being conducted at Princeton University, is proving that consciousness can affect what would otherwise seem to be totally random and inanimate physical events. Edgar Cayce made it very clear that there is a direct connection between the natural disasters that might befall a given geographic location and the collective state of consciousness shared by those who live there.

The information in this book is derived from three primary sources:

1. **Books about the life of Cayce and the readings of Edgar Cayce himself.** Cayce gave quite a bit of detail concerning his own past lives as well as two of his future lives. He established credibility by his thousands of readings, many of which gave clearly verifiable diagnoses of his clients' physical conditions as well as predictions for the future. I draw on this data to see how well it reconciles with information from other sources.

2. **Wilcock's website and my personal connection with Wilcock.** The circumstances of his own life have led David Wilcock, often "dragged kicking and screaming," to the conclusion that he is the reincarnation of Edgar Cayce. He has drawn on information from his own psychic readings, impossibly precise astrological correspondences, dream memories of his life as Cayce,

and more. And of course, one cannot overlook the irrefutable physical resemblance. We will pore through all of these indicators with a fine-toothed comb and see how they match up with our other sources.

3. **The "tuned trance telepathy" channeling of L/L Research.** The Ra Material, also known as the *Law of One* series,[2] was published through the efforts of L/L Research (Dr. Don Elkins, Carla Rueckert, and Jim McCarty, with Ms. Rueckert as channel, Dr. Elkins as questioner, and Mr. McCarty as scribe) during the period of 1981 to 1984. As I read their five books, I realized that I was connecting with a source of wisdom and knowledge regarding the workings of the greater universe that was more profound than anything I had previously been exposed to. It revealed information about events in our cosmos outside any recorded history or geological evidence available to humankind.

The Ra material/*Law of One* series presents an all-inclusive, cosmic perspective of the origins and purpose of life. It contains more pieces of the puzzle that dovetail in an astonishing way with the stories of Cayce and Wilcock. When Edgar Cayce gave his readings, the voice that spoke through him identified itself as the "Source." I theorize that Cayce's Source was not an isolated intervention unique to Cayce. In fact, if my informed assumptions are correct, Cayce's Source was his own Higher Self, which was part of a group soul that identified itself as Ra through both Wilcock and L/L Research. In addition, there may be many other people incarnate on the planet whose Higher Selves are part of the Ra group or possibly other group souls. The Ra group alleges to have been assisting humanity from another dimension for tens of thousands of years. Rueckert and Wilcock, because of their unique abilities to channel, have each been able to give this group a voice.

As Wilcock finally became convinced that he is Cayce returned and prepared to make a public statement regarding same on the Internet, he realized that he was setting himself up to be ridiculed, scoffed at, and shunned. Nonetheless he bolstered himself to stand up against the resistance he anticipated when he put up his website, www.ascension2000.com, making the case public in February of 1999.

The true charade is in making a point of realizing one's own Oneness and then stopping it from becoming anything more than just a hobby. The realization of one's own Oneness comes only with the practice of the eventualities therein, and that very process is, by all accounts, deeply involved with the awakening of said life-force energy within the planet. In these modern times, as you would call them, one needs to focus entirely on the positive energies that seek to manifest themselves.

—Ra/Wilcock, unpublished quote

Chapter

2

David Wilcock: From Academia to Interdimensional Student

The circumstances of David Wilcock's life journey are highly relevant to our presentation and conclusions in this book. There may be those who view Wilcock as an egomaniac and make the judgment that he is craving the limelight, but he has never charged money for people to peruse his readings, articles, or five books (involving many years of dedicated daily research), and I have watched him knowingly sabotage many career opportunities, which almost included this book as well. Over the period of time I have worked on this project with Wilcock, I have also watched him go through immense challenges with those in his immediate personal sphere. His mission has become very real to him. To be effective in his mission, he must sometimes try to lay his human frailties aside, but unfortunately, all too often, people perceive those frailties and use them to judge and discredit him. Wilcock's thirty-year-old (in 2003) persona is barely able to handle his mission, but there's no more time for him to mature. The message is too important, too urgent. Time is passing. He's being forced to rise to the occasion.

Some may think that his readings come from his own consciousness and that he has deluded himself in his own infatuation with Edgar Cayce. After working on this project with Wilcock for two years, I can testify from my own experience that nothing could be further from the truth. Wilcock's "Dream Voice" has consistently demonstrated its prognosticating power, and Wilcock very reluctantly announced his Cayce connection only at the absolute insistence of his Dream Voice. His self-worth is constantly being challenged as he pales in Cayce's long shadow. In taking his position, Wilcock has had to stand up to the resistance of a skeptical world.

Even those who are sure he is Cayce have doubt as to his ability to handle worldly recognition. For a period of time Wilcock stayed at the home of Joseph Myers, who is recognized as an expert on reincarnation. In addition to numerous print articles, nationwide radio shows, and a nationwide television appearance on "PM Magazine," Myers has given lectures on this subject at a metaphysical/spiritual university founded by the Cayce Institute in Virginia Beach. His website www.reincarnation2002.com compares photos and drawings/portraits of famous individuals such as U.S. presidents from one incarnation to the next, showing the remarkable physical and character similarities that can occur. Myers had Wilcock's photo comparison with Cayce up on his site, but eventually he took it down. When one of his web visitors asked why (on his public forum), Myers answered as follows:

> You have asked a question that is not easy for me to answer. Edgar Cayce meant and does mean very, very much to me. And I have no rese[r]vations about the belief [that] David Wilcock is his return. In fact, from the standpoint of supporting evidence, there is not a more evidential example than his. He lived with my wife, Mary, and myself for several months while he was doing some writing. The reason that I took his case off the website was because I became convinced that it was not in his best interest yet for him to try to cope with being recognized as Cayce's return.—Joe Myers[1]

As this book progresses, various aspects of Wilcock's life will be interspersed so that his human side is always taken into account. I include insertions by Wilcock throughout the book, which resulted from telephone interviews or email correspondence, allowing parts of the story to be presented in his own words. The following excerpt documents the period from his college graduation until the time he started doing readings at the demand of his Dream Voice. The subjective voice is David Wilcock's.

I graduated from the State University of New York at New Paltz with a B.A. in psychology in June 1995. I tried to make a quick transition to the Naropa Institute in Boulder, Colorado, for entry into their Transpersonal Psychology master's degree program. This led to me to make a jostling, sleepless, two-and-a-half-day journey via Amtrak train out to hot, dry Boulder, to meet with the Naropa admissions staff in person. I furnished them a list of three hundred metaphysical/spiritual books that I had read throughout college in my spare time, and was quite serious when I said that I could discourse on the contents of any volume in the list—yet they never accepted my challenge. A week later, I was turned down in writing without explanation, though my financial situation appeared to have been a major deterrent.

Feeling quite disillusioned, I returned to New York to my mother's home in Scotia and had a series of gruelingly unpleasant temp jobs, which included an assignment at a fiberglass-producing factory. With glass fibers embedded throughout my entire face, I quit on the first day and came home to a dream of many transparent laboratory mice being microwaved into a puddle of liquid—a metaphor for my own feelings of how the life of my dreams, a marvelous graduate-school experience in Boulder, had dissolved into the reality of toxic, dangerous warehouse and factory labor jobs. The mouse had definitely not found the cheese he was looking for.

Amidst my crushingly depressing labors, my mother strongly and continually pressured me to move out of the house and start my own life. I had lived on campus throughout all four years of college and had a great fear of independent living after hearing the endless stories of college students who survived on bread, peanut butter, pasta, and spaghetti sauce once they got their own place. However, my mother's pressure proved greater than my fear of living on my own, and my dreams continually advised me to move back to my college town. So one day I literally threw all that I owned into my new/used 1988 white Subaru hatchback and drove from Scotia back to New Paltz, spending my first week sleeping on the kitchen floor of my fellow jazz musician friend Adam Makofske.

The very next night after I arrived, my college buddy Eric got me a job working as a deliveryman for My Hero pizzeria, and I soon moved into a boarding house on Innis Avenue, where nine people shared a single refrigerator and the rent was only $220 a month.

After a few months of labor and toil, I scored the first of a series of jobs in mental health, my chosen profession. At this point I was still actively working towards getting a Ph.D. in psychology, and internships were the best way to go. A psychiatric ward seemed to be the best place to start, and $7.35 an hour seemed quite good enough—it was by far the highest wage I had ever received.

After an invigorating, heartbreaking, and highly challenging two and a half weeks, where I was often very glad that I was the one with the keys, I was spontaneously fired for being "too friendly" to the patients. I collapsed into my Subaru and sobbed in the parking lot for over a half hour, looking out one last time at the meandering family of five wild turkeys, which were usually visible from the patients' smoking balcony, their one brief taste of freedom each day. I felt all of my dreams and aspirations sliding away from me—this was my first real internship after the suicide crisis hotline in college, and I hadn't made it past the end of my third week.

I drove back to my parents' home, unemployed, seeking some time to relax and recuperate during the Thanksgiving holiday. Before arriving, I stopped at a bookstore in Albany, where I was strongly guided to purchase the book *From Elsewhere* by Dr. Scott Mandelker.[2] I also perused a copy of Book Three of the *Law of One* series.[3] At that time, the Law of One material did not attract me—it seemed highly complex, arcane, and loaded with specific jargon, so I set it back on the shelf. Little did I know how important it would later become for me.

Mandelker's book brought me to a profound awakening; it discussed the idea that the souls of people on Earth can come from a variety of different origins, and some of them are angelic or extraterrestrial in nature. These so-called "Wanderers" volunteered to be here, perhaps thousands of years ago, and had long since forgotten that they ever made a choice in the matter, having gone through a series of human lives trapped in the Earth's reincarnational pattern. Some one hundred million of them, or one out of every sixty people, had come to Earth to try to help humanity at this crucial period in its evolution. Their home vibrations were in most cases millions of years more advanced than humanity, in terms of linear-time evolution.

I was highly intrigued by the possibility that I might be a Wanderer, but I needed proof. I visited my best friend Jude Goldman, who recommended that I try "automatic writing" to get a message from spirit. Once I became sufficiently deep into meditation, a force seemed to take possession of my writing arm and abruptly scribbled out a series of characters on the paper, without me having any control over the process. It turned out to be a Bible quote, namely Ecclesiastes 2:22 to 3:13. I had never studied the Bible consciously, yet it seemed that some part of me was very well aware of it.

When I finally located the faded black Bible in the late-night darkness, the first words I read were, "For what hath a man toiled and labored under the sun? This too is meaningless." And the cited passage ended with the phrase, "To eat and drink and be happy in one's toil—this is the grace of God." The passage spoke directly to the issue that had just befallen me— the loss of my mental health job and my desires for graduate school—and essentially said that it was "meaningless," so long as I could find something that would make me happy and pay the bills.

My Thanksgiving vacation finally came to an end. I returned to New Paltz and got my first job working with developmentally disabled persons in a day treatment center, earning a regrettable $5.77 an hour for very serious work. Due to my psychology background, I was assigned to the toughest part of the whole center—the "behavior rooms," where the job was often more akin to that of an umpire than an instructor.

That following January, I again came upon very hard times, this time through a phone bill that was far more expensive than I could pay for at my low wage level. I felt that my question "Am I a Wanderer?" had been dramatically answered just a few months ago, but in spite of the mental knowledge that I was a Wanderer, I still felt alienated, and the feeling of being separated from God burned in my soul. I demanded an answer in as open and dramatic a fashion as possible: "If I really am a Wanderer, then I need proof, and I need it right now." Nothing seemed to happen that night, and I went to bed, long before my roommate Eric returned home from his job delivering pizzas.

Little did I know that my question would be answered the next morning. Although he had no idea that I had prayed for an answer the night before, Eric had a dream in which I was present. In the dream, a robed and bearded man emerged from a UFO on a circular platform and spoke of the Earth being transformed into a paradise, and said that his group was our long-lost "brothers" here to assist us. In Eric's dream I approached the man, and we suddenly seemed to know each other. The man threw his arm around my shoulder, looked at Eric, and with a serious expression on his face said, **"It is very important that you know that he is one of us."** I took this to be a confirmation of my status as a Wanderer.

Dr. Mandelker's book had mentioned the *Law of One* series quite prominently,[4] and after this powerful dream suggestion, I decided that it was definitely a good idea to follow Mandelker's recommendation to study the words of Ra/Law of One. I thus began my immersion into the *Law of One* series in January 1996. Then, almost exactly one year after my automatic writing experience, I secured my own intuitive contact with my "Dream Voice" or "Higher Self" in November 1996.

I then spent an entire year developing a daily, working rapport with my Dream Voice source of guidance in private, while publicly working through a long series of low-wage jobs, primarily in caring for developmentally disabled persons. The readings began to associate the mental health jobs with the concept of repeating high school when it was no longer necessary. The readings allayed my fears of academic failure by telling me, "Wearing your cap and gown.... We are peaceful and Ph.D." It was OK to leave mental health, as I would not require any further college education; I was now a direct full-time apprentice with beings of higher intelligence who were transforming the way I ate, the way I exercised, the way I thought about myself and others, and the way I thought about science, consciousness, and the nature of the universe. I would have my Ph.D., but in a course no Earthly institutions could provide.

Once I decided to leave mental health, my Dream Voice precisely guided me how to get a great job at Mohonk Mountain

House, a nearby five-star luxury resort hotel that was absolutely breathtaking. During the day I would be maintaining a composed, sober, and compassionate public persona on the phones in Reservations, while at night I would be reading everything I could about UFOs, metaphysics, ancient civilizations, and the Law of One. And most importantly, each morning I would awaken to another conscious dialogue with my Dream Voice, where I received many startling prophecies of personal and global events, as well as gorgeous streams of poetic, intuitive information.

As one of many examples of personal prophecies, in early 1997 while I was still working in mental health, my Dream Voice told me that my housemate Eric "would be happy to know that his student loan check for New Paltz had come in." This seemed completely off-base, as Eric had already graduated from New Paltz and gone on to graduate studies at the University of Albany. However, about a month later, the New Paltz bursar's office was being remodeled, and while moving a file cabinet from one area to another, a letter addressed to Eric was found behind it. Inside the envelope was an uncashed Stafford Loan check for nine hundred dollars with Eric's name on it. The check was still good. Eric made sure I was sitting down before he told me the news.

Through studying and applying the work of William Buhlman's *Adventures Beyond the Body*,[5] I perfected the art of out-of-body travel in the summer of 1997 while working at the lavish Mohonk Mountain House. This led to a direct meeting with beings "on the other side" who told me with great seriousness, **"You know you have to move, don't you?"** A reading that came through just before this said, **"Strap on your parachute hat; Virginia would be a nice destination."**

Indeed, I had already been considering a move to Virginia Beach, as the Association for Research and Enlightenment, or A.R.E., had the only university on the entire East Coast where metaphysical topics could be studied on the path to a Master's degree in Transpersonal Psychology. This was also, incidentally, a university originally founded by Edgar Cayce in the late 1920s to early 1930s. However, for the moment I had a great job at a top-class resort, which was a prime destination for some of the wealthiest people in the world due to its pristine lakeside setting in the Shawangunk Mountains, its beautiful Victorian rooms, lounges, and verandas, and more than two thousand miles of hiking trails. Although my clerical performance was often quite bad, I was booking more reservations than anyone else in the department. I repeatedly cited the spiritual healing benefits of such a lush setting, and I had no intentions of leaving.

However, just a short time after my guidance to move came through, my entire life in New York started falling apart. Spontaneously my landlady asked for a one-year legal commitment, Mohonk gave me a seasonal layoff with the opportunity to work switchboard over the winter, and my friendship with a woman named Angelica completely collapsed.

With just about seven hundred dollars to my name, I arranged for my pilgrimage to Virginia Beach. Shortly after my arrival, several A.R.E. members (including at least two high-ranking staff personnel) recognized me as being the spitting image of a young Edgar Cayce, and I had almost dared to wonder if it were indeed possible. I queried my Dream Voice in November of 1997 regarding my connection with Cayce and was told that I was Cayce's reincarnation. In this remarkable session, I was told that I was meant to deliver an urgent message to mankind. I was asked to assert my connection with Cayce as a means of getting attention, to get the word out.

It should be noted that this Cayce connection was not an identity that Wilcock wished to declare. Up until this moment, he had never even thought that the words he brought through each morning would be shared with others. Yet it was made clear to Wilcock by his Dream Voice that among many other topics, he was meant to disclose the esoteric significance of the prophecies of Jesus regarding ascension and rapture, and the transition of planet Earth from the third density to the fourth density. He was told that this process is already underway and is scheduled to culminate in the very near future. Needless to say, Wilcock went into a state of shock and disbelief. He began an extensive study of the Edgar Cayce readings and even made acquaintance with some of those still living who had been connected with Cayce when he was alive.

Not only was David asked to validate his Cayce connection, but he was instructed by his Dream Voice to compile his research in metaphysics. The goal was to provide scientific evidence to back up his channeled prophecies regarding the imminent transformation of the Earth and its inhabitants. Although Cayce's work made an impact on humanity and convinced millions of the realities of reincarnation and other dimensions, there was no way to explain the phenomenon of his powers **scientifically.** And yet Cayce himself predicted that in the future there could be scientific verification for spirituality. In a reading done in 1939,[6] Cayce was asked if it would ever be possible to prove psychic and spiritual phenomena by scientific means, i.e., could such phenomena be measured by instruments and proven mathematically. Cayce's Source answered this question with a definitive "yes" and said that when the same interest is shown in spiritual phenomena as is given to material phenomena, then it would become as "meter-able as any other phase of human experience."

David Wilcock believes that the scientific validation for spiritual phenomena to which Cayce referred exists today. In addition to the channeled wisdom that Wilcock is bringing forward, he has freely published online his *Convergence* series[7] of books, in which he compiles and explains this current scientific data. He believes that his data can back up the predicted dimensional shift scientifically as well as explain the miracles of Cayce. In addition, within the context of this new science, Wilcock believes that technologies such as "free" energy, anti-gravity, super-light-speed propulsion, and teleportation are possible, using existing materials available on Earth.

Furthermore, Wilcock offers a scientific explanation for the spiritual significance of pyramid geometry. As our story unfolds, we will make the case that Wilcock himself, in a previous lifetime as Ra-Ta, actually helped to create the Great Pyramid in Egypt, and now in this life as David Wilcock, he's revealing the science behind the pyramid's power.

Little did anyone know in 1939 that Cayce might return to fulfill the very prophecy he made that day in the reading for client number 2012, which interestingly is the end-date for the Mayan Calendar and the year when Wilcock's predicted dimensional shift will culminate.

The physical body is but an extension of the spirit. When it is time for the calling up of those upon your plane to higher frequencies, your body is going to be a part of the past, and your energy body a part of the future.

—Ra/Wilcock, August 12, 1999

Chapter

3

Bainbridge, Cayce, Wilcock: Common Soul, Separate Bodies

This chapter and the next continue to introduce David Wilcock and to compare his manifestation with that of Cayce's. We will see how his present persona could be the next step in the evolution of his prior two lifetimes as the alcoholic womanizer and "wastrel" John Bainbridge and the "seer out of season" Edgar Cayce. Wilcock is certainly not hiding out, waiting for the world to recognize and celebrate him as Cayce. He's cutting his own path and gaining growing recognition for his accomplishments.

The classic picture of the older Edgar Cayce, with the soft loving eyes and the gentle disposition, is familiar to almost everyone who has studied New Age spirituality and metaphysics. Cayce is usually purported to be a very simple person with unusual powers. On the other hand, some see David Wilcock as brash, proud, insecure, complex, and brilliant. In taking his stand as Cayce's reincarnation, Wilcock has often found himself having to endure immense amounts of skepticism, and he sometimes appears defensive. His website is peppered with statements like: "This is true psychic ability in action." Or "This dream was so immediately stunning that it was necessary to post it as soon as possible."

Could the reserved and gentle Cayce really have reincarnated as Wilcock? As I studied Cayce's life, I learned some rather surprising things about Cayce's inner workings. There was frustration and insecurity behind his gentle disposition. According to Harmon Bro in *A Seer Out of Season,* the shadow of Cayce's Bainbridge life hung over him, and if he didn't keep his passions in check, he might jeopardize his ability to do readings. In fact, it seemed to take all of Cayce's will power to stay focused and to accomplish anything at all:

> His own personhood was a battleground, but so were the personhoods of all others around him in daily life.... He knew he was no saint. He could not serve as a model of an ideal spiritual life. At best, he could be seen as a warrior who kept fighting the darkness in himself as long as he could. For many who looked carefully at the story of his life, he knew that would not be enough. He knew he smoked too much, ate too much, lost his temper, criticized others arbitrarily, worried, rode his passions, forgot to put first things first, trusted too much in his own plans, failed to build community as he went.... [According to Cayce's son Hugh Lynn Cayce,] "The real miracle is that Edgar Cayce, with all the problems and tensions inside of him, gave readings and kept on giving them."[1]

As I researched, I found myself intrinsically understanding the process of reincarnation and soul evolution more profoundly, intuiting how Cayce's soul could make the transition from John Bainbridge to Cayce to Wilcock. Cayce did document many of his lifetimes, the Bainbridge one being of particular relevance since it was the lifetime immediately prior to Cayce's own. Many of the personal trials and tribulations of both Cayce and (hypothetically) Wilcock are related to the life as Bainbridge. Before going through an analysis of this, I'd like to present a brief review, in my own words, of Cayce's cosmology of reincarnation.

We develop our personalities on the physical plane based on our upbringing, our culture, and our choices. Beyond our personality is our soul, which represents our actual individuality. The soul, originally part of the Creator, separated out in order to experience its own individuation. According to Cayce, we were originally spirit forms while animal life was evolving on the planet. The spirits would occupy the animal bodies to experience physical existence and sexuality, thinking that they could move back and forth from the physical to the spiritual—but as you might guess, they got stuck. Thus began this process of reincarnation, where the spirit had to keep returning back into the physical. The death of the physical body is also the end of the personality, but the individuality is retained and carried forward in the soul until it once again reincarnates and begins the development of a new personality.

The *Law of One* series and other sources mention the "veil of forgetting" as a natural blockage that stops us from remembering who we were in previous lifetimes. This gives us the opportunity to be "fresh" when the same lessons are presented to us once again. Until we make the choices that our Higher Self wants us to make, the most difficult experiences will continue to repeat themselves. The "rules of the game" are such that we need to go into these experiences just as blindly as we did in previous cases, with the hope that we will now make more optimal choices thanks to our overall increase in spiritual "vibration."

The ultimate purpose of all this spiritual work is to "graduate" from our current "third-density" physical world to a higher plane of existence. Most who "make graduation" will move on to the higher world that Earth is now moving into, but some people will have advanced enough to move on to even higher planes of existence. All souls will eventually grow to the point of again becoming One with the Creator, having no memory, no identity, no sense of past, present or future, just pure Oneness. So, as we travel through our various incarnations, the focus of our lives will change if we are truly taking in the lessons of these lifetimes. We start as isolated beings seeking survival and power. As the progression of our earthly third-density lifetimes gets closer to culmination, we seek spiritual love and the experience of unity, which are characteristics of the "fourth density." This cycle of birth and death can extend over hundreds of lifetimes and tens of thousands of years—and perhaps longer, if you happen to be one of those resistant to life's lessons. The *Law of One* series tells us that most of those on Earth fit this category, as we will see later on.

According to the Cayce readings,[2] John Bainbridge was described as a gambler, drinker, and womanizer who lived in America during the early 1800s. Although Bainbridge had psychic abilities, they were used for self-serving purposes. I would hypothesize that if we follow Cayce's previous lifetime as John Bainbridge through his current theorized lifetime as David Wilcock, we might conclude that the Bainbridge lifetime was a period of worldly experience, the Cayce lifetime was a period of service and atonement, and the Wilcock lifetime is a period of motion towards integration and mastery. We might also see how different the lessons are from one incarnation to the next, noting the extreme swings from Bainbridge the gambler to Cayce the prophet. We could also anticipate that there would a swing in the transition from Cayce the prophet to Wilcock the scientist, scholar, and mystic.

Both Wilcock and Cayce would have probably regarded John Bainbridge's life as a service-to-self existence, where he manipulated and controlled other people for his own gains, without regard for the consequences. According to the Cayce readings, Bainbridge was literally unbeatable at the "shell game," because he was able to utilize telekinetic powers to move the pea from one shell to another and outsmart players. Even the most evolved of souls can be tempted into a negative path, and perhaps all souls must go through lives of self-serving behaviors as they move through their cycles of birth and death on the journey back to God.

According to a Cayce reading, "Bainbridge, the entity, in the material sojourn, was a wastrel, one who considered only himself, having to know the extremes in his own experience, as well as in others."[3] Bainbridge was a charismatic Englishman who was sent into Canadian military service, from which he escaped. He traveled as an adventurer and wanderer, and "many suffered in his wake" through "many escapades that have to do with those of the nature of the relations with the opposite sex." Cayce was warned in his readings that he could sabotage his positive spiritual benefit in his Cayce lifetime if he yielded to his more base desires. According to Harmon Bro in *A Seer Out of Season,* "the legacy of his life in colonial America could detonate within him, damaging both him and others."[4]

On the surface, Cayce lived an exemplary life. In addition to his thousands of readings, he was a regular visitor to prisons, taught Sunday school, and never missed an opportunity to display compassion and caring. (Wilcock also frequently lectured at a New Age church in Virginia Beach on Sundays and worked for two years with the developmentally disabled.) But despite Cayce's positive accomplishments, his struggles with his dark side and negative habits were always apparent, to those in his immediate sphere. His Source gave him complete dietetic regimens, which he ignored, as well as suggestions to avoid worrying, which he was largely unable to carry out.

In spite of his good works and the blessings he bestowed on so many via his readings, Cayce seemed to suffer low self-esteem, which kept him in continuing financial difficulties through most of his life until his death in 1945. He was a chain smoker and a workaholic, often plowing ahead for such long periods of time that his physical health was severely compromised. He never had enough confidence in his own psychic abilities to charge anything beyond a small donation for his readings, and all attempts to use the readings for profit, such as digging for treasure or oil, ended in disaster. Cayce agreed with his readings' perspective that his problems were due to the necessity of balancing the excesses that he had accumulated in his Bainbridge life.

Now we flash forward to the life of David Wilcock. Wilcock definitely has a sense of his destiny. He is a man on a mission. He is clearly a workaholic, often failing to leave his computer long enough to turn on the lights once the room has become dark. He has received numerous instructions and counsels in his readings (to himself), which correlate very well with all the life issues that plagued Cayce. Wilcock speaks candidly about his conflicts in his online book *Wanderer Awakening,* where he reveals the process of his self-discovery in his formative years. Thousands of pages of his online books are downloadable for free. Although he has already done readings for a few hundred people at the time of this writing, he has been told by his Source that readings are not to be his principal service. Planet Earth is in the process of a dimensional shift,* and his most effective role would be as a leader, one of a team of "liberators," who help guide humankind through the changes taking place. Wilcock is presently laying the groundwork for his own part as a liberator with his soon-to-be-published scientific research, his client readings, his Web presentations, international lecture tours, and now the creation of a complete CG-animated DVD series to illustrate his *Convergence* work; but he would be the first to acknowledge that he has personal obstacles to be processed, cleared, and removed before he can fully own this potential destiny.

We can refer to a comment by Harmon Bro[5] about Cayce:

> Evidently real damage to the soul's growth had been done by the suicide [in a previous lifetime, when he was shamed in a position of authority], in the readings' view, leaving a wound of self-doubt which would correspond to what we encountered at times as Cayce's hunger for attention and confirmation just below the surface of his personality. And the self-violence of suicide had magnified, the readings indicated, a tendency to a "quick temper," with its "unexpected" flashing out at even those closest to him.

---

*Earth is in the process of increasing its vibrational rate and becoming a fourth-density planet, where compassion and love will be the operative parameters.

When we perceive David Wilcock expressing self-doubt or diffi-cult financial straits, we can intuit how he's still working out the left-over karma from the life where he committed suicide, as well as his Cayce and Bainbridge lifetimes.

A Seer Out of Season was one of the books that gave me insight into the inner workings of Cayce's persona and helped me to con-nect a lot of the dots between Cayce and Wilcock. Bro actually lived in the Cayce household for a period of time and had direct access to the private life of Cayce. Concurrently with my study of Bro's book, I was also getting to know Wilcock personally, and I was amazed to find that Bro's descriptions of Cayce fit Wilcock perfectly.

Wilcock prefers to emphasize his online books and jazz-influenced musical compositions more than his channeled material. Bro speaks of Cayce's frustration with being recognized only as a purveyor of channeled readings produced in his sleep. Many clients had virtu-ally no interest in talking to him while he was awake but were ready for him to go into his entranced state as soon as they entered the room. The following is quoted from *A Seer Out of Season:*

> Some part of Cayce seemed to yearn for a yet higher level of integration and ego strength, a take-charge person, captain of himself and others in good times and bad.... For the present, his leadership lay in disappearing from view in a trance state which submerged his manhood, his individuality, and his ego.[6]

In Wilcock's online books, he is taking the steps towards this higher level of integration. In many ways, Wilcock's treatises scien-tifically support the Cayce readings' metaphysical descriptions of how our universe functions, though the scientific research was not available during Cayce's life to provide this kind of back-up. Part Three of this book includes a current summary of relevant research, compiled by Wilcock.

When I first read Wilcock's *Shift of the Ages,* I wondered how Edgar Cayce could have possibly transformed himself from the simple, uneducated, sleeping prophet to the dazzlingly brilliant Wilcock. But as I commenced my research, I found that although Cayce may have been uneducated, his thinking processes were intelligent and wise. From *A Seer Out of Season:*

> Though he chose to live simply, he embodied complex, conflicting currents that gave him size and depth sufficient to mark everyone he touched.... [T]his was a mountain of a person, despite his customary soft speech.[7]

From *Mysteries of Reincarnation* by Jess Stearn:

> It became obvious that a good deal of the information in his subconscious had trickled into his conscious awareness and given him a breadth and depth of mind irrelevant to his own education. He had never gone beyond grade school, but he could discourse meaningfully on life with the ease and facility of the greatest of philosophers.[8]

In one of the few books written by Cayce himself, *My Life as a Seer,*[9] Cayce certainly does not present himself as a simple man. His thoughts about his own life reveal his capacity for introspection, intelligence, and wisdom.

From here, it's not a huge leap to sense how Cayce, as Wilcock, would have the need to be recognized for his own conscious creations in the areas of scientific research and musical compositions, and not simply settle for being the front person for his channeled information. Wilcock's online books have already garnered him public respect and acknowledgement, leading to two appearances on the Art Bell international radio program, a two-year job as Research Director for a nationwide, multimedia seminar tour, a university graduate-level lecture and workshop appearance on alternative physics at the pioneering US Psychotronics Association, and a month-long tour of Japan to give lectures, make media appearances, and perform readings through an interpreter.

As of summer 2003, Wilcock finally succeeded in building a complete computer-based, music-sequencing studio, allowing him to compose professional-quality music to accompany his upcoming lecture appearances, as well as develop the *Convergence* DVD series. He composes and records what might be called spiritual/inspirational music in a modern jazz/New Age style. In researching this book, I learned that Ra-Ta, one of Cayce's past lives, composed music to be used for healing purposes in Egypt. When one hears Wilcock's compositions, it's not difficult to picture his free-style rhythms and melodies reverberating in the halls of an Egyptian temple.

Wilcock seldom mentions his Cayce background or his channeled information unless prompted. At different times, Wilcock's Dream Voice (which eventually identified itself as Ra) chastised him for overemphasizing his scientific side and not giving the channeled messages enough attention. At the time of this writing, Wilcock still has a backlog of nine months' worth of tapes of his personal dreams and channeled transmissions, and well over five hundred client tapes in need of transcription:

Let it be known that without these transmissions, we are not fulfilling one of our very basic purposes, and disasters will result. The least that you can do is to honor us this one point by allowing the ego self to step aside once in a while and bring these messages through. That way, there is no separation between your goals and our own.—Ra/Wilcock, July 3, 2002

The philosophy of soul evolution should earn a good chunk of airtime in the book [a reference to one of Wilcock's online books] and to heck with the skeptical crowd. . . .
—December 17, 2000

The book should be designed to pave the way for the realization of the wisdom that is being brought forth by humanity's interaction with the extraterrestrial [interdimensional] forces. And as those forces have kept increasing in size and potency, more and more people will have an innate tendency to accept them, since there is so much publicity at this time.

—February 21, 2000

Wilcock was quite resistant to announcing to the world that he was Cayce. As mentioned, he only did so at the direct demand of his Dream Voice, and his fears of rejection and ridicule were soon confirmed as even those closest to him conveyed their doubt. I can personally testify to Wilcock's resistance to being in the limelight. I found his attitude with regard to fame parallel to Cayce's. Cayce revealed this reluctance in his own words in Harmon Bro's *A Seer Out of Season:*

Man has one answer to every problem—power; but that is not God's way. Then why shouldn't I dread publicity?[10]

However, Wilcock has been instructed that his message is too important and he must put personal issues aside and use the Cayce connection to get attention. When he first published the results of his research on the Wilcock/Cayce connection on his website, he included the following disclaimer:

I, David, do not wish to self-aggrandize or make myself out to be something great through writing all of this. In fact, I dislike the spotlight and the controversy, and that is why I haven't yet written up this article until now, after knowing about this [Cayce connection] for a year and seven months already. I just want there to be a document that states the truth as I see it— both the strong points and the weak points. We are all One in this creation and no entity is any more or less valuable than any other. If I were trying to tell everyone that I was some spiritual super-hero, then I obviously would not have included the information about my losses, relationship problems, and the like. I do not feel that I will single-handedly "save the world" or do anything grandiose. I am simply one of a great team of Light workers, both incarnate and discarnate, all of whom wish to be of service to others. That's it.[11]

The Cayce who lives in our minds and memories no longer has a body or a personality. Cayce's major impact on the world occurred in the period since he left the body. It is very easy to lose sight of his humanness in the shadow of his legacy, but as Harmon Bro describes Cayce: "He had to deal with his passions, his extremism, his moods and doubts and loneliness, while he encountered incredible successes and shattering failures of his dreams."[12]

It's easy to hold Wilcock up to unfair comparisons with "Cayce the legacy" rather than "Cayce the man," and many people do. In many senses, the relationship of a person to his or her own past life is akin to that of a child to its parent—you don't expect the offspring to be a carbon copy of its progenitor. If you evaluate Wilcock's priorities, you will find him to be a young man plowing through his own obstacles, who has dedicated his life to transcending his personal weaknesses, sharing his readings, and compiling the scientific back-up to make credible the theory of a pending dimensional shift.

Wilcock's language is more contemporary than Cayce's archaic-sounding syntax, and he's not bound by the Fundamentalist Christian viewpoint, which seemed to be a limitation that Cayce's Source was aware of. The Cayce readings ultimately presented an updated form of Christianity that shed dramatic new light on a classic story, revealing the cosmic context behind Jesus' mission. Wilcock further expands the scope of Cayce's cosmology by drawing on the "tuned trance telepathy" of L/L Research, as well as his own Ra connection and the abundance of information, research, and wisdom brought forth by many other lightworkers who are now inspiring the world at this crucial juncture of time.

When one looks at the entire picture, the pieces seem to fit. Instead of Edgar Cayce's life being an isolated mystical manifestation, one can sense the flow between John Bainbridge, Edgar Cayce, and David Wilcock. One can intuit how David Wilcock bears both the weaknesses and strengths carried forward from his previous lifetimes. In *A Seer Out of Season,* Bro presents a discourse, based on the Cayce readings, describing how fine the edge actually is between positive and negative, with the guidelines for transmuting the negative:

> ... one's weaknesses could become one's greatest strengths if the energy were properly engaged. Anger and hostility could become boldness and courage. Stubbornness could become leadership, which endures where others quit. Deception could become true inventiveness. Sensuality could turn to healing through rechanneling the life force itself. Pride of wisdom could become genuine understanding used in sensitivity. The changes here envisioned were not through amputation, but through redirection of specific energies and urges ... growth in which impulses and habits were transmuted ... for the purpose of serving others and glorifying God ... evil was not poles apart from good, but "evil is just under good waiting to be lifted."[13]

As the facts come into view in subsequent chapters, the chances of having so many intertwining, evidentiary circumstances tying Wilcock to Cayce would be highly unlikely without the ultimate link of reincarnation. Although being the heir apparent to the Cayce legacy is not a role that Wilcock longs to play, he couldn't avoid the arrows pointing in that direction.

In addition, we are able to comprehend Ra's ongoing master plan to communicate with the human plane through Edgar Cayce, Don Elkins, Jim McCarty, Carla Rueckert, and now David Wilcock, as well as unidentified others around the planet, in present time and throughout history. Through these channels, Ra is giving us a continuity of information with time-stamped clues to inform us of this pending dimensional shift so that we might understand the urgency of connecting with and manifesting our loving and spiritual natures. As I present the case for the reincarnation of Edgar Cayce, I intertwine the story of Ra's intervention and assistance in the evolution of humankind over the past 12,500 years.

We wish to use our inspired messengers to bring these truths out to the public, while simultaneously attempting to tone down their conscious mind's messages quite a bit so as to receive a clean and unfiltered channel. In David's case, we do not have to work very much more on this, and thus the connection is quite good. As to whether this connection is the best one in existence on your plane or otherwise seen as a mode of comparison, there is no point in trying to talk about something like this that way. The fact of the matter is that there are indeed many of those now who are being born into this ability, or who already have this ability, and are capable of great teachings and great tidings.

—Ra/Wilcock, November 11, 1999

Chapter

4

The Cayce Legacy
and the Wilcock Promise

Warner Books published *The Edgar Cayce Reader*[1] in 1967, twenty-two years after Cayce's death. In the introduction, it was noted that the ten books written about Cayce up until that time had "totaled more than a million in sales." In 1998, fifty-three years after the death of Cayce, the State University of New York published a book called *Edgar Cayce in Context* that gave the following opinion: "He exerted a literary influence comparable to the greatest religious innovators of the last two centuries in America."[2] Cayce can also be given considerable credit for inspiring the New Age and holistic health movements of the sixties, which have both become everyday fixtures in today's consensus reality.

The following statistics are found in *Edgar Cayce in Context:* as of May 1997, 646 books were published since 1950 on the subject of Edgar Cayce, compared to 542 books on Ellen G. White (founder of Seventh Day Adventists), 264 on Joseph Smith (founder of the Mormon Church), and 121 on Helena Blavatsky (founder of Theosophy).

It was only during the later years of Cayce's life that he received national attention with the release of Thomas Sugrue's Cayce biography, *There is a River.*[3] His 14,500 documented readings have stood the test of time. He had abilities never before demonstrated or publicly acknowledged in the written history of the world. In his sleeping state, he was apparently omniscient. He could diagnose the medical condition of anyone regardless of his or her location. He could recommend medical experts by name and location, and tune into them psychically. He could recommend undiscovered miracle cures and remedies for physical ailments. Most health food stores now have shelves dedicated to Cayce's unique remedies. He could read someone's past lives and explain how their present circumstance and condition were influenced by their previous experiences. He could explain the spiritual workings of the universe with facts that no one on the physical Earth could possibly have known, and he made startlingly accurate predictions of future events, some of which have not yet come to pass.

In the last chapter I made an effort to note the human side of the man behind the legacy of Edgar Cayce and compare it to the present-day David Wilcock. In this chapter, I paint the picture of what I predict will become the Wilcock Legacy.

Wilcock has been instructed by his Source to put his data online and make it freely available to anyone who wants to peruse it. His website includes hundreds of his dreams and readings, as well as the complete texts of his books, available for downloading. Those who have discovered Wilcock's site visit it often, looking for his latest update or current "prophecy." As of this writing, June 2003, his site has been up for four years and has received more than 350,000 hits, with interest increasing exponentially. Two years ago, his site meter was indicating somewhere around 60,000.

David Wilcock was born on March 7, 1973, in Schenectady, New York, to avant-garde parents who were open to New Age thinking and metaphysics. His mother, presently a college professor and performing musician, was a piano teacher and scholar of the Seth books, and his father a Vietnam veteran and published music journalist. David was interested in psychic phenomena, astronomy, and science fiction throughout his youth, along with Tarot readings, lucid dreaming, and

UFOs. He describes some phenomena and powers that were similar to experiences that Cayce had when he was young. For example, Wilcock could think of someone at a certain time in the middle of the night and wake him or her up, as could Cayce. Cayce at one point did an experiment and found that he could psychically induce someone to show up at his photography studio. Wilcock once psychically summoned his friend Angelica to meet with him at the Mohonk cafeteria, and her anger at Wilcock saying "You're two minutes late" was a major factor in their relationship dissolving, as she did not like feeling controlled. Similarly, and on a more positive level, Wilcock's mother was able to telepathically call young David to return home when he was out playing. When Cayce was seven years old he heard a whirring sound, and a being of light appeared to him. When Wilcock was young, he had an out-of-body experience and later remembered meeting with light beings that he identified as ETs.

Beginning in September 1991, Wilcock attended college at the State University of New York in New Paltz, studying psychology and jazz performance as a percussionist. He planned to be a counselor and therapist, perhaps doing jazz gigs on the side. He started documenting, analyzing, and following the guidance of his dreams each morning as of October 1992, a practice that continues to this day. His passion turned to the understanding of UFO and ET phenomena in the spring of 1993, when a friend revealed some classified information from a source that had worked inside NASA in the 1970s—namely, the reality of the Roswell crash and the artifacts that were recovered were discussed, and the reverse-engineering of those artifacts into usable technology such as lasers, computer chips, and Teflon. This information made Wilcock believe for the first time that such phenomena could be real. The disclosure inspired him to dive into an extracurricular study of various metaphysical and spiritual books, leading him to digest three hundred texts in two and a half years.

As stated, Wilcock's first experience with paranormal communication was with automatic writing at age twenty-two, in November

1995, just months after graduating from college. Exactly one year later at age twenty-three, in November 1996, he initiated a daily communication with what he referred to as his "Dream Voice." As he relates on his website (www.ascension2000.com):

> I became aware of the fact that every morning I could wake up and just start listening. I would be getting messages from a very high spiritual source, and it completely changed my life. They immediately started to talk about my diet needs and my personal needs. I had a very different agenda. So, it was pretty interesting that, here I thought I was contacting extraterrestrials and was going to get all this cosmic information, and they end up being, basically, like my psychotherapist![4]

As Wilcock began to document his Dream Voice readings, he realized that future events were being accurately predicted, both in his personal life and in world affairs. In following the counsel, he noticed his own life patterns changing for the better, as destructive and addictive habits fell away. He began taking his readings very seriously.

Then in September of 1997, Wilcock was asked by his Dream Voice to move to Virginia Beach. His life in upstate New York was falling apart and he had no reason to stay there. He decided to make the move, being aware that Virginia Beach had been the home of Cayce and that Cayce said that it would be a safe haven in the event of Earth changes. By this time David was channeling on a daily basis but he considered it a very private experience, and the thought never crossed his mind that he had any special connection with Cayce.

David called the A.R.E. (Association for Research and Enlightenment, the Cayce Institution in Virginia Beach) from his New York residence to inquire if there were any members with rooms for rent, and they faxed him a list of housing options. In the interim period, before he left upstate New York, his friend Skip called and asked David to stop by, as he had something important to show him. Skip then showed David a copy of *Venture Inward,* the monthly magazine put out by the A.R.E., pointed to a photo, and asked David if he knew who it was. After several seconds of contemplation, David recognized that it was a young Edgar Cayce, but he also noticed with discomfort that the picture bore a striking resemblance to his own features. He didn't mark this as extremely significant at that time but took it as an unusual, even alarming coincidence.

When he finally moved to Virginia Beach, Wilcock had another validation of the prophetic power of his readings. In July of 1997, before the move, he had received the unfamiliar words "Great Neck" during a reading, with the strange word "Scarstahldig" appearing two days later. Eric had studied German well enough to be able to translate this cryptic phrase, which meant "a group of German steel helmets." At the time, Eric thought it might be the name for some sort of punk rock band. I happened to find an interesting correlation with this in *A Seer Out of Season:* "There was a record of an instance in which Cayce had given part of a reading in German (of which he knew nothing)...."[5]

The paragraphs below are David's own words from his website describing his arrival and first months in Virginia Beach:

David used the A.R.E.'s volunteer housing list to find his first rental in Virginia Beach with a woman named Linda, who ended up being off Old Great Neck Road, which was directly off Great Neck Road. Amazingly, Dennis, the other man subletting at the time, was a collector of German steel helmets.

On his second day in Virginia Beach, David remembered his reading having said "Great Neck," and he grabbed the book of transcripts and sat on the sofa to try to see if there were any other examples of prophecy. Before he even had a chance to look at his transcripts, his eyes went to the bookshelf, where he saw a volume entitled *The History of the German Steel Helmet: 1921–1945.* Dennis hadn't even *looked* at the house until August and did not move in until September, though the German phrase had come through in July. In

December, Dennis learned that his entire collection of helmets had been stolen out of storage in his hometown.

Across the street from Linda was a relatively high-ranking A.R.E. employee. He heard about David and wanted to meet him right away, and was astonished at the facial resemblance. He later invited his boss, one of the most powerful A.R.E. staff members at the time, to meet with him and David at the Nawab Indian-food restaurant, and at the end of the dinner the boss told David that he *"nearly fell over backwards"* when he first saw David's resemblance to Cayce. David still wasn't willing to fully believe that there was an Edgar Cayce connection at this point.

Just a few weeks later, the owner of a major business devoted to Cayce's work saw David, and without knowing anything about him said to his friend, *"My God, he looks just like Edgar Cayce!"*[6]

Increasingly, people in the A.R.E. were noticing the similarity, and others also began suggesting that perhaps he might be the reincarnation of Cayce. Wilcock pondered the meaning of it all. Finally, in November of 1997, he asked his Dream Voice if he was Cayce. [The exact question reads as follows: "I would like to incubate a question on [my] identity here, related to Edgar Cayce."]

In Chapter Eight one can read the complete text of the answer, but in short, it says: *"David, the answer is yes; you will need to review the whole life and see the parallels."*

Wilcock went into shock. He was instructed in this same reading that it was something he must make public. He already had hundreds of incidents where his Dream Voice had correctly predicted future events, so he had to take it very seriously. He was told that to not reveal his Cayce connection would be tantamount to a spiritual crime. He absorbed it all but decided not to make a public announcement immediately. He needed to take the time to validate and research this on his own.

Then in July of 1998, Wilcock's readings brought him to a point where they essentially demanded that he give up his three-year stint with minimum-wage jobs and begin earning a living by giving readings for others, or else he would lose the ability entirely. He had already performed readings for some of his friends and they seemed to derive benefit, and he had informally taken two paying clients a few months earlier, both jazz musicians.

All he had to do was to privately announce his new business to a few people at the Fellowship of the Inner Light church, founded on the work of the psychic Paul Solomon. Right away he got two clients, and both of them were very social ladies who quickly spread the word like wildfire. His third client walked in the door not wanting to say anything that would tip him off, and she quickly went into tears as the reading described exactly what was going on with her marital difficulties.

Although the lure of guaranteed income from a "regular job" continued to draw Wilcock in, within the first week he had so many requests for readings that he could not take any normal job, as his days were increasingly filled with scheduled readings. And thus, he crash-landed his way into starting a new business, which began at $65 a client and promised each of them a tape and written transcript. Although Wilcock had the potential to make more money than he had in any other job, transcribing the tapes proved to be quite labor-intensive, so after the first ten clients he discontinued the practice. Furthermore, his flow of clients was inconsistent, leading to a fluctuating financial state of feast and famine. Like Cayce, Wilcock would frivolously spend money when he gained a surplus, thus perpetually returning him to a near-bankrupt state as the requests for readings went into the "famine" part of the cycle.

As David realized how much his readings were actually helping others, it became increasingly important for him to do more. He gave up his other career ambitions and dedicated himself to fulfilling what he was beginning to realize was his larger spiritual purpose and mission.

Finally in May of 1999, nineteen months from the time of the disclosure of his Cayce identity by his Dream Voice and after doing his own extensive research, Wilcock decided to make it public. During the interim period, he thoroughly contemplated the possibility. He had several experienced portrait artists look at photos of Cayce and compare his own facial features from every conceivable angle, and they always pointed out many precise similarities. He compared his astrology chart with Cayce's and noticed highly improbable correspondences, with the inner planets being in nearly identical positions on the two charts. He read and re-read existing Cayce material, comparing and looking for concordances, and much of what he uncovered will be revealed in subsequent chapters. Finally, when all trace of doubt was gone from his mind, Wilcock made the public declaration on his website that he believed he was the reincarnation of Edgar Cayce, putting up a treatise explaining the circumstances which brought him to that conclusion.

In short, Wilcock made himself one of the most controversial figures in the history of metaphysics as he publicly announced his link to Cayce and put up his channeled messages on his website.

As today's world goes through its transitions, and old paradigms of consensus reality fall apart, more and more people are finding meaning and significance in Wilcock's work. Many are coming to the same inevitable conclusion as Wilcock himself.

We've only just begun to present our case, giving an idea of who Wilcock is, what he does, and some of the personality parallels to Cayce. Later chapters present some of the more objective correspondences. As I put the pieces together, I could only conclude that Wilcock must be Cayce returned, and the "social memory complex" that identifies itself as Ra was the intermediary "Source" for both Cayce and Wilcock. This would be a new and controversial piece of data for Cayce scholars, and it is something that each reader must evaluate for himself/herself.

In an interview with Rick Martin, Wilcock shares his ideal and mission as follows:

My ideals are that I do not want ego to get involved. I do not want to think of myself as anything special. I have a mission to perform. I have a job to do. The job is to tell people the reality of life on Earth and the reality of life in the Higher Dimensions, and to make that reality more tangible.... The whole reason why these readings are so intensely focused right now is that we're heading into a frequency shift—and that's probably going to be your next question: what is Ascension? How is it going to happen?... The understanding that I now have is that we are passing from the third level of vibration into the fourth. And when this passage is complete, the frequency of matter on Earth, in vibrational speed, will be seen to increase. As the frequency tries to increase, it creates a great pressure on any person who is not accepting the higher-dimensional energy, because the higher-dimensional energy is the energy of love. So, any place that we are not being loving and alive at this time is going to be forcibly shown to us—and very directly—because this energy is forcing us to be more loving. We have to, if we want to stay compatible. If we're not compatible with it, everything that's holding us back is going to be very forcibly shown to our face.[7]

Among the most compelling aspects of this story are the time-stamped hints that Ra, Wilcock's Source, has been leaving over a 12,500-year period. First there was Cayce's prior incarnation as Ra-Ta. Then we hypothesized that Ra was Cayce's unnamed Source. Next there was the channeling of Ra by Carla L. Rueckert with L/L Research from 1981 to 1984. And finally there is the Wilcock connection. At this point in our storyline, Ra has not yet identified itself to Wilcock, and Wilcock refers to his source as his Dream Voice. In the next chapter we'll learn about the Ra group and its connection with Earth's affairs.

I am part of the social memory complex that voyaged outward from a planet in your solar system, the one you call Venus. We are a race old in your measures. When we were at the sixth dimension our physical beings were what you call golden. We were tall and somewhat delicate. The covering of our physical body complex had a golden luster. In this form we decided to come among your peoples. Your peoples were much unlike us in physical appearance. Thus we did not mix well with the population and were obviously other than they. Our visit was relatively short. This was when we built the pyramids.

—Ra, L/L Research, from Book One (p. 90) of the *Law of One* series

Chapter

5

Ra, Ra the Gang's All Here

This chapter may seem like a deviation from our goal of establishing the connection between Wilcock and Cayce, but as we proceed, it will become obvious how the information presented here is highly relevant in understanding and strengthening this reincarnational claim.

Who exactly is Ra? Where do "they" exist? How did "they" get there? What science makes this possible? Why are they communicating to our planet through Wilcock and others? What's the value for us?

Ra defines itself as a "social memory complex" or "group soul" comprised of potentially billions of individual souls like ourselves who have long since evolved into a unified consciousness in a higher dimension. In the distant past, many of those souls had third-dimensional (or third-density) existences in bodies similar to ours on the planet Venus. Ra is an example of the long-range potential of our own evolution. From their higher vantage point, Ra is available to help humankind through its present period of dimensional shift. Just as many people on our planet choose of their own free will to do God's work as an expression of charity and compassion, Ra, as a group, has chosen of its own volition to assist the "One Infinite Creator" in helping planetary populations evolve.

Some of the individual souls who were part of the Ra group decided to break away with the intention of assisting the evolutionary process of our planet, and entered into a series of earthbound incarnations. One of those souls was Ra-Ta, an Egyptian incarnation circa 10,500 B.C., who happened to be a past life of Edgar Cayce, according to Cayce's own readings. This soul, once incarnate, became trapped in the heavy density of the planet and the "veil of forgetting" that causes those here to lose touch with their true nature. For most of this soul's incarnations, the conscious connection with the group was lost, but Wilcock's work suggests that the Ra group was finally able to establish a communication with Edgar Cayce in his dream state (first when he was under hypnosis and then in his sleep), since Cayce's own Higher Self was of Ra. This concept helps us comprehend Cayce's miracle of omniscience.

According to Ra, each of us has a Higher Self, which acts as an intermediary between our conscious selves and the greater cosmos. Intuitions and inspirations are downloaded through and from our Higher Self to our conscious mind. In a dream state, we can have a more direct, interdimensional connection with our Higher Self. This Higher Self is actually part of our consciousness in the sixth density (the same density as Ra) on an evolutionary track beyond our normal conscious awareness. This is part of the multidimensionality of our being. For some of us, Ra actually takes the position of our Higher Self, with one of the souls within the Ra group fulfilling this role.

According to the *Law of One* series from L/L Research, Ra made a small but pivotal number of direct interventions on our planet, via channeling, dream work, and even physical manifestation. In this chapter, I look at some of these interventions and give an overview of Ra's cosmology as brought forward in the *Law of One* series and expanded upon by Wilcock. I also reveal the evidence that substantiates the claim that this group soul Ra worked with Cayce, L/L Research, and Wilcock. I tie in some of Wilcock's current research that gives credibility to Ra's cosmology and provides a scientific model to explain how reincarnation can actually work.

During the period between 1981 and 1984, L/L Research connected with a stellar* entity that identified itself as Ra and delivered some of the most extraordinary, profound, and intelligent channeled information ever made public. This information happens to be highly relevant to our story of the reincarnation of Edgar Cayce.

Carla Rueckert of the L/L Research Group has hosted meditation groups every Sunday since 1973. She has channeled information consciously and telepathically since 1974, connecting with various discarnate entities. One Sunday, January 15, 1981, something different happened; she lost consciousness and went into a deeper trance than she had ever experienced before. Two others were present at the time: her research partner Don Elkins and Jim McCarty. It was established that Jim would meditate and hold the light during the sessions and transcribe them afterwards, while Don posed questions. As a Ph.D., Elkins' questions were highly scientific queries as to the cosmic workings of the universe. In response to Elkins' first question, a being identified itself as Ra with the following greeting:

I am Ra. I have not spoken through this instrument before. We had to wait until she was precisely tuned, as we send a narrow-band vibration. We greet you in the light and love of our Infinite Creator. We have been called to your group because you have a need for a more advanced approach to what you call seeking the truth. We hope to offer you a somewhat different slant upon the information, which is always and ever the same.[1]

Elkins excitedly prepared question after question, which were answered from a knowledge that no one living on our planet could possibly have. For the next four years, Ra explained in great detail the inner workings of our universe, describing historic events in our

---

*"Stellar" meaning celestial or not of this Earth. Most channels bring in discarnate entities who are still bound to the Earth's collective energy.

solar system that occurred hundreds of thousands of years ago. Ra described the specific ways that creation evolved from formlessness into form and back to formlessness, with great similarities to Cayce's cosmology but in much more detail. Ra described the different phases or cycles of creation and how beings on a higher evolutionary track assist those who are behind, in order to maintain their own momentum and growth. Although Ra is centered in the sixth density, the Ra group fans out into lower densities so they can assist where needed. As Ra evolves through to the seventh density, it is readying itself to reunite with the Creator, such that *"At the seventh level or dimension, we shall, if our humble efforts are sufficient, become one with all, thus having no memory, no identity, no past or future, but existing in the all."*[2]

By combining the work of L/L Research and Wilcock, we are told that Ra claims to be radiating love energy through 90% of all Creation, working specifically with Earthlings via dream work interactions, "subconscious" inspiration, and through direct verbal channels in only five known cases in the last 12,500 years—Ra-Ta, the Egyptian pharaoh Akunhaton, Cayce, L/L Research, and Wilcock. In the density where Ra is centered, one lifetime is equivalent to hundreds of thousands of years, so Ra has been involved with the history of Earth for a very long time.

According to Ra, the entire universe is made up of a spiraling, intelligent light energy coming from the "One Infinite Creator" or God. This spiraling energy is the building block for everything else, from planets to people and all things in between. The universe is divided into eight major *densities* or dimensions. (Cayce's Source also described a universe of eight dimensions.[3]) All life moves through these dimensions as part of the evolutionary process. The densities themselves are composed of living, intelligent energy, and they correspond to planes of existence. Each density has a particular grade or quality of consciousness associated with it, which all entities must attain before they can graduate to that density. We on Earth are involved in the "third density" part of our evolution, where the lessons to be learned build on an initial awareness of self, which pulls one into third density. To enter the fourth density, one must have an experience of love and the unity of all life, and the lessons build on that. Until we have the beginnings of the experience of unity (not a belief, but an experience), we must keep re-embodying, in the process referred to as reincarnation, within the third-density world.

In Ra's model of creation, originally (prior to a physical universe) there was nothing but undifferentiated potentiality, and eventually, in some inexplicable way, "nothing" became intelligent and aware of itself. This awareness and intelligence gave what Ra termed "intelligent infinity" the ability to reproduce itself, and thus began the process of intelligent infinity (also referred to as the "one infinite creator" or God) separating itself into many parts, which eventually became galaxies such as our Milky Way. Each galaxy (or *Logos*, as Ra called it) is a perfect part of the One Creator, but it also has its own "personality" and identity as a conscious being. It can make its own choices and create its own set of natural laws for the planetary systems within its domain. Each Logos creates a basic outline for "archetypes" of evolution that all of its members will follow. If the Logos represents the galaxy, then the members in the domain of those Logoi will include the solar system, the stars, the planets, and, of course, individualized life forms on the planets. Every soul in the galaxy will probably experience, at some point in its development, each of these aspects on its journey back to the original Oneness.

Ra refers to the many millions of stars in a galaxy as *"sub-Logoi,"* meaning that they also are spiritually united with the galaxy. In this cosmology, stars actually have a consciousness and are aware of the entire Octave of densities, and they also have some degree of "personality" and free will in terms of how they carry out the galaxy's plan of soul evolution. This allows them to "set up the game" by, in turn, designing planetary systems that must progressively evolve through the Octave of densities. The Solar Logos sets up exact timelines for when each planet will progress through each density; and thus, as per the Cayce readings, each planet has its specific marching orders from the divine (the Solar Logos); humankind alone is given free will and can choose to defy the will of God.[4] As we will expound on later, our planet is at the end of a 75,000-year cycle, following its "marching orders," and is in the process of undergoing a shift from third density to fourth density.

So, the One Creator separates into galaxies, and the galaxies have some control over how life, such as the stars, evolves within them. Also, each planet has a certain degree of free will in terms of how it will follow the guidelines of its parent star and galaxy. This means that each planet has some say-so in how intelligent life such as us will evolve. (Ra sometimes refers to humans as *"sub-sub-Logoi"* along these same lines, indicating the Oneness of the energy fields of our souls with those of the planet, Sun, and our galaxy.) Throughout our own Galactic Logos and several of its close neighbors, the human bodily form has been chosen as the vehicle for conscious life to express itself on any given planet, hence "The Logos (God) created humans (Man) in Its own image." (Genesis 1:27)[5] The Sun and Earth both have some control over the exact nature of the energy that forms DNA and the humanoid bodies that have now been created as a result.

When Wilcock was first exposed to these communications from Ra, he experienced incredulity. He began researching to see if this idea of a dimensional shift could somehow be validated by current science. In an interview I conducted with Wilcock, published by *The Spirit of Ma'at* in January of 2002, entitled "A Scientific Blueprint for Ascension,"[6] he explains that current scientific research implies that the DNA molecule is "gathered together" from the basic elements on a given planet by this spiraling, intelligent "light" energy that permeates the entire galaxy. We will hear directly from Wilcock about this research in Part Three.

Russian scientists have actually discovered and measured this spiraling energy field in the laboratory, and it is frequently referred to as "torsion *[i.e., twisting, spiraling]* radiation."[7] This radiation has qualities that distinguish it from electromagnetic radiation. Torsion radiation has been shown to be responsive to consciousness, far more so than electromagnetic energy, and it has very healing and spiritually enlightening effects on an organism exposed to it. If you have ever been in the presence of a spiritual healer, visited a sacred site, or walked into a room that had "good vibes," you might have had your own experience of this "spiraling light energy" or torsion radiation.

Ra's cosmology, as presented by both Cayce and L/L Research, was outside the realm of conventional scientific understanding at the time it was originally expressed. But Wilcock believes that this cosmology can be validated today. In Part Three of this book, Wilcock contributes an essay on this subject, "The Evolutionary Engine of Evolution," presenting scientific evidence that can explain Ra's basic outline of planetary evolution.

In describing scientifically the cosmic workings of reincarnation, as well as how dimensional shift affects DNA, Wilcock draws from the work of two Russian scientists, Peter Gariaev and Vladimir P. Poponin.[8] This correlates the relationship between spiraling light energy and the DNA molecule. Their research demonstrates that DNA has the unique property of attracting light (photons) into itself, causing the light to spiral through the molecule instead of traveling in a straight-line path, as one would expect. Gariaev et al.'s major discovery, now known as the "DNA Phantom Effect," is that *once the DNA molecule itself is removed from its holding chamber in Gariaev's laboratory, the light will continue to spiral, all by itself, held by some invisible force field, for up to thirty days thereafter. This "invisible force field" is created by the spiraling torsion wave that originally gathered the DNA around itself.* Even more importantly, the research of Yu V. Dzang Kangeng showed that the spiraling energy forming the DNA could be transferred from one organism to another. In this experiment, a duck was bombarded with high-intensity torsion waves, which were then redirected into a separate chamber. This second chamber contained a hen. In as little as five days of exposure, the eggs in the pregnant hen would undergo changes that created hybrid duck-hen creatures upon hatching. Though these creatures were formed from a hen's body, they had many typical features of a duck, including elongated necks and beaks, larger internal organs, and webbed feet. Gariaev has now replicated this effect by using energetic waves with the "information fields" of DNA in them to transform frog embryos into salamander embryos (also described in Part Three). The discovery of torsion wave radiation and its ability to hold the imprint of DNA (the DNA Phantom Effect) for the first time scientifically substantiates the nebulous abstract concept of spiritual energy—metaphysically referred to as aura, shakti, prana, or chi—as well as creates a scientific model by which reincarnation can operate. Dr. Wilhelm Reich,[9] a contemporary of Sigmund Freud, tried to scientifically explain this energy, calling it "bioenergy fields," which led unfortunately to his condemnation by the scientific community.

Most microbiologists are aware of the existence of transposons or "jumping DNA." These small segments of the DNA molecule can detach from one area and re-attach to another, thus rewriting the code. From this, we can see that our DNA functions somewhat like a computer chip, with different sections that can either be "on" or "off." We can imagine how the torsion-wave energetic pattern of the human soul could, by analogy, actually program DNA, in a manner similar to a computer operating system. One can buy two of the same computers, but by loading different operating systems and software, they will "look" very different on screen and have very different functions once you turn them on.

As a human soul reincarnates from lifetime to lifetime, its torsion-wave "energetic signature" will alter the DNA inherited from the parents. This creates similarities in facial appearance, personality, and body characteristics. It also sets the body up with the necessary physical attributes so that the soul can gain the requisite karmic experience to continue to evolve. The research efforts of Joseph Myers, P.E. (Professional Engineer),[10] and Dr. Walter Semkiw[11] have explored these connections extensively through demonstrating the possible reincarnations of many famous people in history by comparing their current facial characteristics with their presumed historical counterparts. This gives new meaning to the old saying about how married couples start to look more like each other the longer they are together. As they continue to be exposed to each other over time, their individual soul vibrations intermingle, and the resulting torsion waves that they radiate will subtly rewrite the other's DNA. Wilcock's model helps us to understand how similar facial features can be passed down from one lifetime to another, in this way leading to the striking physical similarities between Wilcock and Cayce. Their commonly shared soul would carry the uniquely coded torsion wave that would ultimately program Wilcock's DNA.

According to the Russian findings, this spiraling "torsion" energy could actually be the substance of our human souls, and is therefore the precursor to the DNA molecule itself. It already exists in the fabric of space and time before any physical life emerges on a given planet. In the evolution of life forms, the gentle, organized spiraling pressures of "torsion waves" on physical matter will naturally gather the available elements into the basic building blocks for life—for example the amino acids, which eventually form into "de-oxy-ribo-nucleic acid," or DNA. This could explain how the chain of command operates from the original Logos to our individualized souls and bodies. Interestingly, one of the scientists who first described the DNA molecule, Prof. Francis Crick,[12] has proven that DNA is far, far too complex to have evolved by random chance. This new model put forth separately by Wilcock and L/L Research gives us a feasible explanation as to how the DNA would have been formatted.

An understanding of this model also allows us to grasp how certain metaphysical systems may work. For example, this could explain how the planets' astrological positions can actually impact an entity. Each planet is a sub-Logos of the galaxy with its own unique intelligent patterns and archetypes as a conscious entity.

At any particular moment of an entity's birth, the torsion waves emanating from the galactic center are passing through the energetic field of the Sun and on through each of the planets. As an entity leaves the protective shell of its mother's energy field in her womb through the birthing process, it receives an imprint of that exact planetary configuration at the moment of birth into its DNA/energy body. Thus, a chain of causality links each of us, via our DNA, to the consciousness of the entire cosmos. Our souls time our births so as to incarnate during a planetary configuration that is most auspicious for our body/mind/spirit development, in relation to the lessons we then choose to learn/master in that incarnation.

According to Ra, empty space is not really empty but is filled with this invisible torsion wave energy at different degrees of concentration. Then, as a star or planet drifts through the galaxy, it passes through different concentrations in very exact intervals of time, with precise cycles that can vary in length from thousands to millions of years. As a planet moves through periods of high concentration of these torsion waves, a transformation is effected in the DNA structures on the planet, which causes more highly evolved forms to rapidly replace less evolved forms of life. Ample evidence of this is seen in the fossil records, where evolution has been shown to occur in sudden jolts rather than as a gradual process. This effect has been named "punctuated equilibrium"[13] by mainstream scientists, even though they are unaware of the causes behind the effect.

In this context, it is notable that we have never found the "missing link" in human evolution that could support the Darwinian model of gradual evolution. For some reason unknown to mainstream science, about 75,000 to 100,000 years ago the human organism had a massive increase in the size of its brain and the elegance and usefulness of its body. According to Ra, this was brought about by spontaneous DNA evolution, caused by our Sun passing into an area of higher energy in the galaxy, comparable to the increased energy of the current "solar cycle" which is creating a dimensional shift and supposedly reprogramming human DNA. Some modern channelers have explained this phenomenon as resulting from a "photon belt," which according to Wilcock is conceptually an approximation of the truth.

When this energetic "upgrade" occurred in our own history, the cycle of third-density life began on Earth. In our galaxy, third density represents the beginning of the self-aware humanoid form, whereas the "second density" animal kingdom operates on more of an instinctive group consciousness. In the *Law of One* series, Ra said that third-density experiences for any given planet occur in *"major cycles"*[14] of approximately 25,000 years each. This length of time corresponds to how long it takes a star to pass through a given zone of energy as it orbits the galactic center, and Wilcock believes that his scientific research validates this concept. At the end of each of these 25,000-year cycles, the highest possible grade of vibration is reached for the third density. At this time, entities going through their reincarnational process can graduate into higher densities via a transition that Ra refers to as "harvest" if they have attained a sufficient grade of loving vibrations within themselves and are ready and willing to give up attachments to their third-density experience.

The longest period of time allotted for an entity to graduate from the third density is three "major cycles" of 25,000 years each. After these three "major cycles," the energy of the entire planet automatically becomes upgraded by the new zone of galactic energy and moves into the next density. This change occurs whether the inhabitants are ready for it or not, so beings from higher densities, like Ra, make an effort to prepare people for the change without infringing on their free will, such as would occur if they were to make a direct, formal announcement of their presence. As we said previously, third-density humans experience themselves as separate from each other and are preoccupied with issues of survival and self-awareness. Fourth-density humans have the conscious awareness that they are part of each other and connected by love. Supposedly, a third-density body could not live on a fourth-density planet, as its DNA would no longer be supported by the torsion waves in the area. Wilcock's own readings have often said that our bodies will simply disappear from third density as we transmute into fourth, similar to the ascension of Jesus, and that this is what could be thought of as death, even though we perceive a continuous experience the whole time.

Of course, each major cycle of experience for a given entity, such as a human being, will include many separate lifetimes or physical incarnations. If a third-density planet has reached the end of a cycle and is about to shift into fourth density, then those inhabitants who are not ready to graduate will end up reincarnating on a different third-density planet. This does not happen "by accident" or simple conscious intention, but rather involves an intelligently guided transfer of the souls themselves and the appropriate genetic material for the creation of physical bodies that will match up with the souls. This "planet-hopping" process is managed by groups of interplanetary cosmic beings such as Ra. Because star systems are continually moving into different zones of energy throughout the galaxy, there is always work to be done. From the reference point of Earth, these beings are known as angels, celestial beings, brotherhoods of light, ascended masters, or perhaps the Lords of Karma.

Ra has identified a group of these beings as "The Confederation of Planets in Service of the One Infinite Creator,"[15] and they govern a section of our galaxy that we now inhabit. They are collectively responsible for managing the transfer and evolution of souls from one planet to another. Typically, those who evolved together on a certain planet are kept together when moved to a new planet. If a certain percentage of entities in third density did not make graduation after three major cycles, then they would be moved to this other planet as a group. However, at the time that Earth was being populated, the members of this Confederation saw that there were several leftover groups from various planets of third-density "cycle repeaters" that were too small in number to justify terra-forming an entire planet just for them.

Therefore, Earth was chosen as a unique experiment, wherein "cycle repeaters" from many different planetary populations would be combined together under one roof. It is uncommon for a planet to have as much racial diversity as we do on Earth; for example, just within the Caucasian races there are broad differences in appearance that can be seen among Slavic, Mediterranean, and Western European peoples. The same is true in the Asian races, with Chinese, Filipinos, and Japanese as three of the clearest examples. The reason for all of this genetic diversity is that these souls have come here from different planets; the Chinese people, for example, are said in the *Law of One* to have come from a planetary system surrounding the star Deneb. Thus, their souls originated from stars and planets that had slightly different "personalities" in terms of how the DNA was structured to form the appearance of the human being. These basic differences cannot and should not be erased, since according to Cayce they are all aspects of the inner character and harmony of the soul. This information on the origins of Earth's population is derived from the Cayce readings, the *Law of One* series, and Wilcock's subsequent investigations.

Ra explains that this great "experiment" went awry, in the sense that not a single entity graduated after the end of our first major cycle some 50,000 years ago.[16] Normally, it is expected that perhaps 10 to 20% of the people make it after the first cycle. At the end of our second major cycle some 25,000 years ago, only 120 entities were ready for graduation, and they chose to stay behind and help out the others. Normally, at least 60% of the people would graduate after the second major cycle on a third-density planet, leaving the small remaining percentage of people to finally get clear about the importance of love before the end of the third and final cycle.

By the end of the second major cycle on Earth, it became alarmingly clear that the "experiment" of combining all the cycle repeaters was not working. Great spiritual suffering was occurring, and a dramatic form of assistance was required in order to try to turn things around. As a result, massive numbers of entities from the fourth, fifth, and especially the sixth density—including those from the Ra group itself—volunteered to take on human incarnations in order to help. Ra refers to these souls as "Wanderers," and if you feel an intuitive connection with this idea, then you might be one of the nearly 100 million "wanderer souls" who now walk the face of the Earth. Wanderers are not necessarily expected to "do" anything or to "save the world" by their own efforts, but by simply remaining in a physical body and preferably by maintaining a joyful state of mind, they have a tremendously beneficial energetic effect on the mass consciousness of humanity. This, in turn, can dramatically increase the number of souls who will qualify for graduation from third density to fourth.

Earth is actually the fourth planet in our solar system to have hosted third-density life forms. Venus, Mars, and Maldek all had third-density life in the past.[17] Maldek was a planet that ended up exploding into fragments that exist now as the Asteroid Belt. At some point millions of years ago, Venus was the first planet to be populated with humanoid life forms. The inhabitants were going through their third- to fourth-density transition and were being assisted by a group soul that had already completed this same evolutionary step. About 17% of those third-density inhabitants of Venus graduated or "ascended" and went on to evolve through the fourth, fifth, and sixth densities. This un-named sixth-density "social memory complex" or group soul continued to assist the Venusians in their ascension process in the same manner as Ra is assisting planet Earth in present time.

"Ascension" is another name for the process that beings go through as they change densities. As the Venusians ascended through the densities and got closer to merging their essences with the One Infinite Creator, they also started to lose their separateness and the need for individuated physical bodies. This same group of ascended Venusians now exists in the sixth density as the "social memory complex" Ra.[18]

The second planet to host third-density humans was known as Maldek, which exploded, according to the *Law of One* series, in a freak worldwide nuclear catastrophe brought about by war. Normally such events are regulated by the Confederation of Planets and are not permitted to occur, since they violate the free will of many innocent beings throughout the entire planetary system, but not even the Confederation is perfect. In this case, the nuclear conflagration occurred spontaneously and unexpectedly, and the planet's explosion created fragments that formed comets and the Asteroid Belt, causing huge damage throughout the solar system.

The severe trauma of the inhabitants of Maldek from this disaster caused them to go into a "social memory complex knot or tangle of fear"[19] that lasted for more than 200,000 years before it could be broken. As a group, they then decided to take on a series of incarnations in bodies with drastic physical limitations, which would create "karmic alleviation" by preventing them from having the ability to produce any advanced civilization capable of self-destruction. These were the first entities to people the Earth in the form of the Neanderthal humanoids.

The third and final planet to host third-density humanoids before the Earth was Mars. Ample evidence of an advanced civilization still rests amidst the red sands there, including pyramids and monuments with precise geometric relationships to each other and to the planet itself, as documented in the work of Richard C. Hoagland,[20] among others. The Martians were progressing fairly well until they too had a worldwide catastrophe caused by war. In this case they did not destroy the planet itself but rather blew off its atmosphere, creating the parched, desolate wasteland that we now see. The souls and genetic material of the Martians were moved forward thousands and thousands of years in time for placement on Earth at the beginning of its first third-density cycle about 75,000 years ago. Prior to that time, second-density life existed on Earth. "The second density is the density of the higher plant life and animal life which exists without the upward drive towards the infinite."[21] At this time, Ra existed in the sixth density, the level of "compassionate wisdom," and was beginning its service to Earth, as it assisted in the genetic "packaging" and transmigration of the Martians.

Aside from helping with the Martian transmigration 75,000 years ago, Ra has intervened in Earth's history in quite a few other circumstances, as per the *Law of One* channelings. Ra has proclaimed: "In the remaining part of this cycle we have never gone from your fifth dimension."[22] Ra extends into the lower densities from the sixth, are able to work more directly with humanity.

yce's readings were delivered to him by what he identi-
the "Source." Throughout the 14,000 Cayce readings
there were 386 references to the "Law of One." The books released
by L/L Research were called *Ra, the Law of One,* because the Law
of One is an intrinsic principle of Ra's cosmology. At the outset of the
Law of One sessions with L/L Research, there was a specific reference to an intervention where Ra, the social memory complex, con-
tacted an entity who became an Egyptian high priest in 10,500 B.C.
Ra had a telepathic connection with this high priest, and together
they built the pyramids from levitation of rock. Over time, with
humanity's tendency to put spiritual teachers on pedestals and to
worship heroes, this entity became recognized in Egyptian history
as Ra, the Sun God. The following passages are taken from *The Law
of One,* Book One:

> The covering of our physical body complex had a golden lus-
> ter. In this form we decided to come among your peoples. Your
> peoples were much unlike us in physical appearance. Thus we
> did not mix well with the population and were obviously other
> than they. Our visit was relatively short. This was when we
> built the pyramids. When we chose this mission among your
> peoples, we would have been perceived as light had we arrived
> on Earth in our natural form.[23]

> We now feel a great responsibility for helping remove certain
> distortions that have been given to the Law of One. We, as
> social memory complex or group soul, made contact with a
> race on your planet that you call Egyptians. We spoke to one
> who heard and understood [this is the reference that ties Ra
> to Cayce's previous life as Ra-Ta] and was in a position to
> decree the Law of One. However, the priests and the peoples
> of that era quickly distorted our message, robbing it of the
> compassion with which unity is informed.[24]

Thus according to the *Law of One* series, Ra takes credit, via a series of direct physical manifestations in Egypt, for building the Great Pyramid (for use as a healing chamber) by levitating the rocks:

> **Ra:** One can speak to more well-tuned higher bodies, be they rock or human. With this connection made, a request may be given. The intelligence of infinite rock-ness communicates to its physical vehicle or body, and that splitting and moving which is desired is then carried out.

> **Questioner:** Why not create it as a whole instead of with blocks?

> **Ra:** We did not want to be worshipped as builders of a miraculous pyramid. Thus it appears to be made, not thought.[25]

In Book Three, Ra describes the function of the pyramids as an initiation chamber to help open the energy centers of those inside:

> **Ra:** The concept of initiation demands the centering of the being upon the seeking of the Creator. The initiation in the Queen's chamber [of the Great Pyramid] involved the abandoning of self to such desire to know the Creator in full that the purified instreaming light is drawn in balanced fashion through all energy centers, or chakras, meeting in the inner eye chakra and opening the gate to intelligent infinity. Then true life is experienced, or, as your people call it, resurrection.[26]

The connection with Cayce, established in the *Law of One* series, is quite specific and extraordinary. Cayce, in his own readings, refers to one of his early lives on Earth as Ra-Ta, an Egyptian high priest, during whose life the pyramids were built by levitation of stone in 10,500 B.C.

When Cayce was asked exactly what the construction technique was for the Great Pyramid, his Source gave the following answer: "By the use of those forces in nature as make for iron to swim. Stone floats in the air in the same manner."[27] According to the reading, the purpose of the pyramid was as a "hall of initiation."

This was the first significant clue I uncovered that linked David Wilcock and Carla Rueckert to Edgar Cayce. The correspondence between the readings of L/L Research and Edgar Cayce was very precise. Both set the time period of the construction of the pyramids as 10,500 B.C., both talked about levitation of rock, and both referred to an Egyptian high priest. My heart skipped a beat as Wilcock's story became more plausible. The existence of Ra was seemingly validated by two completely separate sources of channeled information. I began to seriously consider that Ra might have been Cayce's "Source." I did a search on the Cayce CD-ROM, and to my surprise I found numerous incidents in the lifetime of Ra-Ta where Ra-Ta and a being named Ra existed concurrently. The Cayce references and examples of these incidents are documented in Chapter Nine.

The Egyptian priest referred to by Ra in the *Law of One* series seems to have been Ra-Ta, one of Edgar Cayce's earliest lifetimes on this planet. If Ra was Cayce's main Source, it couldn't be revealed to him in his own readings due to his conservative Christian upbringing. The *Law of One* series never named the Egyptian high priest, but when compared to Cayce's past-life reading on himself, it would be a logical conclusion that the priest in the L/L Research channeling and Cayce's Ra-Ta were one and the same. Carla Rueckert herself was never aware that Cayce had a past life as Ra-Ta, and how this corresponded with the Law of One material, until this author brought it to her attention twenty years after the information came through.

Notably, unlike her prior channeling work, Rueckert fell into a completely unconscious state during the Ra sessions and did not remember anything that transpired once she came back. As part of my own due diligence, I had to find out whether Rueckert might have uncovered this bit of obscure information concerning Ra-Ta in the

Cayce readings, and then remembered it subconsciously during her channeling. I made it a point to meet her personally when she was giving a lecture in Laughlin, Nevada, in March of 2002. When I queried her about the Cayce correspondence to her channeled Ra information, I learned that she never knew that the Cayce readings referred to the time period of the creation of the pyramids or the manner of their construction by levitation of rock. She related to me that her only exposure to Cayce was connected to his alternative medical remedies.

It is important to mention here that Wilcock's research has shown that the *Law of One* series has a great deal of scientific credibility and coherence, far outside the scope of a person like Rueckert to have produced by her imagination alone. In most cases, there was no way to scientifically validate any of the Ra material twenty years ago, as the scientific back-up simply did not exist then. It is virtually impossible that Rueckert could have produced the sophisticated answers of Ra from her own consciousness to the inquiring mind of the Ph.D. who was questioning her, and thereby create such a far-reaching, internally consistent, and specific cosmology over the course of three years. She was not even allowed to read any of the results of the first twenty sessions, as Dr. Elkins wanted to maintain scientific controls. Only after L/L Research finally asked Ra if it was OK for Carla to read the words was permission granted.

Furthermore, Wilcock's compilations and research have revealed answers to many of the unsolved physics questions that boggled the minds of the original L/L Research team, such as the meaning of the term "the spiraling line of light." Ra often used words (correctly) that no one in L/L Research had ever heard of, which required an unabridged dictionary to verify. In Book Five of the *Law of One* series, especially in Session #102 on March 22, 1983, Ra displayed the ability to perform "medical readings" that were similar to Cayce's, using technical medical terms unknown to Rueckert consciously. This session reads almost exactly like a traditional Cayce reading, giving a precise diagnosis of Rueckert's own medical condition and supplying suggestions for treatment, including the exact name of the local doctor to go to—Dr. Arthur Schoen, MD. Though it took some time, as no one in L/L Research had heard of this man, they were able to find him once they figured out how to spell the last name from its pronunciation in the reading. Dr. Elkins then wanted Dr. Schoen to consult Ra's words as part of Carla's treatment, but Schoen was spooked by the whole thing and refused to read it, though his experience proved useful.

Many more parallels unfold in the next chapters as we plunge deeper into the life of Ra-Ta, who apparently was "the one who heard and understood" in the *Law of One* series. We will also show how well Wilcock fulfills Cayce's own prophecy regarding the return of Ra-Ta in 1998.

Summary of important points

1. Ra is a group soul or social memory complex who evolved from a group of 17% of the third-density inhabitants of Venus, who ascended into fourth density and higher densities thereafter.

2. Ra exists in the sixth density now, increasingly approaching Oneness with the Creator. Ra is in service to humankind in its evolution to higher density, just as another higher-density group soul assisted the individuated souls of the Ra group on Venus when Venus went through its dimensional shift.

3. Most of Ra's participation has been through psychic and dream interaction with Earthlings, although in 10,500 B.C., according to the L/L Research data, Ra assisted a priest who had an affinity with the "Law of One." This priest, never specifically identified by L/L Research, appears to have been Cayce in a previous incarnation, according to Cayce's own readings. Ra

built the pyramids during this period by levitation of rock. Cayce also said that the pyramids were built by levitation in this same time period and for the same purpose as described by Ra, though Carla Rueckert was unaware of these connections until the author revealed them to her, some twenty years after her channeling of Ra's words on the subject.

4. According to the L/L Research material, the creation of the pyramids and the teaching of the Law of One, implemented by Ra, did not work out as planned. Those in power abused Ra's teachings, as expressed through the high priest, and used them for self-serving purposes. As a result of creating distortions in the evolutionary track of Earth, Ra has felt bound by their sense of honor to hang in with us and make reparations.

5. Ra apparently manifested a series of bodies in Egypt different from a normal-looking human body; those of Ra were tall, delicate, and had a golden luster.

The fact of the matter is that Ra is the collective Over-soul of which David is a part. There! We have said it.

Now that essentially means that Ra has always been the guiding principle behind David's works. Based on the history of his past incarnations, this should not be difficult to see, and we do not need to explicate on these matters any further, for our purpose is not to aggrandize David, merely to illustrate the point.

—Ra/Wilcock, November 11, 1999

Chapter

6

The Story of Ra-Ta

The Edgar Cayce readings detailed Cayce's incarnation as an Egyptian high priest named Ra-Ta in 10,500 B.C. As I researched the Wilcock/Cayce connection, I learned some fascinating things about Ra-Ta that were not revealed in the Cayce readings. This additional information was uncovered by comparing the data from the *Law of One* series, the Cayce readings, the Egyptian myth of Ra the Sun God, and the hypnotic regression of Anne Holbein by Jess Stearn, as related in Stearn's book about Cayce, *Intimates Through Time: Edgar Cayce's Mysteries of Reincarnation*.[1] (Anne Holbein had a reading by Cayce where it was revealed that she had a past life with Ra-Ta.) The comparisons among these various sources strongly imply that Ra-Ta the man was unfortunately deified into the legend of Ra the Sun God, since the Egyptian priesthoods "quickly distorted" Ra's message and "robbed it of the compassion with which unity is informed" [*Law of One*, Book One, Session 1, p. 66]. Ra never intended to be worshipped as a god; he was entirely focused on the Law of One, which states that all entities are manifestations of the One Infinite Creator, and hence no entity is above or below any other, regardless of their density of origin.

If my conclusions are correct, Ra, the sixth-density "social memory complex" channeled by L/L Research, was also the oversoul or

Higher Self of Ra-Ta. Hence, if Ra was the oversoul or Higher Self of Ra-Ta, then Ra would continue to be the oversoul for future incarnations. This would include Edgar Cayce and David Wilcock. Ra, the social memory complex, is a common thread running through the stories of Ra-Ta, Cayce, Rueckert, and Wilcock. This chapter explains the progression of knowledge that led me to draw these conclusions.

The Story of Ra according to Egyptian Mythology

Ra was considered one of the great gods of heaven, one of the creators of our universe. According to legend, Ra created the rivers and mountains of our planet, and lastly he created mankind. Then Ra took the form of a man and became a great pharaoh in Egypt who reigned for thousands of years. He was called a sun god, said to command a chariot that rode across the sky during the day.

Isis was a woman who was desirous of Ra's power, which was said to be in the form of a secret word that gave Ra the ability to perform miracles. Isis caused a serpent to bite Ra and make him ill. She had the remedy for Ra's illness, and she cajoled him to share the secret word with her in exchange for healing him, which gave her miraculous powers as well.[2] In researching Ra the Sun God, I discovered the following quotes from the Internet referring to the mythological story of Ra:

> Thus we see that even to the great god Ra were attributed all the weakness and frailty of mortal man; and that "gods" and "goddesses" were classed with beasts and reptiles, which could die and perish.[3]

As Ra grew older:

The time was drawing near when he must leave the Earth to reign forever in the heavens, letting the younger gods rule in his place. For dwelling in the form of a man, of a Pharaoh of Egypt, Ra was losing his wisdom; yet he continued to reign....4

The Story of Ra-Ta:
The Edgar Cayce Readings

According to the Cayce readings, Ra-Ta was a hybrid birth, a cross between the "gods from that area" (perhaps the "golden" manifestations of the Ra group in human form?) and a human mother. He was born in a "less civilized" area ruled by the tribe of "Zu" near the Caspian Sea, which appears to have been Sumeria. As a result of his hybrid parentage, he was an unusual-looking child with pale white skin and blue eyes. Because of his striking appearance and the fact that his mother was not married, the elders of the tribe eventually exiled the two of them.

Ra-Ta and his mother left with a group of assistants to protect them. Over time, they made their way to the slopes of what is now Mount Ararat in Turkey. As Ra-Ta grew up, it became clear that he had prophetic abilities and could channel very accurate psychic information. At twenty-one years of age he had a prophetic dream that a worldwide cataclysm and pole shift would occur in the not-too-distant future. Most of the island continent of "Poseidia" (part of Atlantis) was going to be inundated, and his own area would also suffer cataclysms. His prophetic abilities suggested that Egypt would be the safest place to go for weathering these Earth changes. When the Earth's poles shifted, Egypt would be the balance-point for their movement.

Ra-Ta communicated this prophecy to the King's son, Arart, and a pioneering group of nine hundred people led by Arart with Ra-Ta as their spiritual leader made the journey from Turkey to Egypt.

After a long and arduous trip, they arrived in the Egyptian city of Luz, where eventually the local people accepted and exalted them. Arart was proclaimed King, and Ra-Ta was accepted as their high priest.

Ra-Ta was able to perform many miracles of healing in special temples dedicated to this purpose, and became beloved by the people. Over a period of time, he instituted spiritual and moral reforms, including a code that supported monogamous marriages.

As part of what was "really a very busy life" [Cayce reading 294–148],[5] Ra-Ta traveled [apparently in an Atlantean anti-gravitational aircraft, the existence of which the Cayce readings often mentioned[6]] and interacted with the Atlanteans and other cultures over a ten-year period. By this time, many Atlanteans had received visions of the coming inundation and were emigrating in droves from the island continent of Poseidia. Furthermore, the Atlanteans wished to create a storehouse of their accumulated knowledge and wisdom so that it would not perish, and three places were chosen to move these records to, Egypt being one. Ra-Ta had a close liaison with the Atlanteans, as he himself had previous lifetimes in Atlantis.

On one of his return trips from Atlantis to Egypt, Ra-Ta found that his sacred temples had been converted into sexual playgrounds. He vehemently condemned these actions as being against the Law of One. Certain individuals became very angry with him and started planning a way to bring about his removal from power. They hatched a plot to discredit him by having a temple dancer named Isris seduce him, which would cause Ra-Ta to violate his own moral code of monogamy. The plan ultimately succeeded, except that Ra-Ta and Isris fell in love in the process.

Jealousy and the desire for revenge led to the banishment of Ra-Ta, Isris, and 231 followers who decided to go with them. They ended up in what now is called Ethiopia and what was then called Nubia. Ra-Ta reflected with regret on the monumental consequences of his dalliance. But regardless of where Ra-Ta lived, he carried his quiet strength and compassionate nature, and he became a beloved teacher of spiritual principles in his new home in exile.

Meanwhile, King Arart was losing control of his people without the calming influence of Ra-Ta. There was discontent and mob rule, and the Atlanteans' hopes and dreams for the future of Egypt were crumbling. The King, having regrets over his banishment of Ra-Ta, finally rescinded the banishment decree after nine years. Upon return-ing, Ra-Ta was once again exalted, and the King willingly allowed himself to become just a figurehead. Ra-Ta became an inspiration for all; Isris, who was now his wife, was treated as a queen and his spiritual equal. Those who wanted an audience with Ra-Ta had to make their appointments through her.

During this period after the return from banishment, Ra-Ta built the pyramids. By some esoteric means, the stones were levitated and set in place. Peace and harmony reigned once again in Egypt. Ra-Ta went on to live an unusually long life. The Cayce readings attrib-ute his unusual lifespan to the time he spent inside the pyramid rejuvenating himself. Ra-Ta was now known as Ra, and Isris was known as Isis. Ra-Ta continued to create scandal, as once he was allowed to return to Egypt, he ignored his previous decrees of monogamy and had many sexual partners. This would prove to be his undoing, karmically bonding him to continually reincarnate on Earth until the end of the 25,000-year cycle.

> Then there came the period when all the pyramid or memorial was complete. Ra, having finished his work, ascended into the mount—and was borne away. [Cayce reading 294–152][7]

Hidden within another Cayce reading [5755–1][8] is the obvious inference that Ra-Ta was, in fact, the same entity recognized in Egypt-ian mythology as Ra the Sun God. Ra-Ta is said to have come from the infinity forces or the Sun, and in their ignorance his followers became "sun worshippers."

Ra in the *Law of One* Series

Ra's origin and influence according to the *Law of One* series were explained in detail in the previous chapter.

Ra and Ra-Ta as per a Regression Experience

Jess Stearn, author of *The Sleeping Prophet,* released a book in 1993 called *Intimates Through Time: Edgar Cayce's Mysteries of Reincarnation.* Stearn decided to find someone who had previously lived in the time of Ra-Ta and had been informed of this in a reading from Cayce. His subject was Anne Grey Holbein, a friend of Cayce's as well as a close associate in his past Ra-Ta incarnation. Stearn's plan was to hypnotize and regress her back to the time of Ra-Ta and get some "eyewitness accounts." What follows is excerpted from that regression when Stearn asked her what Ra-Ta had come for:

> To bring about a unity of minds, to establish a oneness, to have all races know they were one and the same. For to that land he built, there came people from all over to study with one who knew the secrets of the universe.... He wanted everyone to develop their inner capacities, for as the individual grew, so did the nation. No leader in Egypt had thought like that before. He was Ra then. He shortened his name to one syllable. It mated his energy to the sun.[9]

She also talks of Ra's building of the pyramid:

He was able to move the great stones of the pyramids as if they were made of cork.... He talked to the stones. He would point and say, "I want you there" and the stone moved there.... The thought of death never bothered him; he never spoke of it.[10]

Then one day Ra was gone. No body, no ashes, no funeral:

The older people said not to fret about it. His energy would always be with us.[11]

I believe that the parallels among these four separate sources validate my conclusions.

Isis and Isris: According to Egyptian mythology, Isis coaxed a serpent to bite Ra the Sun God and poison him. In the Edgar Cayce story of Ra-Ta, Isris was the temple dancer who seduced Ra-Ta and caused his fall from grace. The serpent's connection with temptation and seduction is apparent. The similarity of the names Isis and Isris is obvious, and in the Cayce story, Ra-Ta eventually became known as Ra, and Isris became known as Isis.[12]

The physical appearance of Ra-Ta/Ra: In the Cayce readings, Ra-Ta was described as "a very unusual child, in that he had pale white skin and blue eyes in an area where the others did not look this way."[13] In the *Law of One* series, Ra said that "We were tall and somewhat delicate. The covering of our physical body complex had a golden luster. In this form we decided to come among your peoples."[14] In the Jess Stearn regression of Anne Holbein, Ra-Ta "... had a magnetic power, enhanced by a striking appearance. He seemed to give off a golden aura."[15]

The connection between Ra-Ta and Ra the Sun God: In *A Seer Out of Season,* Harmon Bro indicates that Cayce was actually aware of his connection to Ra, the Sun God:

He [Cayce] appeared to take the Egyptian epic seriously, though not obsessed with it, it seemed to be a burden on him. The saga made him a figure of world history.[16]

It is definitely not the intention of Ra, the group soul, to be recognized and worshipped as a god by humankind. They would define themselves as a partner/friend in assisting us, as a group as well as individually, in the evolution of our consciousnesses. The Cayce readings were very careful not to overly aggrandize Ra-Ta's importance. In Reading 281–43, Cayce said that the fact that Ra-Ta might have been looked upon in an exalted way was due to a misunderstanding as to the nature of his more advanced spiritual evolution. But, the specific connection between Ra-Ta and Ra the Sun God was implied in a more obscure Cayce reading: "[T]he activities of that entity [Ra-Ta] were turned into that influence called the sun worshippers." [Cayce reading 5755–1]

Ra's reparations according to the *Law of One* series: In the *Law of One* series, Ra, the group soul, indicated that their/its manifestation in the physical had been a mistake and did not bring about the intended results:

It was our naive belief that we could teach by direct contact. These cultures were already closely aligned with an all-embracing belief in the live-ness or consciousness of all. We came and were welcomed by the peoples we wished to serve. We attempted to aid them in technical ways having to do with healing of mind/body/spirit complex through the use of the crystal. Thus were the pyramids created. However, it turned out that those in power reserved this technology for themselves. This was not intended by the Law of One. We left your peoples. However, we have never left your vibration due to our responsibility for the changes in consciousness we first caused and then found distorted in ways not relegated to the Law of One.[17]

Ra, in making reparations for the "distortions" created during their association with Ra-Ta, continued their work with Edgar Cayce and was the Source (my postulate) that brought Cayce his dream information. Ra did not inform Wilcock that he was Cayce's reincarnation until an entire year after Wilcock had perfected his channeling, including having issued scores of accurate, documented future prophecies. In the Wilcock reading that revealed the Cayce connection, there was a strong suggestion that Ra had also been working very closely with Cayce. This can be seen in the following excerpt from the reading where David's Source announced that David was the reincarnation of Edgar Cayce, on November 26, 1997. (A greater portion of this reading is included in Chapter Eight.)

> Be it known that you are not as configured this time for medical readings and for individual one-on-one counseling. This is one of the involvements that we have wished to change.
> —Ra/Wilcock[18]

This reading makes it quite clear that Ra was in control of the "configuration" of Cayce and Wilcock's connection to the other side. Ra couldn't identify itself to Cayce. And Ra didn't identify itself to Wilcock for a period of well over a year after he was told that he had been Edgar Cayce in a past life.

Ra, Ra-Ta, Cayce, Wilcock — A Possible Scenario

Each of the above sources brings its own clues to the actual story of Ra, Ra-Ta, Cayce, and Wilcock and helps us build a possible scenario to explain these correspondences as Ra-Ta's incarnational track on Earth. Beginning 25,000 years ago, a variety of individuated souls from the Ra group volunteered to separate from the complex and take an incarnation on Earth to attempt to speed up humanity's evolution, with the foreknowledge that they would very likely become karmically bound into the reincarnational cycles of the planet. According to L/L Research:

> The desire to serve must be distorted towards a great deal of purity of mind and what you call foolhardiness or bravery. The challenge and danger to the Wanderer is that it will forget its mission, become karmically involved, and thus be swept into the maelstrom and turbulence which it had intended to avert.[19]

One such volunteer soul incarnated in Egypt around 10,500 B.C. as Ra-Ta and apparently was more successful at penetrating the "veil of forgetfulness" than most other Wanderers of his time. Ra-Ta had an unusual physical appearance due to his hybrid genes. He had the ability to prophesy, perform miracles, and heal. One of these miracles was the creation of the pyramids by "levitation of rock," in conjunction with other manifested feats of Ra.

Because of his unnatural abilities, he became recognized historically as Ra the Sun God. Ra-Ta was able to teach esoteric knowledge and advanced technology, but those in power later tried to keep his teachings secret so they could gain advantage over the general population and thus use the teachings for self-serving purposes. Eventually Ra-Ta became caught in the reincarnational trap of the Earth's third density. The Cayce readings largely attribute this to his affairs with women. Wilcock related to me that when he was under hypnosis with his friend Skip, he obliquely mentioned a former life in Atlantis where he had become karmically bound to the Earth by having too much pride in his scientific achievements, considering himself intellectually superior to others. Wilcock received this information nearly half a year before he was made aware of a connection to Edgar Cayce and had no idea that Ra-Ta was the entity under discussion.

As a result of this karmic entrapment, Ra-Ta lost the memory of his origins. Ra "the group memory complex" kept a monitor on Ra-Ta as he commenced his Earth incarnations. They were looking for opportunities to interface and reconnect.

Ra, the group soul, was finally able to make contact with Ra-Ta when he was born as the entity we know as Edgar Cayce. They appear to have been able to communicate with Cayce from their higher dimension when he slept and could be responsible for his psychic and prophetic powers. The Cayce Readings made the prediction that the priest—Ra-Ta—"would enter" in 1998. In 1992 David Wilcock began recording his dreams. Four years later, Ra, the group soul, once again made conscious contact, which Wilcock called his "Dream Voice." David recognized his connection with Edgar Cayce just prior to 1998, on November 26, 1997. David Wilcock is taking on a role in the present similar to that which he had in the past when, as Ra-Ta/Ra, he gave the warning for coming inundations and led his small group from Turkey to the safe land of Egypt. After Wilcock's many land-bound incarnations on Earth, he is far removed from the powers he had as Ra-Ta, but his psychic connection with Ra, the social memory complex, is still intact, allowing him to bring forth essential, specific information to assist in humanity's future. In this incarnation, Ra/Wilcock is giving us notice of the impending dimensional shift and explaining how to approach it in the most positive manner.

Before I go more fully into the life of David Wilcock and how his own process of self-discovery brought him to the realization of his connection with Ra and Cayce, I've inserted a chapter on the Great Pyramid of Giza. Both Cayce and Rueckert independently channeled the incredible claim that the pyramids were constructed by "levitation of rock" in 10,500 B.C. I decided to research the creation of the pyramids and see how the historical view compares to the fascinating intent and meaning of Rueckert's and Cayce's entranced words.

He was able to move the great stones of the pyramids as if they were made of cork.... He talked to the stones. He would point and say, "I want you there" and the stone moved there.

—Anne Holbein, from the Jess Stearn book
Intimates Through Time: Edgar Cayce's Mysteries of Reincarnation (pp. 84–85)

The Great Pyramid at Giza

The Great Pyramid is composed of over 2 million blocks of limestone which weigh from 2 to 70 tons each. Its base covers over 13 acres and its volume is around 90,000,000 cubic feet.

Chapter

7

The Great Pyramid of Giza

This chapter presents some background information on the Great Pyramid of Giza (Egypt), from historical, mythological, scientific, and esoteric perspectives, allowing us to evaluate how these perspectives interface with the information from Cayce and the *Law of One* series. According to the channeled utterances of Rueckert and Cayce, Ra built the pyramids by the "levitation of rock" in 10,500 B.C.[1]

Conventionally, it is believed that the Egyptian Pharaoh Khufu built the Great Pyramid in approximately 3000 B.C. The Association for Research and Enlightenment or A.R.E. (the foundation established to perpetuate the Cayce body of data) did a carbon-14 test on the pyramid to determine its age in an attempt to reconcile this discrepancy. The result seemed to validate the historical age of approximately 5,000 years, but as I researched this further I found an interesting article, posted June 21, 2001, on the BBC's Internet site, which I quote below:

> A complete rewrite of the history of modern humans could be needed after a breakthrough in archaeological dating techniques. British and American scientists have found radio carbon dating, used to give a rough guide to the age of an object,

ng by thousands of years. It means humans may
on Earth for a lot longer than previously thought,
ted versions of early history could need a radical
Experts have known for years that carbon dating is
me... but until researchers from Bristol and Harvard completed their study no one knew by how much.[2]

So therefore, we could say that the carbon-14 test on the Great
Pyramid is not conclusive, and the historical date of the pyramid's
creation cannot be validated from such a study. Furthermore, we are
talking about dating the stone through organic material that is found
in and around it. It is all too easy for 5,000-year-old decaying organic
matter to have covered the rocks and thus skew the results of such
a study.

In the third century B.C., Plato wrote about having been told that
Atlanteans invaded Egypt after their continent was inundated nine
thousand years before Plato's time, or about 11,300 years from today,
which would be pretty close to the 10,500 B.C. date assigned by Cayce.
Plato's account also fits in with the Cayce story of the exodus from
Atlantis and the subsequent occupation of Egypt, where Ra-Ta would
become involved in the affairs of Atlantis. For many years, Plato's
reference was the only known historical mention of the existence of
Atlantis.

Also, according to an article by Robert Sheer,[3] water marks were
found on the sides of the Great Pyramid at a level 400 feet higher
than the Nile River is today, and deposits of sea salt inside the Great
Pyramid corroborate the theory that it and the Sphinx must have
been built before the end of the last great Ice Age, about 12,000 years
ago.

According to Zecharia Sitchin in his book *The Stairway to Heaven*,[4]
the common view that the Pyramids of Giza were actually tombs for
pharaohs cannot be supported. No pharaoh's body has ever been
found in the Great Pyramid. Sitchin took note of the fact that there are
no hieroglyphics on the inner walls of the pyramids. He hypothesized

that this was because they were built prior to the written language of the Egyptians.

Conventional archeologists date the Great Pyramid primarily by a series of painted red "quarry marks" that were found in passages above the King's Chamber. Yet these "quarry marks" were all written at the only appropriate angle for the arm of a person who had just broken into these very narrow "relief chambers" through tunneling in from the King's Chamber. This is indeed what the explorer Col. Howard Vyse had just done before the markings were allegedly found. Compelling evidence suggests that Vyse deliberately hoaxed the quarry marks, attributing the building of the pyramid to the Pharaoh Khufu, since workers' morale was very low, his funding almost completely exhausted, and no substantial archeological discoveries had yet been made. There were several mistakes in the way that the quarry marks were written that were identical to the mistakes in Budge's seminal work of the time for decoding the Egyptian hieroglyphics. Vyse had a copy of Budge's book, and all evidence suggests that the quarry marks were a deliberate forgery, since Vyse created a message that combined hieroglyphics from different periods of Egyptian history that were separated by hundreds of years.

Sitchin believes that the pyramids were healing chambers, and according to the *Law of One* series, Ra states that the Great Pyramid was a healing chamber used to concentrate aetheric energy. Napoleon was said to have spent a night in the Great Pyramid. When he emerged, he was reportedly "pale and dazed," and when questioned about his experience he replied, *"You wouldn't believe me if I told you."*

The actual method of construction of the pyramids has historically been a bone of contention and controversy, even among conventional Egyptologists. The technology to put together sixty-ton blocks of granite with the precision that is found in the pyramids just doesn't exist, even today. On March 2, 1999, Fox News presented a TV show exploring the mysteries of the Pyramid. Fadel Gad, an Egyptologist, conjectured:

Were the Egyptians thinking of UFOs at that time? Yes! [They wrote of] A very sophisticated, highly intelligent species that had intercepted this planet Earth and had caused the evolution and the exploration of the human consciousness.[5]

David Pratt posted an intriguing article on the Internet called "The Great Pyramid":

The Pyramid is an unrivaled feat of engineering and craftsmanship. It is aligned with the four cardinal points more accurately than any contemporary structure, including the Meridian Building at Greenwich Observatory in London. The 350-foot-long descending passage is so straight that it deviates from a central axis by less than a quarter of an inch from side to side and only one tenth of an inch up and down—comparable with the best laser-controlled drilling being done today. The casing stones, some of which weighed over 16 tons, are so perfectly shaped and squared that the mortar-filled joint between them is just one-fiftieth of an inch—the thickness of a human nail. Egyptologist Sir Flinders Petrie described such phenomenal precision as "the finest opticians' work. Work of this caliber is *beyond the capabilities* of modern technology." The casing stones show no tool marks and the corners are not even slightly chipped. The granite coffer in the King's Chamber is cut out of a solid block of hard red granite—so precisely that its external volume is exactly twice its internal volume. Engineer and master craftsman Christopher Dunn rejects the theory that it could have been cut and hollowed using bronze saws set with diamond cutting points, because when pressure was applied, the diamonds would have worked their way into the much softer copper, leaving the granite virtually unscathed. In his opinion, the evidence shows that the Egyptians would have to have possessed ultra-modern tools, including tubular drills that could cut granite 500 times faster than modern drills.

But that is not all. The Great Pyramid embodies an advanced knowledge of geometry, geodesy [the science of earth measurement], and astronomy.[6]

The pyramids that were built for fifth-dynasty kings—supposedly just a few decades after those at Giza—were vastly inferior in terms of size, materials, and workmanship. One wonders why, if the Egyptians actually had the ability to build with the precision demonstrated at Giza, would there have been such a startling loss of construction skills in the later pyramids.

And then we must consider a series of geometrical proportions associated with the Great Pyramid that indicates a precision of workmanship and a knowledge of the Earth and the solar system beyond any information that should have been available to the ancient Egyptians. For example:[7]

- The base length of the Great Pyramid x 43,200 is equal to the equatorial circumference of Earth, with better than 1% accuracy.

- The height x 43,200 is equal to the Earth's polar radius, accurate to 0.2%. (**Note:** Whoever built the pyramids knew that Earth wasn't a perfect sphere, for there were different measures for the equatorial and polar circumferences.)

- 4,320 is the number of years for Earth to move through two zodiacal signs, or one sixth of the precession of the equinoxes, the 25,000-year cycle referred to in the *Law of One* series.

- The three main pyramids at Giza mimic the stars of Orion's Belt in size and arrangement, and they are time-encoded to form a perfect alignment with their celestial companions, but only in 10,450 B.C.—almost the same date given in the Edgar Cayce readings and the *Law of One* series.

- Each of the Pyramid's four walls, when measured as a straight line, is 9,131 "Egyptian" inches long, for a total of 36,524 inches. The exact length of the solar year is 365.24 days.

- The Great Pyramid's perimeter-to-height ratio is exactly 2 pi. The pi constant in mathematics was not discovered until much later.

- The Pyramid is located at the exact center of the Earth's land-mass. Its East-West axis lies exactly on the longest land parallel—passing through Africa, Asia, and America. The longest land meridian, through Asia, Africa, Europe, and Antarctica, also passes right through the Pyramid.

- The sides of the Pyramid are very slightly and evenly bowed in, or concave. A pilot taking aerial photos discovered this effect around 1940. Today's laser instruments show that perfect concavity precisely duplicates the curvature of the Earth.

In 1932, Edgar Cayce gave his reading on the story of Ra-Ta, including Cayce's description of the construction of the pyramids by levitation of rock. Some other facts about the construction of the pyramid were also provided. Amazingly, though Cayce never read much other than the Bible, his reading actually referred to some of the parameters listed above that were incorporated in the design, some of which had not even been discovered at the time of the reading!

Compare this: "[The pyramid] was formed according to that which had been worked out by Ra-Ta in the mount, as related to the position of the stars about which this particular solar system circles in its activity." [Cayce reading 294–151]

With this: "The three main pyramids at Giza mimic the stars of Orion's Belt in size and arrangement, as they would have appeared in 10,450 B.C."[8]

John Zajac, scientist and pyramid expert, made the correlation between the Old Testament Book of Isaiah and the Great Pyramid:

There is strong evidence that Isaiah spoke of the Pyramid: "In that day there shall be an altar to the Lord in the midst of the Land of Egypt, and a monument at the border thereof to the Lord, and it shall be for a sign, and for a witness unto the Lord of Hosts in the Land of Egypt" (Isaiah 19:19–20). In the Hebrew language, each of the original thirty words has a numerical value because each Hebrew letter is also a number. When the thirty words are added up, the total is 5,449, which is one of the most significant and dominant numbers [utilized in the construction] of the Pyramid. It is the exact height of the Pyramid in sacred Jewish inches.

Although the first books of the Old Testament were written after the Pyramid was built, the height of the Pyramid could not have been measured when the book of Isaiah was written, because the geometry required to make such a measurement had not yet been developed. Also, the base of the Pyramid was obscured by shifting sand.

Of course, being located both "in the midst" of Egypt and at the same time "at the border" seems to be a logical impossibility. However, in ancient times before the unification of the country, there was lower Egypt (north) and upper Egypt (south). The borderline between the two Egypts goes right through the Pyramid, thus placing the Pyramid both in the center and at the border of Egypt.

A few years ago, the Japanese reportedly tried to duplicate the 4,600-year-old Great Pyramid of Giza at ¼ scale, employing today's technology and knowledge. They couldn't do it. Indeed, the Great Pyramid seems to resist all efforts to comprehend how it was built, by whom, and for what purpose.

Each year the North Star shines further down the Descending Passage. It will illuminate the entrance to the Well Shaft (sometimes called the Point of Last Escape) in 1997. The North Star will shine on the floor of the Subterranean Passage seven years later in 2004. What is the significance of these events?

Some people speculate they may be related to "the signs in the stars" that the Bible mentions with regard to the Second Coming of Christ.[9]

In an ancient system where certain numbers are assigned word meanings, the dimensions of the inner passages of the Pyramid have encoded the exact years of significant planetary events, including the time of the Jewish exodus from Egypt and the birth, baptism, and crucifixion of Jesus. More recently, the major wars of the twentieth century also appear to have been indicated.

I quoted from Zecharia Sitchin's book *The Stairway to Heaven* earlier in this chapter. In that book, Sitchin makes a scholarly evaluation of a great deal of evidence concerning Biblical and early Egyptian periods and comes to the conclusion that the Egyptian Gods were not mythical beings, but actually extraterrestrials with extraordinary powers. The bottom line is that there are a great many reasons why the normal historical viewpoint regarding the construction of the pyramids makes less sense than the story presented by Ra in the *Law of One* series. To continue with physicist John Zajac's 1995 talk:

Who built the Pyramid? We have to conclude that it was somebody who was very knowledgeable about the Earth and who had technology beyond what we possess today. The Pyramid's designer could also see, and more likely control, the future. The builder knew when and where the most significant person in history was going to be born and when he was going to die, and what impact that would have on the people of the Earth....

Could the builder of the Great Pyramid be a space visitor from another planet? Possibly, if we focus on his advanced knowledge. However, being able to see and/or control the future precisely is what we would recognize as supernatural. Dedication of the interior of the Pyramid to the history of the Jews, prophecy, and especially to the life and death of Christ indicates that the Pyramid must have been designed and built with supernatural help as a prophetic monument able to endure through the ages, despite millennia of natural and man-made assaults against it.[10]

Compare the last sentence above with this Cayce reading: "As the changes came about in the earth, the rise and fall of nations were to be depicted in this same temple, that was to act as an interpreter for that which had been, that which is, and that which is to be in the material plane." [Cayce reading 294–151]

The mythological Ra, the Egyptian Sun God, was able to create things by thought, according to Michael C. Carlos of the Museum of Emory University:

> All Ra had to do was think of a thing and it existed.... Of course the people needed a leader, so Ra took human form and ruled Egypt under the name of Pharaoh. His kingship was long and prosperous, and lasted thousands of years.[11]

And in another Internet reference to Ra:

> The film [*Stargate,* 1994, starring Kurt Russell] is obviously suggesting that this is essentially what happened in ancient Egypt: that Ra and the other gods were extraterrestrials who made a profound impression on the pre-dynastic Egyptians, who then memorialized a catalogue of religious rituals based on these early experiences. These rituals then eventually became solemn and sacred ceremonies carried out by the priests and pharaohs for thousands of years afterwards. According to at least one researcher, this scenario is uncannily close to the truth![12]

From the Cayce readings (Ra was never described as a Sun God in the Cayce readings; it is assumed by Cayce scholars that the Ra referred to below would have been Ra-Ta):

Then there came the period when all the pyramid or memorial was complete. Ra, having finished his work, ascended into the mount and was borne away. [Cayce reading 294–152]

The *Law of One* series gave us the channeled words of Ra quoted earlier about ancient Egypt and the Law of One: "the priests and the peoples of that era quickly distorted our message, robbing it of the compassion with which unity is informed." How does the "distortion" of Ra-Ta's mission affect us today? Ra-Ta incarnated to bring the message of the "Law of One" to our planet. Because of his interdimensional connections, he was able to manipulate the physical plane in ways that appeared miraculous. Many of the elite at the time of Ra-Ta attempted to learn how to activate these advanced abilities for self-serving purposes rather than as a manifestation of the "Law of One." Access to the healing powers of the pyramid was closed off to the masses of the people and reserved for the elite. Teachings about the importance of exercising one's own free will were distorted, and the masses were subjugated by the elite who held the secret belief that the extremes of both positive and negative behaviors needed to be experienced in order to spiritually evolve. Occult rituals were devised which misused the knowledge of the Law of One in an attempt to gain power over others. Many of these rituals are, in present time, part of the agendas of various secret societies, some of which are engaged in the practice of "magic" or what might even be called "black magic," where spells and invocations are used to gain power over others without their free-will choice. If one researches these secret societies, one will find that they incorporate many symbols and rituals of Egyptian origin.

In the next chapter, the evidence is presented how this same Ra is currently in communication with mankind through none other than David Wilcock, who if my premises are correct, is still working diligently to reinstall the same information that was given 12,500 years ago and then subjected to endless distortions throughout history thereafter.

Entities enter our solar system from other systems, bringing with them the development and influences from these systems. Such influences are seldom understood, for the laws of this three-dimensional sphere become too binding, limiting our understanding. One importance of these more vast influences lies in their relation to the entrance of great leaders and teachers at periods of world change.

—"Source," Edgar Cayce readings, File 2265–1

Chapter

8

Enter Wilcock ... Prophecy Fulfilled

Edgar Cayce died in 1945, leaving a cryptically worded prophecy regarding his alleged return in 1998:

> Is it not fitting, then, that these [a reference to Ra-Ta and his associates] must return? As this priest may develop himself to be in that position, to be in that capacity as a liberator of the world in its relationships to individuals in those periods to come, for he must enter again in that period, or in 1998. [Cayce reading 294–151]

From a Cayce dream, documented in *Many Happy Returns* by William Church, we have this information: "He saw himself back in Virginia Beach."[1] Another dream documented in the same book offers: "Surrounded by many of those who had been with him at that earlier time."

The exact choice of words in reading 294–151 is very interesting. Cayce's Source did not say *Cayce* would return in 1998. He said *the priest* must enter in that period, meaning Ra-Ta or Ra. Edgar Cayce predicted that he *may* develop himself to be a "liberator of the world," ostensibly one of many involved with such tasks, so his destiny is not preordained. The implication is that he would have obstacles to overcome before he could become "a liberator of the world," because he would have to "develop himself." He would live in Virginia Beach, and many who had been with him earlier would again surround him.

This chapter reviews some of the events in Wilcock's life that brought him to the conclusion that he has to be Cayce. As the story of Wilcock's life unfolds, we would expect to find evidence that would nominate him as a candidate to fulfill the Cayce prophecy of Ra-Ta's return. We would also expect to find evidence validating the Ra oversoul connection of Cayce, Wilcock, and Ra-Ta.

If Wilcock is in fact the reincarnation of Cayce, we could hypothesize that there would be indications of that in his childhood, such as interests in healing, psychic phenomena, and spirituality. And that's exactly what we find. Wilcock still has some of the books that he read between the ages of seven and ten years old which dealt with hypnosis, ESP, and healing—all of the most important features of Cayce's gift.

Curiously, Wilcock was inspired to put an American Lung Association Christmas fund drive sticker from 1981 in Harold Sherman's book *How to Make ESP Work For You,*[2] thus documenting that he was reading the book by age eight. Both his choice of reading materials and the fact that he put special, time-stamped attention on the chapter of the ESP book related to healing ability demonstrate Wilcock's early interest in healing and psychic ability.

Wilcock's parents and grandparents were/are talented and educated. His father, Don Wilcock, is a music columnist and writer who authored a mass-market biography on the blues guitarist Buddy Guy (*Damn Right, I've Got the Blues,*[3] released in 1993). Don frequently went to concerts in the area to review artists and their performances for his local newspaper, and David often attended these shows. David and his brother were both accustomed to being surrounded by celebrities as a result of receiving backstage passes through their father's work.

David's mother, Marta Waterman, is a college professor and professional musician who performs in New York, Florida, and Europe. Marta was a devoted student of metaphysics, and young David had full access to the books from her library, tucked away on shelves under the cellar stairs. He gives her the credit for first exposing him to spiritual principles. She had a sense that David was special and believed that his ESP was genuine and that he could have out-of-body experiences.

His grandfather, Dr. Don F. Wilcock, was an engineer and inventor with many patents to his name, including a bulletproof helicopter turret that is now standard issue. David's great-grandfather, Frederick (Fredy) Wilcock, had a Ph.D. in engineering and a Master's degree in law and was the chief architect, engineer, and legal advisor responsible for the design and construction of the original eastern portion of the New York City subway system. David has noticed a curious connection to his own life as Ra-Ta, as the Cayce readings asserted that there is an extensive array of underground rooms and tunnels beneath the Giza plateau, including the so-called "Hall of Records." David thinks that his great-grandfather might have been a collaborator in designing this elaborate tunnel system.

David Wilcock's unusual childhood prepared him much better than Cayce's upbringing for the paranormal experiences yet to come. David's formative years were peppered with mystical, spiritual experiences and phenomena. He compiled a list of some of these early experiences for inclusion in this book:

- David's desire to induce an OBE (out-of-body experience) led him to read his first adult-length metaphysical book at age seven, *How to Make ESP Work For You* by Harold Sherman.

- Within the first week of reading the book, David remote-influenced his friend Eric to wake up in the middle of the night and think of gold as his first thought. Eric reported bolting awake in the pitch-blackness of the night, feeling a strong presence in the room. The first thing he thought of was his watch,

ıs gold. David had no idea that Eric used a watch, not
ᵤs a timepiece, since he had never visited Eric's bed-
ᵤm in waking life. Eric did not wear the watch, only using it
on his bedstand. David confirmed all these details at lunchtime
before telling Eric what he had done.

- David got a team of friends together who would go around the
corner of the kindergarten building and select a number between
one and ten. David had 100% accuracy in guessing the numbers correctly. This experiment was only conducted once, as the
other boys were spooked by it.

    Note: I found the following story about Edgar Cayce in *Many
    Happy Returns* by W.H. Church.[4] It has a rather direct corre-
    spondence to David's psychic abilities discussed above: "His son
    [Edgar's son], Hugh Lynn, once remarked to me that his father
    always regarded his chronic financial problems in the present
    lifetime as a direct karmic result of his gambling activities as
    Bainbridge, who was able to use his innate psychic abilities to
    cheat the other players at the table. In fact, in a dramatic illus-
    tration of this point, Edgar responded to Hugh Lynn's insistent
    demand that he join them in a game of cards by tersely order-
    ing his son to deal out the various hands. Then, going mentally
    around the table, he called out the cards in every hand but his
    own. This last, he slapped down, face up on the table. 'Now you
    know why I never play cards,' he said unsmiling, as he pushed
    back his chair and stalked away from the astounded players."

- As a child David had the undying conviction that he could put
a jump rope under his feet and then pull up very hard on either
side and he would levitate. He spent hours trying to do this in the
driveway or on the playground, since it worked effortlessly in
his dreams.

    Note: There's an interesting parallel (aside from the levita-
    tion of the Egyptian pyramid's building blocks) in the life of
    Cayce, which might explain one of the reasons David had this

conviction. Cayce, early in his career, was doing a reading conducted by a dentist named Blackburn, who couldn't understand the words coming out of Cayce's mouth. As reported in *A Seer Out of Season* (p. 305), Blackburn put his hand over the center of Cayce's body, and in order to better understand his speech told him, "Up up—not so fast" attempting to get Cayce to speak louder and slower. The entranced Cayce took his command literally as his body floated up off the table, "completely unsupported," towards Blackburn's hand and remained in a levitated state until the astonished Blackburn pulled back.

- David gave a classroom demonstration of his psychic ability in second grade with the same friend Eric, using a handmade deck of cards that had numbers, words, or images on them.

- The second and third books that David read at age eight were both about hypnosis. David felt that hypnosis and psychic ability were somehow strongly connected. He brought these books to school with paper covering them so he could read them secretly in his free reading time while the other children read 22-point picture books like *Clifford the Big Red Dog*.

- David was convinced that other people could hear his thoughts as well as he heard theirs, and thus he worked very hard not to think negative thoughts about anyone.

- At age eight, David overheard his brother talking in his sleep and felt that important information would be conveyed. He tried to set up a tape recorder to catch these fragments on voice-activation and had some measure of success. He felt that in this state, Michael could potentially answer any question he was asked, although they only slept in the same room while on vacation, so David was never able to "catch" it at the right time. (Perhaps this was a hidden memory of his Cayce experience.)

- Also at age eight, David took a walkie-talkie and set it next to his father's ear with the volume knob set to 1 while his father napped on the couch in the living room. David then went upstairs and broadcast through the walkie-talkie at a soft volume messages about how delicious a sausage and mushroom pizza would be. When he came back downstairs, his father woke up from his slumber and said, "OK boys, how about we go get a sausage and mushroom pizza?" This confirmed scientifically to David and his brother that hypnosis and the power of suggestion really did work.

• David was able to repeatedly come home at the exact minute that his mother asked him to when he went on bicycle trips with his friends, without ever wearing a watch or checking the sun's position. His friends would be very surprised when the clock indicated exactly 5:00 as they walked into the house. This was the norm, not the exception. Such precise timing would become far more apparent later in David's life with the "clock synchronicity" phenomenon, where he is often influenced to look at a clock just as its digits are all repeating, such as 3:33.

• On other occasions, when his mother wanted him home but had not specified a time, she would walk out to the end of the driveway and "Send" to him, as she called it. Both he and his brother would feel these calls and come home within five minutes.

• David could throw sticks up into the air and then decide on the direction to make them point in as they fell. As they hit the ground they would point in the direction that David intended about 90-95% of the time. One end of the stick would be broken so as to provide a pointer, meaning that there was only one 360-degree position that would constitute an accurate result.

• On several occasions David and his brother believed they were able to use psychic ability together in order to create rain or sudden gusts of wind.

• David was enrolled in the Pyramid Program for Gifted Children in school and carried out independent projects in chemistry, astronomy, stargazing, computer programming, crystals, and multimedia planetarium presentations, all before the sixth grade.

• David experienced many accurate psychic results using Ouija boards, palmistry, and Tarot, beginning in seventh grade. By ninth grade he discontinued any use of the Ouija board due to its potential for abuse and focused his efforts on studying the Tarot, which consistently provided powerful accuracy and insight. (According to the *Law of One* series, Ra introduced the Tarot in Egypt in 10,500 B.C.)

• David's diet was poor and he became overweight beginning in sixth and seventh grade after his parents' divorce. His favorite food at the time was pork hot dogs. (Cayce also was known for his poor diet and had a particular weakness for pork.)

• David read Julius Fast's best-selling book *Body Language*[5] in seventh and eighth grade, which was his first major introduction to the idea that human beings have a subconscious mind that can tell the truth through body language even while the person's words are telling a lie. David was fascinated by how easy it was to "read" people's real emotions based on these techniques, and this was his first inkling that he wanted to have a career in psychology.

• When David was sixteen, he went on a strict diet and rigorously lost eighty-five pounds in nine months, never gaining any of it back.

• At age sixteen David read *Lucid Dreaming*[6] and *Exploring the World of Lucid Dreaming*[7] by Dr. Stephen LaBerge. He was quickly able to use one of LaBerge's techniques, "The Mnemonic Induction of Lucid Dreaming," to gain access to fully-conscious dream states where he could levitate, fly, travel through solid objects, perform astounding feats, change his entire surroundings at the snap of a finger, and temporarily fulfill his biggest wishes. He would have the experience, real or imagined, of talking to higher beings and being out-of-body. Several of these experiences brought him to the main deck of an advanced spacecraft.

• David read *The Secrets of Shamanism*[8] and became aware of how seemingly random events could actually be communicating messages in a symbolic language, once properly understood. This was his introduction to the phenomenon of synchronicity.

• At age sixteen, David experienced his first "ear blast" (actually a sudden, overwhelming energetic pressure in the frontal lobes of the brain, supposedly caused by an energetic activation from his Higher Self) exactly as the clock turned 3:33. This still happens to him about every other month on average. The experience is completely de-personalizing, with massive kundalini energy shooting up the spine. Historic Catholic accounts of "flying saints" reported that they would get this exact same sensation before they were able to levitate, but David has never demonstrated such ability.

• From early childhood through the beginning of college, David would occasionally have experiences of walking and talking while asleep. David sat up in bed several times during his first year of college and talked directly to his roommate while still asleep, going on about "the water" on one occasion—a metaphor for spiritual energy. David recalls many occasions where he would wake up, take a shower, pack his book bag, eat breakfast, and leave by the side door to go to school, only to realize that it was pitch-black outside. Only then would he notice that he had been in trance and did not register the times that he was seeing on the clocks.

• In his senior college year in New Paltz, New York, David began dating a Japanese girl named Yumi, who woke up in trance on several occasions and gave him messages. Two of these messages involved telling him that he was "Shining" while he was reading books such as *Aliens Among Us* by Ruth Montgomery.[9]

- In December 1994, Yumi went back to Japan over winter break and showed David's picture to a very trusted and highly accurate Shinto priestess and psychic. The woman immediately said, "This man will be a very famous spiritual leader." David was very surprised to hear this.

- David and Yumi separated after college graduation in June 1995, as she returned to Japan. David quickly moved back to his college town after graduation, as almost every dream he had while he was with his family featured that area. He then found the book *We The Arcturians,* by Dr. Norma Milanovich,[10] and it was the first time that he took "channeled" material seriously. He was surprised when the Arcturians advised a strict diet of no meat, no dairy, no white flour, no refined sugar, and no preservatives, but he nevertheless began doing it, which took about two years to really sink in as habit. He had already been heading in that direction, having given up dairy and meat a year earlier.

The next period of David's life was outlined in Chapter Two, where he attempted to gain admission to the Naropa Institute and ended up as a pizza delivery boy. But his interest in metaphysics, extraterrestrials, and spirituality continued as he discovered Dr. Scott Mandelker's book *From Elsewhere*[11] and the idea first occurred to him that he was a "Wanderer" soul from another dimension. Mandelker gave extensive descriptions of the personalities and characteristics of Wanderers in his book, and David realized that he matched these personality traits perfectly. It was in the Mandelker book that he first found written reference to the *Law of One* series from L/L Research. By January of 1996 Wilcock owned all of the *Law of One* books and was intensively studying the data, finding a great affinity with it. In fact, he referred to the Ra Material on his website as the "ultimate source of UFO [interdimensional] wisdom."

Wilcock began the habit of recording his dreams in 1992 while he was still in college, but in November of 1996 something different happened. In a telephone conversation with his associate Joe Mason, he learned about a technique of writing down or recording whatever stray words went through his mind as he awakened from sleep. The process itself was rather tedious and nothing seemed to make any sense to his deeply entranced conscious mind, but when he reviewed what he had written, he saw a series of sentence fragments that seemed to be coming from intelligence outside of him, speaking to him directly and commenting on his progress through life. Wilcock became fascinated and preoccupied with this process each morning, improving his ability to bring in longer fragments of communication until finally he was recording pages and pages of perfectly composed, complete texts, dictated into a tape recorder.

He describes his information-gathering method as somewhat akin to lucid dreaming, where he is being spoken to in a dreamlike state by entities outside physical view, but he also remains conscious enough to speak while this is taking place. In Part Two of this book, David's intuitive work is explored more extensively, with examples of his first attempts at documentation of his Dream Voice. Unlike Cayce, Wilcock doesn't have to fall into a deep sleep to receive his information. There is a reference in Edgar Cayce's own readings that in his future lives, he might not have to go into an unconscious trance, and that this would represent a higher level of development of his ability.

Interspersed with counseling Wilcock, his dream source frequently offered premonition-type material, such as correctly predicting events that would happen to him later in the day or week and making prognostications regarding upcoming world events. The readings also gave information pertaining to a dimensional shift that had already commenced and would be increasing in intensity on planet Earth in the years to come. As Wilcock found himself making accurate predictions concerning his personal affairs, world events, and politics, his readings became a very important part of his life, although he never anticipated any recognition or prominence for this talent. In fact, he thought of himself as an intellectual with a scientific bent, and, for the most part, his dream communications were a very private happening that he was even embarrassed to talk about with others.

David was well aware of Edgar Cayce through the books he had read on Atlantis, and in the spring of 1997, still in New Paltz, David joined an Edgar Cayce "Search for God" study group. He felt a strong affinity with Cayce's work and actually contemplated attending the A.R.E.'s Atlantic University in Virginia Beach. Skip Weatherford, an early pioneer in psychic research and a hypnotherapist, led the group. David showed an uncanny ability to interpret and understand passages in the "Search for God" textbook when no one else could. Weatherford's house was only five minutes' driving distance from David's house on country roads, even though it was one of only two local centers for the A.R.E. in the entire Northeast.

During this period of time, David's "Dream Voice" suggested that he move to Virginia Beach. It should be noted that up to this point David had no idea that he resembled Cayce. I did a telephone interview with Wilcock in 2002 regarding this part of his life; below are his words:

Two weeks before I moved to Virginia Beach, my friend Skip called me up on the phone and said, "You've got to come over to my house. You've got to see something."

I didn't want to go but he said, "You really need to come over and see this right now." I had attended a couple of "Search for God" study groups at his house, which are based on Edgar Cayce's channeled material in his later years. So I walked inside, and he brought me to a table, whereupon he slapped down this magazine with a white piece of paper on top of it. A square was cut out in the middle of the paper, and inside the square is an image of a person's face. As he slapped this magazine down on the table, he said, "Who is this?" I looked at it and said to myself, "Oh, my God! That's my face," but I obviously knew it couldn't be my own face for two reasons. First of all, it was on a magazine cover, and I had never been published, and second of all, it was rendered in this sort of artistic style where it was partly a photograph and partly done over with colored pencil.

Inside my mind I said, "Obviously, that's not me." I then continued by saying to myself, "Okay, well, he's obviously an A.R.E. member. This is typical of the type of artwork that you would see on the cover of the A.R.E.'s *Venture Inward* magazine. Therefore, this must be a picture of Edgar Cayce when he was young." So I finally responded, "Well, that's Edgar Cayce," and he replied, "Well, yeah, but who else does it look like?" And after a long pause, I said, "Wow, that's pretty weird."

After I moved to Virginia Beach, people who were working in the A.R.E. in various capacities would come up to me and be astonished at my physical resemblance to Edgar Cayce, which is quite stunning, as anyone can see in the comparison photograph on my website.[12]

Without going into all the details, let me just say that more and more people started to comment on the similarity between Cayce and myself. It eventually built up to a crescendo where I had to ask my Dream Voice: "You've got to tell me. Is this true or not? What's going on?" I asked two or three times before I really got the answer. When they finally answered, they said, "Well, we're willing to tell you, but you have to understand that with this answer comes great responsibility."

It's funny, because when you actually read that reading where they are telling me, there is sort of an argument going back and forth between us where I'm saying, "Man, if this is true, then I'm in for some real rough times. Nobody is going to accept this. Nobody is going to believe this." I had always disliked hearing about people who claimed to be someone famous in their past lives, and then tried to use that alleged data to give themselves some sort of credibility to others in the metaphysical community. I was already aware that Cayce had been through some very grandiose past lives, including

Ra-Ta, and that Ra-Ta was predicted to return in 1998. Never in a million years could I have imagined that I would be that person. On the one hand it was rather exciting, but on the other hand it felt like a death sentence.

However, they basically told me that if I didn't let people know about this, and if I didn't start publicizing my private channeling work and trying to get it out into the world, such as by the Internet, then I was basically committing the equivalent of a felony in the spiritual realms. So all of a sudden I felt like I had all this responsibility thrust on me, and I can't really say that I enjoyed it. What had always been my own novel little secret had suddenly taken on earth-shaking importance.

I was no longer just David Wilcock, I was a reincarnated historical figure whose previous work was known and revered by millions of people worldwide. Though I was indeed quite psychic and would receive all sorts of information that I was not aware of until after I transcribed my cassettes, Edgar Cayce was widely considered to be "the most accurate psychic of all time" outside Nostradamus, and those were some very big shoes to fill indeed. This created the possibility that my own work, character, purpose, and destiny would be perpetually judged against Cayce's, instead of being accepted on its own merits. I felt that I could already see the scornful faces and hear the howls of protest as I followed up on my instructions to publicize this information.

The text below is a verbatim transcript of Wilcock's Dream Voice from November 26, 1997, in response to his question concerning his connection with Edgar Cayce.[13] The Dream Voice had not yet identified itself as Ra to Wilcock at the time.

David: I would like to incubate a question on [my] identity here, related to Edgar Cayce.

Source: ... This is our boss. We will have to move over, as he is in charge. [Author's note: Perhaps this is a group soul at work, and they are having a meeting.] What we are doing here is staring each other in the face. Sometimes, you will need to do that. It should be very easy to take a guess at this point, but with that guess comes responsibility; enormous responsibility. Furthermore, as you are well aware, your connection with us will need to be dramatically strengthened. **In short, David, the answer is yes; you will need to review the whole life and see the parallels.** Someone else came along, and it is important that you know this. [Author's note: Probably a reference to souls within the Ra group.]

David: What do you mean by that?

Source: The words that we speak are inspired by sources we have not yet particularly identified; though this gives us great concern, it is not a matter of impending importance at this point.

David: But this is such an important finding! It is very difficult for me to completely accept this.

Source: To bury this concept in time would not be wise for you, as it is very important that you make those aware around you. We do not have the time for you to hide this. We understand that you will be tested, and we feel it imperative that you take the necessary precautions to ensure that you are ready for said involvements. Be it known that you are not as configured this time for medical readings and for individual one-on-one counseling. This is one of the involvements that we have wished to change. We would like to see you progress in the direction of spending more time teaching universal concepts to the masses; this would be the highest utilization of your creative forces. As you have seen before, this process works quite well in a controlled situation, wherein you have the time and patience to pay attention to these words as they come through you. You are correct in discerning that part of the conscious channeling process is for us to provide organization to the words which you speak, and vice versa.

To comment on this again, it is no longer necessary to keep up with the Joneses. [Author's note: Wilcock has to start thinking about creating his life outside of consensus reality.] Now that you are aware of the part that you are playing, you may grow into the role with a greater responsibility and understanding of its purpose. Did you not think that there was a reason why you were never influenced to undergo a broader-scale study of the life of Edgar Cayce? This is because it concerned us that deep memories might be triggered before their time.

David: Are you really serious about this? It just seems to be so overwhelming.

Source: You forget that there is light in the darkest of places. Though yours was one of many difficulties, it is a lifetime replete with examples of a person born ready to unfold his natural abilities, almost as if from birth. Thus, you have had a very strong predilection towards this, and we do not wish you to use this as a means of asserting power over your associates, but simply be aware of the great responsibility that this entails. You will need to focus diligently on the questions and concerns at hand with why you are here and what your ultimate mission is. To that end, we wish to see you go forward and promote these concepts of unification with one's Higher Self, and alignment with the Law of Love so that others may prepare for the impending problems and/or ascensions that wait.

From our perspective, you can clearly see the difficulty that we have had in terms of preparing you for this moment and making the necessary arrangements in order that it be realized. So just be calm, David; you will use our abilities well, and together we will go forward and hopefully teach the world that which needs to be taught.

Our love is here with you now, David, surrounding you, becoming you. We do not want anything bad to happen to you. We want you to be aware that protection and guidance exist. Now you understand why all of our prophecies were geared towards December, as this is the month when you would first be fully aware of your identity therein. It is a very exciting time. You are correct in that we will be able to go further with you if you meditate and get yourself deeper into trance than you are right now. We also wish for you to go much further with your out-of-body experience, and in so doing a massive amount of information can be compiled in a very short amount of time. Peace be with you in the Light of everlasting Love.

Understandably, this reading rocked Wilcock to his core, and in many senses he very much wished that it weren't true, since he knew that it would expose him to extreme ridicule. Nonetheless, in a shuddering way, all the pieces suddenly fit together. Here he was living in Virginia Beach, in a room that he was introduced to via the A.R.E., attending Cayce study groups, and suddenly his source tells him he was Cayce. In spite of the credibility already established by his Dream Voice, Wilcock couldn't just accept this disclosure at face value. So he began a study of the Cayce material, attempting to validate the truth of this revelation. As he studied, he realized that his own readings had dropped strong hints of this connection long before it was made explicit, even including a visual image of him lying and doing a reading with the text *Edgar Cayce: The Sleeping Prophet* floating above him. At the time he thought this was because his work was similar to Cayce's, not that he had actually been Cayce.

As he researched the Cayce archives at the A.R.E., Wilcock was able to compare photographs of associates in his present life with those who had been close to Edgar Cayce, and he found startling facial similarities. He eventually posted examples of these on his website. [14] Wilcock believes that he has identified the recurrence of such Cayce comrades as his financiers Morton and Edwin Blumenthal, his most trusted friend David Kahn, his first business associate Dr. Wesley Harrington Ketchum, his wife Gertrude Cayce, and his father Leslie Cayce. This is a good moment to remind the reader of the Cayce prophecy at the beginning of this chapter where he had returned to live in Virginia Beach and was surrounded by associates from the past lifetime.

As part of his due diligence, David began a study of current scientific data that might validate the dimensional shift that his Dream Voice prophesied. In February 1998, David deliberately avoided taking any new temporary jobs for three weeks and put together the first edition of *Convergence*. This book compiled David's scientific research into Atlantis, the Global Grid, Ascension, and extraterrestrials. It was first published on the Great Dreams (www.greatdreams.com) website in March 1998 and received very positive public recognition. Three major revisions later, this text is now posted on Wilcock's website, entitled *Convergence, Volume One: The Shift of the Ages.*

After *Convergence* was completed, David returned to his "miserable" temp-jobs. He had done some readings for his friends and they seemed to get value out of them, so in July of 1998 he was influenced to begin performing readings as a paid service. Literally within a week, he had enough clients to support himself financially.

By early 1999, David followed the guidance of his readings and established a web page online, http://ascension2000.com, where he featured his scientific research, articles, readings, and dream interpretations. The site quickly grew in popularity.

David began to realize that he was having dreams about his clients on the mornings before he was to do their readings. The dreams had extraordinary detail about the clients' issues. This led David to realize that every client would be dreamed about before the session like clockwork, and in almost every single case there were startling psychic connections clearly presented in the dream, which David could analyze and interpret. He thus began soliciting clients on his web page, where the client would get to talk to David on the phone for at least an hour in an "intake" conversation, while David typed everything the client said, followed by David getting a dream for the person at an appointed day shortly thereafter. He would awaken from this "incubated" dream, dictate and analyze its contents into a tape recorder, and then perform a psychic reading, filling a 90-minute tape. That same day, the client would get a 15-plus-minute follow-up conversation where Wilcock shared the dream and whatever themes he remembered from the reading itself. His initial rate was $65, then $80, then $100 when he began doing the dream readings, and he was finally influenced to go up to $150 by several of his own clients. He made enough money from this to eke out a living. Without exception, every dream reading that David performed for his clients had remarkable accuracy and picked up on many pieces of data that he had not been told consciously.

One man was flying out to California to apply for a new job and wanted to know if it was a good idea. David's dream went into extremely specific detail, including the structure and mirrored appearance of the building, its position next to a body of water with a small footbridge, the yellow backhoe seen outside the building, what the woman interviewing the man looked, sounded, and acted like, what food would be offered to the man, what the office looked like, what the bathroom looked like, and the fact that he would walk through a party on the way out. At the end of the dream, out of the lake came a monster that looked like a cross between Godzilla and a hippopotamus, which destroyed the building entirely. The man was so shocked at how accurately David's dream came true that he became quite concerned about the destruction prophecy and booked a flight out of California just hours after he left the interview in haste. The business he was applying to in 1999, which at the time seemed "too good to be true," ended up collapsing in the dot-com stock market crash of 2000–2001.

In another dream-reading case, David's client awoke from a dream where he had trouble setting up a tripod. Still remembering his dream, he then went out, found the tape from David in the mailbox, and listened to it. David's dream also featured a person having difficulty setting up a tripod. After a standard opening statement, the reading stated, "The tripod represents ..." et cetera. The client was so impressed with this that he paid for David to fly to Knoxville, Tennessee, to do a lecture and workshop at Pellisippi State University. This was David's first paid public appearance as a scientific researcher.

In 1999, David's then-companion Sabrina stopped him while he was transcribing his dreams and readings to tell him a story. At this point David was about three months backlogged in transcriptions. She had visited the A.R.E. over the weekend and met a man who showed her pictures of a building where the top floor had been designed to look like a UFO. David continued transcribing right after Sabrina told him this, and less than a minute later the dream was describing a building where the top floor was designed to look like a UFO. David called Sabrina into the room and played her the tape immediately, and they were both astonished. This is but one example of many where David's audiotaped dream transcriptions referred to events that were just about to unfold in his life at the time he transcribed them, regardless of when the actual dreams or readings were dictated. Almost every time David sat down to transcribe, this would occur—it was the norm, not the exception, throughout the entire time that David worked with cassettes between December 1996 and December 2000. (In 2001 he switched to entering his dreams directly into his computer upon awakening, thus eliminating the potential for massive backlogs.)

The Wilcock readings are quite different from Cayce's. First, they are much more coherent. They come out in perfectly crafted English, utilizing metaphor in bringing a person's life issues to the forefront of their consciousness. They don't usually dwell on past-life or health circumstances, but rather offer a soul-level perspective on what an individual needs to do to transcend his or her third-density karma. The question often comes up as to why, if Wilcock is Cayce, can't he do the same kind of readings that Cayce did. By way of an attempted answer to this question, I will repeat the passage from Wilcock's website relating the incident in which his Cayce connection was verified by the Dream Voice, which said: *"Be it known that you are not as configured this time for medical readings and for individual one-on-one counseling. This is one of the involvements that we have wished to change. We would like to see you progress in the direction of spending more time teaching universal concepts to the masses."*

In my own consideration of this, I formulated three reasons why it would not be advantageous to allow Wilcock to do the kind of readings that Cayce did:

1. Most of Cayce's life was lived in relative obscurity. He couldn't display his powers without calling undue attention to himself. It wasn't until the end of his life that he started to become well known, after the release of Thomas Sugrue's book *There is a River.* If Wilcock were able to have Cayce's on-demand omniscience, he would now be instantly recognized worldwide due to the Internet and a far more open-minded intellectual climate. This kind of recognition might actually put him in personal jeopardy with respect to those who might want to control this kind of psychic ability for self-serving use. We can assume that Ra would know this and protect Wilcock from this potential outcome. Even when he makes future predictions, they are usually couched in metaphor and cryptically encoded so that they only become obvious after the event has occurred.

2. If Wilcock were able to do medical readings with the same acumen as Cayce, he would be caught in a perpetual crisis of conscience. He would have to turn down hundreds of thousands of requests. The best use of his gifts in this period of time, with the urgencies of the predicted dimensional shift, is as a world teacher, bringing "universal concepts to the masses" and making the wise words of Ra available to all, assisting the greatest numbers of people and backing the claims up scientifically. We will learn in Parts Two and Three of this book that this is exactly what Wilcock is doing, using the Cayce connection as a means of getting people's attention, which his readings instructed him to do. This is part of the reason why this book was written, as David had no desire to do it himself and inevitably be accused of an "ego trip." It was allowed only at the persistence of the author that such a book could help many people. Wilcock had certain aspects of his own karma to work out in this lifetime. If he were able to do readings with past-life and health information available on demand, as per Cayce, and became accepted and celebrated as Cayce by the A.R.E. and

others, the recognition and immediate fame could have impeded his ability to work out his own personal issues.

3. In this lifetime, because he emphasizes empirical scientific validation, Wilcock has chosen to focus a larger part of his intuitive abilities on the creation of scientific/spiritual models to explain Ra's cosmology. Cayce, on the other hand, was almost entirely configured to do medical and, later, spiritual readings.

As an interesting aside, in January 1999 David befriended Dr. Hideo Izumoto, a Shinto teacher and acupuncturist who was psychic himself. Without knowing of David's Dream Voice revelation, his own angelic guidance informed him that David had been Edgar Cayce. So, he went to the A.R.E., bought a book that had pictures of a young Cayce, came back, opened them up on David's kitchen table, and said, "Exactly the same, exactly the same," and then informed David that he was Edgar Cayce's reincarnation. Quietly, and with a note of resignation in his voice, David reluctantly chimed in, "Yeah, I know."

Nearly fourteen additional months would pass after the Cayce/Wilcock disclosure reading before it would be revealed that Ra is his Source. Had he been given such information any earlier than this, it would have only added to his feelings of overwhelm, since Wilcock was already aware of the connection between Ra-Ta and Ra and the fact that Ra had apparently worked with Ra-Ta during the Egyptian/Atlantean period. On January 3, 1999, it was revealed to him that the ultimate source of his readings was none other than Ra, the same group entity whose teachings were preserved in L/L Research's *Law of One* series, which had been so pivotal to his own growth. Ra told Wilcock the following about their group:

Ra: The planet Venus was made as our starting point, designed to open and unfurl an opportunity wherein the source body of a new race could be had. The identity Ra is our identity. We are that social memory complex that you have been striving for. We have desired to speak through this instrument with a maximal desire of increased accuracy in contact for some period of time. We now feel that it is okay for you to be knowledgeable about the nature of the source. As you are aware, we stated that we would be in the fifth dimension, eagerly awaiting any further attempts at service that we might make.

David: If this is indeed Ra, why don't I need to go into a deep trance to get your unfiltered guidance? Why is it that I have to do this consciously, when it seemed so impossible for Carla to have done that?

Ra: The curvature of space and time is not yet something that you understand, and yet we were capable of grossly manipulating its distortions so as to produce a whole new affair. This new affair centered around the notion of immaculate seniority, creating a feeling within that is vibrationally compatible with those realms of energy that are inherently all around you. Periodically speaking, we find that we have the opportunity for an entity to come along who is able to engender such a maximal desire to serve, and it is at this time that we are then able to produce the greatest results.

... This also has proven to be a venue wherein we are able to continue allowing ourselves to have the messages without needing the elaborate process of deep unconscious trance work. Of course, as you are aware, our messages are filtered somewhat (through your own personality self), and thus the end product is not always the same as what you see in said Ra Material. However, do not doubt yourself in knowing that you have indeed produced much comparable material with us, and that it also is a representation of the blending of foci between our own level and your own. It is through this melding of dimensions that we have been able to take off some more of the scholarly edge that we possessed in the Ra Material and instead turn it into a more completed form in the here and now.

—Ra/Wilcock, January 3, 1999

Viewed from the greater perspective, it's easy to see how Wilcock's mission is completely congruent with Cayce's, albeit with a different form of expression. Those who have studied Cayce's work tend to believe that psychic ability is real. Cayce's high degree of accuracy would make plausible the compelling suggestion that the Earth is gearing up for a massive energetic transformation beginning in 1998. However, in spite of the coherence and credibility of Cayce's work, it was still unacceptable to science. There was just no research during the time of Cayce's life that could scientifically explain his abilities. One might imagine Cayce's frustration and his desire to return in the future when scientific validation would be possible.

Wilcock's online book *Convergence, Volume III: The Divine Cosmos* draws on known, published, credible scientific data to create a unified model of the cosmos that he believes can validate the work of Cayce, the *Law of One* series, and his own channeling as well. The perspective of Ra, first implied by Cayce then expanded upon by the work of L/L Research, is finally ready for the mainstream with Wilcock's scientific back-up of Ra's metaphysical cosmology. In Part Three you can read "The Energetic Engine of Evolution" for a first-hand exposure to Wilcock's scientific compilation work.

Even after six years of being aware of his connection with Cayce, Wilcock is still not overly concerned with convincing anyone that he was Cayce. He's much more comfortable with presenting his scientific side than being a recognized prophet. At the time of this writing, Wilcock has received more recognition for his scientific work than his channeling, and he seems to prefer it that way. One of his personal challenges is to bridge the gap between science and spirit by solving the enigma of how what we usually refer to as God or the "One Infinite Creator" actually interfaces with the physical world via the "spiraling torsion field." Wilcock's treatises lend credibility to the dimensional shift and explain how the ascensions prophesied by Jesus might scientifically occur. The majority of his media appearances at the time of this writing focus on his scientific data, and, unless asked, he doesn't bring up his Cayce connection.

His website has received more than 350,000 hits as of the middle of 2003. Wilcock has written five books available for free download online. He appeared two times on Art Bell's Coast-to-Coast radio program, ostensibly with millions of listeners in the audience. He was also the Research Director and a principal lecturer for The Time of Global Shift seminar tour. In these presentations, he never mentioned that he had done any channeled work or that he was connected to Cayce, even though Carla L. Rueckert, who was the "instrument" for the *Law of One* series, was a featured speaker at the last two events in Louisville, Kentucky, and Huntsville, Alabama, along with her husband Jim McCarty, the scribe for that series.

Let's review how well Wilcock's life actually fits the terms of the Cayce prophecy,[15] which was introduced at the beginning of this chapter:

"He must enter again in that period, or in 1998"—Wilcock was informed by his Dream Voice in November of 1997 that he was the reincarnation of Edgar Cayce; in July of 1998 he began doing readings professionally; and in January of 1999 his source identified itself as Ra. Perhaps the Cayce reading referred to the "priest" in the prophecy because the priest had a more direct and conscious experience of Ra as his source, similar to Wilcock's experience, as opposed to Cayce, whose source never identified itself and was only available when Cayce was in his sleeping state.

"He saw himself back in Virginia Beach"—Wilcock was instructed by his Dream Voice to move to Virginia Beach before he had the slightest idea about his Cayce connection and his resemblance to Cayce. He thus "returned" to Virginia Beach just two months before 1998 and began giving readings the following July. By Ra giving Wilcock the direction to move to Virginia Beach, they made sure that he would fulfill the prophecy.

"Surrounded by many of those who had been with him at that earlier time . . . "—Wilcock identified many of his past Cayce associates to be present once again in his current life. There are correspondences of both appearance and personality traits. Wilcock has comparison photos posted on his website.

"As this priest may develop himself to be in that position, to be in that capacity as a liberator of the world . . . "—Wilcock is obviously working out many of his own "distortions" this lifetime and makes no pretense that he is perfect or better than anyone else because of his unusual connections or karmic history. He describes Ra in the initial period of their connection as his personal "psychotherapist." He candidly reveals, on his website, many of the issues he has faced, including women problems, anger, weight problems, and financial difficulties. He "may develop himself" and become one of a team of world liberators *if* he can overcome his own obstacles. He understands very well his mission and is dedicated to succeeding. In the author's estimation, Wilcock is already laying the foundations for being this liberator by having the courage to put up his website and tell his experience, in spite of his own insecurities and the ridicule he has endured.

I would like to take a moment and address the skeptics. There are many aspects of Wilcock's story that are undisputed fact. He definitely had an interest in healing, psychic phenomena, and metaphysics as a child, before he ever knew who Edgar Cayce was. He is definitely psychic. He has done hundreds of readings for people where his Source displayed an awareness of the intimate details of their lives with no prior knowledge. I have personally referred a number of people to Wilcock for readings, and in almost every case they were in awe of his psychic awareness and the wisdom from which their life issues were evaluated.

Wilcock's Source has made a number of very specific and documented predictions regarding his personal life and the world at large that have come to pass. The records of many of these predictions and the associated dates have been posted on his website and the websites of others. His physical resemblance to Cayce is undeniable.

Even though his Dream Voice has implored him to use his connection with Cayce to get attention for their message, his association with Cayce has not been easy, mostly bringing him scorn and ridicule. As the author of this book, I can speak of my first-hand experience with Wilcock regarding his resistance to telling this story so explicitly. It took six months of negotiation before he was willing to trust the author's motivation and to perceive the element of service in allowing the story to be released. He does not look forward to the controversy, celebrity, and notoriety that this book might create.

On the other hand, there are many aspects of Wilcock's connection to Cayce that belong in the category of circumstantial evidence. In my initial exposure to Wilcock I had to evaluate him from the position of my own skepticism. I learned that prior to the time that he became aware of his connection to Cayce, he had studied Cayce and even went to Cayce study groups. He had also studied and was greatly inspired by the Law of One material long before it was revealed to him that Ra was his own Source. I considered the possibility that he had programmed his subconscious with data about Cayce and Ra, and that his subconscious incubated this information to be released later in his "Dream Voice." These were all possibilities that crossed my mind as I did my initial diligent research for this book.

The opposite side to this position is that if Wilcock were Cayce in his past life, and if the same Ra of the *Law of One* series were his own Higher Self/Oversoul, then of course he would gravitate towards an interest in Cayce and Ra. If the only indication of his Cayce connection was his Dream Voice telling him so, then our case would be very weak. If he could be clearly identified as seeking fame, glory, large profits, and recognition, then one might be inclined to think that he concocted this story. But when all the other circumstances are added, the Cayce connection becomes much harder to dispute.

Then there's the A.R.E., which is the organization dedicated to the propagation of the Cayce readings. This is probably one of the biggest bones of contention for those enamored with the Cayce legend as they evaluate Wilcock's authenticity. The A.R.E. has not been willing, at the time of this writing, to endorse Wilcock as Cayce's reincarnation, and this is an issue that deserves to be analyzed rather carefully. During the time Wilcock lived in Virginia Beach (he has since moved), he made a concerted effort to get the attention of the A.R.E. in 1998 and present his case. In the W.H. Church book *Many Happy Returns*, there was an interesting reference to the A.R.E.'s policy regarding "far out" phenomena:

> Anything bordering on sci-fi or UFOlogy is strictly frowned upon by all of the official spokesmen for the Edgar Cayce Foundation and its affiliate organization the Association for Research and Enlightenment, in Virginia Beach. (The critics of parapsychology research are strident enough as it is, without providing them with additional grist for the mills of malice and mockery.)[16]

Taking into consideration the A.R.E.'s policy, it's easy to understand the organization's difficulty with endorsing Wilcock as Cayce, particularly at the time when Wilcock made his initial insecure and nervous introduction. Since the time of Cayce's death, Cayce's credibility has become firmly established, due largely to the efforts of the A.R.E. Accepting Wilcock would have to be seen as an extreme threat to the good reputation built for Cayce over so many years. Wilcock would jeopardize the status quo with his talk of E.T.s, dimensional shifts, and "social memory complexes" from Venus.

In addition, there was a test that Cayce himself created from his own waking state, without the endorsement or guidance of his Source. Anyone who made a claim to be his reincarnation was asked to pass this test in order to receive the "official" A.R.E. stamp of approval. The test consists of a series of five questions that only the "true" reincarnated Cayce would pass, purportedly dealing with such single-word answers as Cayce's mother's middle name, the name of his first pet, et cetera. Since he was not consciously aware of the "veil of forgetting" discussed in Chapter Three, Edgar's idea was that he would be the exact same person the next time and still in possession of memories from his former life that no one else would know.

Wilcock refused to take this test. Although he has consistently demonstrated the ability to bring forth accurate psychic information regarding his clients as well as prophecies, this information has never been available to him on demand as it was for those who would ask the sleeping Cayce questions and always receive specific answers. As Ra said, via Wilcock:

> Please note that we are not here to provide what you would call the "feel-good, curiosity-feeding" psychic readings. We are here to give those messages that may seem rather brutally intense at first, but they are, however, exactly what you need to wake up from.—Ra/Wilcock, November 11, 1999

To expect Wilcock to be just like Cayce is as absurd as judging a child by its parent, or expecting Cayce to be just like John Bainbridge. Cayce could never have anticipated what his higher self was planning for his next life or the karma he would have to work out, just as John Bainbridge could never have imagined that in his next life he would be recognized as the most accurate prophet of the Western world.

I mentioned earlier how if Wilcock had the ability of omniscience on demand, it could be detrimental to him. Because of Internet exposure, his reputation would grow very quickly and he could not possibly satisfy the demand for readings, which could lead to a crisis of conscience and possibly endangerment.

Another factor is that being recognized as Cayce by the A.R.E. might impede Wilcock's own growth, in the same way that certain musical artists lose their creative connection once they become famous. Wilcock's Higher Self might block this recognition until he is able to work out his own personality distortions so that the recognition would not affect him in a negative way. Also, without the official A.R.E. stamp of approval, we are allowed the free-will choice to discern our own truth on the matter.

If such an identity test were to be performed accurately, then the de-facto equivalent of "proof" would be given. According to Wilcock, this would directly contravene Ra's Law of Free Will, which implies that entities must always have the free will to make up their own minds about their spiritual beliefs. If absolute proof were available for Wilcock's connection with Cayce, there would be an opening for negative influences, with the potential for creating blind followers. Though it may seem frustrating, this Law of Free Will is the only way in which the higher forces can ensure that we make our own decisions about what to believe.

Ra has already noted all the problems that resulted from the Egyptian incarnation where Ra-Ta was recognized as the "Sun God" and performed miracles. Humans show the consistent propensity to give their power away to authorities outside themselves rather than accept the challenge of making their own direct connection with the "One Infinite Creator."

It is also Wilcock's experience that the accuracy and depth of his readings are greatly impacted by those present when a reading is conducted. In a situation where the thought forms of those in the room were expressing doubt and judgment (such as the A.R.E. test), his ability to bring forward accurate data would be greatly impeded. Edgar Cayce himself had exactly the same response to the influence of those present in a room where he was giving a reading, according to Harmon Bro in *A Seer Out of Season:* "... there were plenty of signs that he had to constantly guard his mind against intrusion by the thoughts and feelings of others because of his psychic gifts.... All of this information could aid him when he needed it to counsel troubled visitors or friends outside of trance. But uninvited, it gave him clutter."[17]

I believe that the A.R.E. is not aware of all the circumstances of the Wilcock/Cayce connection as presented in this book, and particularly in the next chapter. But as time passes and the story of Wilcock's life becomes more widespread, the A.R.E. might well accept his lineage.

Moving on from the A.R.E. endorsement issue, I also considered the possibility that Wilcock is under the control of a negative being from the other side who is masquerading as positive. With some malevolent plot for mankind, this being could dupe Wilcock and make him an unknowing pawn in the plan's execution.

These are issues that you must evaluate for yourself, just as I did, and make your own decision. History gives us example after example of great people who were persecuted or even killed in their own time, from Socrates to Jesus to Nelson Mandela. Even Cayce went to jail for fortune telling. When Cayce had his first experience of his own prognosticative ability, he himself went into doubt about whether he could trust it. He asked himself if it could be a dark force masquerading as positive. His Christian fundamentalism was being challenged. But every person he did a reading for was helped. Cayce said that if his readings should hurt one person, he would stop doing them. Jesus gave the criteria that "by your fruits you shall be known." Similarly, this will be Wilcock's greatest test. Part Two of this book focuses on Wilcock's Ra readings. It is in that section, I believe, that the most compelling evidence is found. It is the wisdom and compassion that I perceived in those readings that created Wilcock's ultimate validity for me, in addition to the value his readings have created for his clients. Regardless of how many facts and correspondences I might present between Wilcock and Cayce, these readings are the "fruits."

Although I recommend that you withhold your final judgment of the Wilcock/Cayce connection until you read Parts Two and Three, there are many striking additional factors linking Cayce and Wilcock that are further detailed in the next chapter.

Don't let the scorn and derision of others stop you from being effective in your goals. Keep a clear head and remain relaxed, knowing all the while that there is indeed a final conclusion to these words as they now stand, and that this moment does indeed approach with the unwavering certainty of the clock striking on the hour.

—Ra/Wilcock, February 21, 2000

Chapter

9

Common Threads

There are numerous correlations, as already indicated, tying Wilcock to Cayce. I discussed the connection between the *Law of One* series and the Cayce readings; the Wilcock fulfillment of the Cayce prophecy; the correspondences in their life patterns; and the eye-witness evidence of their close physical resemblance.

Wilcock painstakingly researched the Cayce material after his Dream Voice's shocking disclosure, and every piece of evidence that he uncovered fully supported his Dream Voice revelation. This chapter presents some of the additional supporting evidence that surfaced. We will see the statistically improbable correspondences between Cayce and Wilcock's astrology charts. We will take another look at their physical similarities and the precedents for similar appearances being indicative of a reincarnation. We will continue to note congruencies in the information brought forward by Wilcock, L/L Research, and Cayce. If Ra has been the source of information that inspired all three, we would expect to find common perspectives threaded through each of their unique spiritual wisdom teachings.

Astrology

One the most amazing points of correspondence between David Wilcock and Edgar Cayce is the relative positions of the planets at the time of their births. In looking for indicators that could support a claim of reincarnation, obviously there are no scientific criteria to go by. One can only conjecture as to the significance when confronted with the statistically improbable correlations that show up in the comparison of the astrology charts of Wilcock and Cayce. In researching this angle, I looked for some precedent in which similar astrology charts point to an incident of reincarnation, and I found none. But there is indication according to Cayce himself that when one is between lives, there is a degree of choice regarding the next lifetime. An evolved soul like Cayce might choose a moment to be reborn where the astrological alignments match those of his previous life. Both Cayce and Wilcock were born in the Year of the Ox, according to the Chinese Zodiac. Furthermore, the positions of the Sun, Moon, Mercury, Venus, and Mars at the time of Wilcock's birth are almost identical to their positions at the time of Cayce's birth. The Moon in both Cayce and Wilcock's charts is in thirteen degrees of Taurus. A cursory comparison of the similarities of the two charts is outlined on the facing page.

For astrologers who would like to validate the Cayce/Wilcock correspondences for themselves, Cayce's birthday is March 18, 1877, at 3:00 P.M. in Hopkinsville, Kentucky; Wilcock's birthday is March 8, 1973, at 11:16 P.M. in Schenectady, New York.

Astrologer Brian McNaughton has independently concluded that there could not possibly have been a more favorable day for Cayce to reincarnate in a 127-year period than at the exact date of Wilcock's birth, March 8, 1973, provided that the goal in the reincarnation of a more evolved soul was to attain character similarity through natal

Parameter	Chart of David Wilcock	Chart of Edgar Cayce	Probability
Position of Sun	Pisces	Pisces	1:12
Position of Moon	Taurus	Taurus	1:12
Position of Mercury	Pisces	Pisces	1:12
Position of Venus	Pisces	Pisces	1:12
Position of Mars	Capricorn	Capricorn	1:12
Chinese Year	Ox	Ox	1:12
Degree of Moon	13 degrees	13 degrees	1:360

astrology. The chances of having the Sun, Moon, Mercury, Mars, and Venus simply appear in the same sign of the Zodiac for both lifetimes are one in two hundred fifty thousand. That doesn't even take into account the fact that they are both in the Year of the Ox, with a probability of one in twelve. Furthermore, many of the overlaps are quite exact, leading to an average variance of 7.1 degrees for the inner planets, which diminishes to about 2.4 degrees if the planet Mercury is excluded. Though the outer planets are not directly covering each other, they exist in very precise geometric relationships to each other such as 30, 60, and 90 degrees, which is by no means a common occurrence when studying two combined astrology charts. Furthermore, the position of the Moon, which is considered a key determinant of one's character, is so exact between the two charts that there is only a small percentage of one degree between their two positions. David informed me that his mother and father both state that they were getting frustrated at the time of his birth, since he seemed to be waiting too long to emerge. Now we know why.

If we simply look at the overall probability of having all the personal planets in the same sign, both entities born in the Year of the Ox, and the Moon being in exactly the same degree on both charts, *the chance of all these circumstances occurring randomly becomes at least hundreds of thousands to one, if not millions to one, depending on the parameters of the probability calculation.* Once we factor in the similarities in facial appearance with the astrology, the probabilities of all this being pure chance are ... well, "out of this world."

The following information is a verbatim summary based on comparison of the two charts made by professional astrologer McNaughton. The text is excerpted from Wilcock's website, www.ascension2000.com.[1]

The fact that Edgar Cayce worked himself to such an early demise most likely accounts for the incredible number of contacts between his chart and Wilcock's. The implication is that Cayce had unfinished business in his Cayce life and he would attempt to reincarnate in a similar astrological pattern.

I [McNaughton] searched the period from 1873 to the year 2000, to find another year in which the personal planets (Moon, Mercury, Venus, and Mars) were in the same signs as Cayce and Wilcock.... In that entire 127-year period, Wilcock's exact birthday, March 8, 1973, was the only date where **all four planets were in the same position as in the chart of Cayce.**

Similar Appearance

It is not just Wilcock's dreams that tell him he is Cayce reborn. It is his mirror: his jaw is slightly less undershot, and his earlobes are bigger, but otherwise Ed and Dave could be twins.

—Uri Geller[2]

David Wilcock is the spitting image of any of a number of photos in the A.R.E. archives of a young Cayce, depending on which angle of the head is considered. Edgar Cayce, Plato, and H.W. Percival all made statements about the correspondence of facial appearance and characteristics between lifetimes.

The soul returns to earth in a body similar to its last one and has similar talents and inclinations.—Plato[3]

Pictures of the average person taken at corresponding periods of two or even several lives would show little difference. The physical parents may or may not be the same, but the features furnished by heredity no matter from what parents are the same for a string of lives, with the ordinary person.
                          —H.W. Percival, *Thinking and Destiny*[4]

The senses ... are registered in our physical bodies in such a way that they are stamped upon our very faces.
                          —Edgar Cayce, *A Search for God*[5]

Dr. Walter Semkiw's book *Return of the Revolutionaries*[6] is based on the premise that many significant figures from the Revolutionary War period have reincarnated in the present period of time—only now, instead of trying to change the world through politics, many of them have reincarnated as popular figures of New Age spirituality.

The book is filled with comparison photos and drawings demonstrating extreme facial resemblances carrying through from one lifetime to the next, with many case studies including Bill Clinton, George Bush, Marianne Williamson, and even Oprah Winfrey. When Semkiw was researching his book, he had the help of Kevin Ryerson, a trance channel who claims to have powers similar to Edgar Cayce's. In certain cases when Ryerson had indicated the past lifetime of a given individual, Semkiw found that the facial features of the person indicated by Ryerson were similar to the person whom he inquired about.

In doing a comparison of the two pictures of the young Edgar Cayce and David Wilcock, I had some amazing realizations. On a surface level the similarities are obviously striking, but as one looks a little deeper, the differences between the two pictures are even more striking, particularly as one considers the life experiences of Cayce as they would have transferred into Wilcock.

One may describe Cayce's look and mood as innocent, perhaps slightly passive, while Wilcock looks very intense, aggressive, and a bit angry. If one were going to assign a song to the pictures, Cayce might be singing "What's It All About, Alfie?" while Wilcock's song might be "Hey You, Get Off of My Cloud." We must keep in mind that this is a young Edgar Cayce prior to going through the experience of his amazing life, whereas young David Wilcock would have come into this life having completely internalized the life experiences of Edgar Cayce at the time of his death. So what could have happened in the course of Cayce's life to cause this transformation?

As I studied Cayce's life, as opposed to his readings, two things stood out as recurring themes. One was his inability to make himself comfortable financially. Although he made fortunes for others via the information he provided in his readings, no one looked back and made sure Cayce was taken care of. He never made specific business deals and arrangements ensuring that he would be guaranteed to share in the profits; he would depend on others' good will. And his greatest dream was finally sabotaged—that of having a hospital, which would treat patients according to the information brought forward in his readings. Cayce was responsible for the Blumenthal brothers becoming millionaires. They had promised to back the Cayce hospital, but when it was finally up and running, they withdrew their support and let it fall into bankruptcy. So Edgar was left feeling stymied and betrayed by the end of his life.

> For Cayce, it was the end of a 20-year quest. His world, like so many others, finally collapsed into a puddle of evaporating dreams, which would never be realized or seen again. During the ride on the bubble, he had never been paid more than $3,400 a year, thus he had never accumulated any tangible assets. Now he was, once again, totally broke. In the depth of the depression, he finally abandoned the idea of the hospital.

He became aware of his own mismanagement and owned the failure. Essentially, he gave up trying to manage anything.[7]

Cayce's one respite was his service to others via his readings, which is the second recurring theme. He tirelessly gave readings, and as his fame grew, the demand was overwhelming. His readings implored him to cut back. He was told that his health was in danger, but Cayce paid no heed and eventually died prematurely.

Self-repression and denial ran strong right up to the end. He was clearly warned more than once to stop working and rest. Eventually the readings turned sardonic, telling him it was pointless to give him more information about his health because he wouldn't attend to it. At the annual A.R.E. meeting in June of 1944, his public reading asked people to pray daily for Cayce's health, and then gave in effect a last will and testament for how to sustain the work. The reading advised A.R.E. never to promote publicly, to keep the work as an unpretentious shadow exhibiting the patient work of the divine. And so they have. In August of 1944, at the age of 67, Cayce suffered a stroke and never gave another reading. After slowly recuperating in the mountains, he returned to Virginia Beach in December, only to die on January 3, 1945.[8]

If Cayce has returned to the world as Wilcock, it would make sense that he should have to work through feelings of anger. He doesn't want to let anybody screw him around. He's watching his back. He's watching his diet. He's very disciplined. He's staying in control of his life and he's providing service, but on his own terms. Wilcock might appear intractable to some, but in view of his Cayce life experience, it fits together perfectly.

Personality

The correlations continue with a review of the personalities of Cayce and Wilcock. In Chapter Two I gave many references to Harmon Bro's book *A Seer Out of Season,* where Cayce was presented as someone who felt emasculated in the sense that his greatest gift to others occurred when he was in an unconscious state. Cayce had an unfulfilled need for acknowledgment of his conscious creations. It is easy to see how this steps down into Wilcock's emphasis on his scientific research and music over his readings. Bro writes:

> Was Cayce the waking man in competition with Cayce the entranced man? . . . Even though it was time for him to go unconscious, and the conversation stumbled into awkward pauses [when those present wanted him to begin his unique process], he might extend a story as if to say, "Look, I matter as a conscious person too."[9]

Many other characteristics step down as byproducts of the Bainbridge lifetime, whereby both Wilcock and Cayce could easily be taken over by feelings of rage, frustration, moodiness, and/or withdrawal.

Dreams

The significance and interpretation of dreams are extremely relevant to both Wilcock and Cayce. I realize that this is a rather unique point of comparison between the two, as I am not aware of very many psychics who utilize dreams in their work as extensively as Cayce and Wilcock. Cayce's Source interpreted dreams similarly to Wilcock's Ra, as Harmon Bro tells us in *A Seer Out of Season:*

> The scope of what his trance counsel could accomplish with dreams was breathtaking ... [T]he major task was interpreting the meaning of dreams, which the *unconscious* Cayce did so well that his dream study became one of the first areas to win his work wider recognition after his death.[10]

Wilcock's readings, which are posted on his website, show that in most cases, the reading is preceded by a dream of Wilcock's, and Ra uses the dream as a foundation for the reading. As mentioned earlier, Wilcock will even have a dream on behalf of his client prior to delivering the actual client reading:

> Note: Your reading consists of a personalized dream where David acts and lives through your own life's issues, sealing off any conscious mind overlay from the data and answering your questions with remarkable effectiveness. Once the dream is completely dictated onto the tape and analyzed, a reading from positive Confederation sources [Ra] then follows it.
> —from Wilcock's website[11]

Fear of Water

According to Cayce's readings, John Bainbridge died while marooned on a raft. In *My Life as a Seer,* Cayce speaks of his intense fear of water:

> As a child, Edgar was not as fond of playing in water as some children and really he would avoid water especially when it was cold. And if he could get to the breakfast table without

washing his hands and face he would do so.... He just hated water or hated to bathe his face in cold water especially.[12]

When I queried Wilcock via email about his attitude regarding water, without mentioning anything about Cayce's phobia, he sent me the following response:

For years as a child I absolutely could not stand to be in the rain. One of the single most terrible experiences in my early childhood was when my brother and I went to Clifton Country Mall with my father to see a movie. When we got out of the movie, we could not find the car and it was pouring rain. I suffered abominably.

Another similar situation occurred as a teenager when I went on a "vacation" with my buddies. The car broke down in the middle of nowhere and we managed to get a ride to the gas station, but had to walk back in the pouring rain with a gas can that had a bad seam and would cut into your hands. I suffered so powerfully when I was the one who had to carry the gas that my mother woke up in the middle of the night.

Probably the single scariest moment of my childhood was when my brother and I got stuck in a boat with my father and his friend Rick in the middle of Lake George when a storm came up. The boat was tilting so much that there was water in the window on the far side of the cabin inside the boat—it was darn near 90 degrees. I totally thought I was going to die—then my father and Rick told me afterwards that they were far more worried about lightning than about capsizing.

Ra-Ta, Cayce, and Wilcock Were All Channels

Obviously Wilcock is a channel. He defines himself as such. I don't believe the word "channel" was used during the lifetime of Cayce. We've already hypothesized that Cayce was, in fact, channeling Ra as his own Higher Self but couldn't be aware of it because of his fundamentalist Christianity. His information was usually revealed as coming from his "Source." But there were specific instances where Cayce did identify sources other than his normal Source. At various times, Cayce acknowledged that other beings were present, including Confucius, during the course of a reading.

Interestingly enough, Cayce's much-quoted "Earth changes" prophecy was not given by Cayce's Source but rather by an entity that identified itself as Halaliel. I include an excerpt from that reading below where the events referred to were supposed to transpire around 1998:

> The earth will be broken up in the western portion of America. The greater portion of Japan must go into the sea. The upper portion of Europe will be changed as in the twinkling of an eye.... I, Halaliel, have spoken. [Cayce reading 3976–15]

In studying the Cayce readings, I learned that the Cayce study groups as well as Cayce's scribe, Gladys Davis, had doubt and concern as to whether they could trust Halaliel, and eventually decided not to allow him to come through.[13] In *A Seer Out of Season,* Harmon Bro addressed this subject as follows:

> After breaking into his readings with messages several times, a source which called itself Halaliel, who proclaimed that it

never had been incarnated but could bring Cayce much-needed wisdom, asked them to place the reading process under his guidance. The event occurred during study group meetings and the group went through much soul searching and division before the majority won out who felt the only attunement Cayce should ever seek directly was the Christ.[14]

Ra, in a Wilcock reading, identified Halaliel as an entity from the negative realms and even referred to the Cayce reading numbers in making his point. Ra commented:

Cayce was not immune to negative readings, as such. And thus, the entity Halaliel did indeed contact him, and gave prophecies of a more vitriolic nature. Messages of doom are not necessarily intended to inspire hope, but rather fear. This fear, as a restrictive complex originating in what you would term as the past, did indeed hang over Cayce's head as it later did in David's own. Said Cayce Readings also predicted a major earth movement in 1936. This also did not come to pass, as anyone can see.

There is an important distinction that can be made between the messages from the positive contact, such as 1602–3 question 8, as opposed to the negative information such as that found in 3976–15. It is important to remember that any of the entities upon your plane who would choose to channel do indeed open up the requirement of the invitation of a negative greeting, if their own actions invite such a greeting. Both Cayce and David in the past have been depolarized by their own freewill decisions to maintain certain attitudes in their day-to-day existence, evoking emotions of fear and worry.... If you look closely at reading 1602–3, it says very, very clearly that the events in 1998 would be gradual and not cataclysmic. Also, if you look to the reading which speaks of Japan going beneath the sea and of the inundation of

California and the like, you see at the end of the reading, 'I Halaliel have spoken.'

We have covered this ground previously with Cayce's workings, as he was eventually able to realize through our guidance that Halaliel was sort of a trickster entity, designed to depolarize the contact somewhat.—Ra/Wilcock, July 29, 1999

Those who are still living in fear of the Cayce Earth-change prophecies can rest easy, at least for the moment. In one reading seldom focused upon by pre-1998 Cayce doomsday scholars, Cayce clearly stated that Earth changes would be gradual and not cataclysmic, from roughly 1998 onward. [Cayce reading 1602–3]

In Cayce's description of his past life as Ra-Ta, we see another indication that Ra-Ta was channeling.

Ra-Ta gradually gathered about him those who would hearken to his words pertaining to relations with an outside world or to those divisions in the body which represented the intermission from an experience to an experience. The natives held more strongly to the necessity of materialization for the enjoyment, as may be surmised from the high materially developed civilization which had been reached at this particular period. [Cayce reading 294–153]

When one reads this section for the first time, it might seem a bit obscure, but upon considering that the Cayce reading is describing Ra-Ta's channeling, it makes sense.

"hearken to his words pertaining to relations with an outside world"—Ra-Ta had people gathered around him listening to his words pertaining to "relations with an outside world," a possible reference to the group soul—Ra.

"... the intermission from an experience to an experience"—possibly a reference to the space between two experiences where the channeling could come through, or perhaps a reference to so-called torsion radiation energy.

"The natives held more strongly to the necessity of materialization for the enjoyment"—Most people of the Earth at that time were more interested in the material world than in spiritual messages such as those of Ra-Ta.

In the Cayce readings, File 294–198, there was an analysis of the origins of Cayce's powers by his wife, Gertrude, where his psychic abilities were attributed to the training he had in his past lifetime as Ra-Ta.

In the Cayce readings, File 254–063, Cayce's Source was described as being "conversant with many dimensions" and had to condense the information brought forward into "three-dimensional terms."

Harmon Bro, in *A Seer Out of Season,* refers to a Cayce reading that foreshadowed Wilcock's semi-conscious channeling abilities:

It was natural to wonder why he needed to be entranced at all when he was so sensitive to people when he was wide awake. His readings observed that because of his past life excesses, he was too vulnerable to those who sought his help. Perhaps in a future life, when he had regenerated himself, he might do counseling without trance.[15]

Interdimensional Science?

Edgar Cayce, L/L Research, and David Wilcock were and are on the cutting edge of insights linking science and spirituality.

Wilcock's work is guided by Ra to correlate current scientific breakthroughs with the advanced models of cosmology introduced to the modern era by L/L Research and Cayce. In the book *Edgar Cayce, An American Prophet,* Sidney Kirkpatrick gives new evidence in support of the thesis that advanced technological information came through Cayce:

> From hundreds of pages of sensational documents and correspondence that have never before been made public, it is now clear that such luminaries as Thomas Edison and Nikola Tesla had trance readings by Cayce, as did engineers at RCA, IBM, Delco, and the president and founder of the Goodyear Tire and Rubber Company. Inventor Mitchell Hastings credited Cayce with helping him to develop FM radio. NBC founder David Sarnoff and his family had secret readings. Remarkable technological and electronic designs provided by Cayce in trance are now used in almost every large hospital and airport in the world.[16]

Was Cayce downloading advanced technology from Ra and giving it to the technological pioneers of the period in the context of the readings he did for them? Sidney Kirkpatrick was the first writer to be given access to the private correspondence and other written materials of Cayce. In an interview with Phenomena News, Kirkpatrick disclosed some of the details:

[Questioner:] That is so amazing. How were you able to have the privilege of getting into some of the archives that have never before been seen? Tell us the story about finding out some of the stuff that hasn't been divulged until now, about who some of his clients were.

[Kirkpatrick:] As I said earlier, synchronicity wasn't even in my vocabulary. I didn't see, but looking back my mouth drops at how many doors were opened for me. I'm so surprised and feel so privileged. The identities of the people who had Cayce readings have always been kept a strict secret, strictly confidential. George Gershwin didn't want it being known that he had hemorrhoids, for example.... So many important names, and Cayce himself didn't beat his own drum. He wasn't out there selling readings. He believed that when you came to him, what he said and the requests he received were confidential—sort of like a patient-physician or attorney-client relationship. Enough people have died now that I could be given the list of names to correspond with the readings. A much richer story about Cayce emerges when you know the names. On one level, it's all the famous people—e.g. Thomas Edison, Nikola Tesla, inventors, scientists, Marilyn Monroe was even using beauty aids that Cayce had recommended. Ernest Hemingway's mother, the presidents of various companies—Goodyear Tire and Rubber, for example—it's a shame Firestone hadn't gotten a reading, engineers at IBM, a man who became a computer expert for IBM had had readings. That in itself was wonderful. It opened new vistas and you could see how many important people put great faith in Cayce.[17]

Wilcock and Ra-Ta

There are some interesting miscellaneous correlations between Wilcock and Ra-Ta. The Cayce readings [including 294-153] said that truths would be preserved in the pyramid not only for the current generation of Ra-Ta's own time (10,500 B.C.), but for the period when the Earth's position would change, causing an inundation in our present time. This could very likely refer to the position of the Earth in the galaxy and the energetic changes that are "inundating" us with new consciousness and social shifts—though most Cayce scholars only interpret such mentions as a reference to pole shift.

Cayce reading 294–153 spoke of Ra-Ta having preserved records in the pyramid for future generations. Keep in mind that the pyramids were built in the period of the inundation of Atlantis. The stored records would be safe until the Earth was in position for another inundation—which would be in the present period according to Ra and Wilcock's predicted dimensional shift. This will manifest as an increased intensity of Earth changes with a possible pole shift. These changes would be gradual, with an anticipated increase in intensity after 2008. There is an implied connection between the vibration of our collective consciousness and the intensity of the changes. Edgar Cayce said in one of his readings that just a few people of pure consciousness in an area could protect that vicinity from disasters.

In Cayce reading 295–150, it was revealed that Ra-Ta was the first person to introduce astrology to this planet during his Nubian exile period and was aware of the connection between celestial archetypes and earthly existence. Wilcock, in his online books such as *The Divine Cosmos,* demonstrates his own ability to research and deeply comprehend the nature of stellar events scientifically. You can read excerpts from *The Divine Cosmos* and *Divine Nature* in Part Three.

In Cayce reading 295–151, there is a reference to initiation during the reign of Ra-Ta and initiates who were "to act in the capacity of leaders":

... for the place of initiation of the initiates who were to act in the capacity of leaders in various activities.... Is it not fitting, then, that these must return?

These initiates that Ra-Ta was developing would become leaders in ancient Egypt and help to spread awareness of the Law of One.

Those initiates are somewhere on our planet right now, waiting to be reminded of their mission once again by lightworkers such as the priest Ra-Ta, in his current incarnation as David Wilcock.

Within the Cayce readings, when the names Ra and Ra-Ta appear, most Cayce scholars assume that they are referring to the same entity. However, in three instances, the Cayce readings clearly refer to Ra and Ra-Ta as being present at the same time, making it patently obvious that they were separate entities. In reading 966–001, it was indicated that the spiritual guidelines associated with the sun god were "later set up by Isis, Ra, Hermes, Ra-Ta." In reading 444–001, the entity for whom the reading was conducted was described as being in association with "... Ra-Ta, [and] with those of Ra...," implying that there were multiple beings at work separate from Ra-Ta. "Those of Ra" could very well be another way of expressing the idea of a "social memory complex" as given in the *Law of One* series. The phrase "those of Ra" appears four additional times throughout the Cayce readings. (Refer to files 294–152, 378–014, 897–001 and 219–001.) And finally, in Cayce reading 5756–10, both Ra and Ra-Ta were indicated as being simultaneously present on the other side at the time of the reading.

There were two additional instances in the Cayce readings where Ra was indicated as being a separate entity from the "priest" who would have been Ra-Ta. (Refer to file numbers 2067–001 and 3347–001.) To my knowledge, most Cayce scholars have never considered these indications of Ra-Ta and Ra being two distinct entities, but a close study of the Cayce readings shows that they are separate and supports the history of this period as outlined in the *Law of One* series by L/L Research.

Metaphysical Congruencies

The Concept of Wanderers

We introduced this term in Chapter One. In Book One of the *Law of One* series in 1981, Ra describes a Wanderer as an advanced soul from another dimension who voluntarily chooses to incarnate on the Earth plane to assist with the evolution of consciousness here.[18] It is a dangerous mission because the Wanderer will almost certainly forget his purpose once he incarnates, due to the "veil of forgetting." If Wilcock is one of the Ra group who separated out and took on a string of Earth incarnations, he is by all definitions a Wanderer.

From Ra/The Law of One Series (1981–1984)

Question: Who are the Wanderers?

Ra: Imagine, if you will, the sands of your shores. As countless as the grains of sand are the sources of intelligent infinity. When a social memory complex has achieved a complete understanding of its desire, it may conclude that its desire is to serve any entities that call for aid. These entities that you may call the Brothers and Sisters of Sorrow move towards this calling of sorrow. They come from all reaches of the infinite creation. They are not sorrowful themselves, but come to aid those that are in sorrow. They are the Wanderers. There are approximately 65 million on Earth. [Book One, p. 127]

Ra: Few there are of 4th density. Most are of 6th density. The desire to serve must be distorted towards a great deal of purity of mind and what you call foolhardiness or bravery. The challenge and danger to the Wanderer is that it will forget its mission, become karmically involved, and thus be swept into the maelstrom and turbulence which it had intended to avert. [Book One, p. 127]

Carla L. Rueckert's comment: "It is no wonder that Wanderers have some difficulty waking up within the illusion we call consensus reality. There is always the fear, as one enters incarnation, that one will not awaken at all, but be lost for the whole life experience." [Book Five, p. 58]

To my knowledge, this is the first time that the word "Wanderer" was expressed in writing with this cosmic connotation, but it has now become a fairly popular concept among UFOlogists. Many websites are based on or refer to Wanderers. (We include some reference to these websites in Part Three.) As mentioned previously, Scott Mandelker wrote a best-selling book—*From Elsewhere*—based on the idea of Wanderers, which he was first exposed to in the *Law of One* series. This book was of pivotal importance in the growth period of David Wilcock, who began seriously considering that he might be a Wanderer when he took Mandelker's quiz. In the story of Ra-Ta, Cayce described an early incarnation on the planet as a hybrid birth between a god and a human, and I drew the conclusion that Ra-Ta was a member of the higher-dimensional group soul Ra who volunteered for a mission on Earth, i.e., a Wanderer. Cayce in his readings said that he originated from Arcturus. Wilcock read *From Elsewhere* prior to his dream messages and described his response to the ideas presented in the book as follows (this is excerpted from Wilcock's website):

Mandelker explained that "Wanderers" were those who had a soul that was extra-terrestrial, a soul that had originated in a higher dimensional level and had then compressed its vibrations to volunteer to be human. This volunteer mission was supposedly geared towards a "lightening of the planetary vibrations" so as to help everyone become more attuned. The long story short is that I read these thirteen questions in Mandelker's quiz and I could hardly even breathe by the time I got to the last one. Somehow, some way, Mandelker's list had described my personality so well, with such accuracy, that I could hardly even believe my own eyes! It was as if I had sat there and told him all of the deepest, most personal secrets of my life, and he had then compiled them into a list of twelve main characteristics that defined me.

I found a very specific reference to this idea of "Wanderer" in a Cayce reading. Although Cayce never used the word "Wanderer," his meaning was clearly the same as the concept introduced by Ra through L/L Research some forty years later.

Entities enter our solar system from other systems, bringing with them the development and influences from these systems. Such influences are seldom understood, for the laws of this three-dimensional sphere become too binding, limiting our understanding. One importance of these more vast influences lies in their relation to the entrance of great leaders and teachers at periods of world change. [Cayce reading 2265–001]

According to Ra, as per the Wilcock readings, there presently are 100 million Wanderers on the planet to assist in our dimensional-shift transition. Most are not aware of their origins or mission. The most common problem that Wanderers encounter is alienation. Until they learn to identify their true natures and begin fulfilling the original contract of service they made at the soul level, prior to incarnating, they will feel out of place on Earth.

And only a being with the celestial wisdom of Ra could even suggest this idea, since it is based on knowledge that is not available to earthbound humans.

Planetary Cycles and the Dimensional Shift

One of the keystone concepts of Ra's cosmology, as expressed through both L/L Research and Wilcock, is the idea of planetary cycles. Our solar system has a 25,000-year cycle and a 75,000-year cycle. We are at the culmination of the 75,000-year cycle right now.

As described in Chapter Four, empty space is not really empty. It is filled with spiraling bands of torsion-field energy. Contemporary metaphysical scientists, such as Gregg Braden, call it zero point energy, the photon belt, or aetheric energy. Braden's book *Awakening to Zero Point*[19] gives his own scientific research backing up this premise of a dimensional shift. The density of this zero point energy varies in empty space, and it is the movement of the Earth and the solar system through this that creates the planetary cycles. So as the solar system passes through this increased density of energy, significant changes are translated down to the physical level.

I actually recall learning about these cycles in the Cayce readings twenty years ago, and I didn't understand them at the time. What I didn't realize was that most likely, no one else understood what a solar cycle was, either. Pondering on what Cayce's Source meant by a solar cycle was pure speculation. But with the expansion provided within the *Law of One* series, Wilcock's intuitive material, and Wilcock's scientific research, the original Cayce references now make more sense and are further supportive of the postulate that Ra was the source of information for all three.

In Cayce reading 1603–2, he refers to a "cycle of the solar activity" regarding the change from the Piscean to the Aquarian Age. In reading 2265–1, "a period of change, a period of trial, the completion of a cycle" is referred to as "the time draws near for a folding up...." Compare this with the information from L/L Research and Ra/Wilcock:

Ra/The Law of One Series (1981–1984)

Ra: This sphere ... has not made an easy transition to the vibrations that beckon. Therefore, it will be fetched with some inconvenience.... This inconvenience, or disharmonious vibratory complex [i.e., the disharmony of the peoples creating Earth changes] began several of your years in your past. It shall continue unabated for a period of approximately thirty of your years.

Question: In thirty years this will be a 4th-density planet. Is this correct?

Ra: This is so.

[Author's note: This channeling session was held in 1981, so the transition to fourth density would culminate in 2011.]

Ra/Wilcock reading, December 22, 1998

"There has never been a greater time in the entirety of your human history as this moment now. Every action that you perceive and perform in your daily life and your larger global life will be forever remembered. As we speak, the actions that you go through are indeed being recorded on the skein of space and time, by the pen or the quill of the Christ self, revealed through your own inner desire to perfect yourselves in Light and in Love."

[Author's note: In doing a scan of the entire Cayce file of 14,500 readings, another one of those strange correspondences showed up. The phrase "skein of time and space" occurs fifty-five times with the word "written" or "recorded."]

"When these concepts are made clear, the fundamental edifice upon which much of humankind has been built will be seen to change. There is a discrete boundary shift wherein the quanta that make up human consciousness and physical matter will be seen to leap the gap in vibrational potential and accelerate themselves into the fourth-density vibrations."

Ra/Wilcock reading, March 19, 2001

"The transformation is indeed the shift of the ages, and the overriding influence that the master cycle brings to usher in a new era of prosperity and peace. There has been so much war, so much dissension, so much foul-minded behavior and action and thought in your world, and it needs counterbalancing. The times today were as those spoken of by the Hindus when they referred to the last days of the Kali Yuga, and the bickering and fighting that would occur between various factions of humanity is indeed being seen.

"We want to again remind you, as we have often stated before, that prior to the time of ascension there will be that of the shifting of the poles."

For the first eight chapters of this book, I focused on the subjective correlations between Cayce and Wilcock and included the cosmology of Ra. I felt it important to set the stage before offering the more objective indicators that are presented in this chapter. When (and if) one comes to his or her own realization that Wilcock is Cayce, there is a definite tendency to want to know the secret knowledge of what's to come. As I immersed myself in the process of writing this book, I realized that knowing what's to come is not nearly as important as getting in touch with one's own divinity and one's own immortality, and even developing one's own personal connection with the interdimensional sources. But our logical minds need to first accept that this is real. I hope that this chapter has helped to anchor the reality of the connection between Wilcock and Cayce. If this connection is genuine, then this dimensional shift might also be real, with the future of your own incarnations being determined by the amount of love you can maintain in your actions and conduct towards others each day.

Please note that we are not here to provide what you would call the "feel good, curiosity-feeding" psychic readings. We are here to give those messages that may seem rather brutally intense at first, but they are, however, exactly what you need to wake up from.

—Ra/Wilcock, November 11, 1999

Chapter
10

Predictions and Prophecies

The story of the link between David Wilcock and Edgar Cayce would not be complete without a chapter on prophecy. Those who are familiar with the work of Edgar Cayce are well aware of his moniker, "the Sleeping Prophet." Although Wilcock has made numerous specific predictions that have come to pass, the manner in which Wilcock's predictions are worded constitutes an interesting phenomenon. The predictions are usually cryptic and incomprehensible at the time of the reading, making perfect and specific sense only after the prophesied event takes place.

In my opinion, Ra is attempting to create credibility, without making everyone dependent on Wilcock to reveal the future. The one exception to this would be the topic of the dimensional shift, where Ra has been more specific as to what we are to expect. These predictions are laid out in Part Two and scientifically supported by Chapter 19 and Part Three. If one examines Wilcock's website, it becomes obvious that Wilcock himself is often frustrated at the proposition of having his work constantly compared to the impeccably credible readings of Cayce. But, underneath it all, the credibility of Ra is established as more and more of the cryptic Wilcock prophecies come to fruition. Ra's words to Wilcock on May 29, 2002, address the form of his prophecies:

We understand that you have become disillusioned with chan-neling, as it is rife with speculation and inaccurate informa-tion. However, instead of seeing this as a curse, see it as a blessing, as an opportunity to shine in an area that should be accessible to all. Only then do you have the ability to function in truth, knowing that you are a being of love and light who is capable of healing conflict in many souls who would read these words.

The best way that you can help us in this process is, again, not to get overly engaged into reading everything you can find about the politics and changes that are going on. Rather, we encourage you to realize that the prophecies are coming true and sit with that knowledge, including all of its far-reaching implications for the nature and existence of the Divine Cos-mos and your role within it as a being of light and love with infinite, multidimensional potential.[1]

When I first discovered Wilcock's www.ascension2000.com web-site and considered his Cayce connection, it crossed my mind that I could get a glimpse of the future so I could know when California would have its big earthquake. Edgar Cayce had predicted a Cali-fornia quake for the year 1998, which never occurred. Like count-less others in anticipation of Cayce's inundation prophecies for California, New York, Florida, Tokyo, and Europe, I watched 1998 come and go without a shudder. But in the back of my mind, I was still thinking that the quake was coming, just delayed. As I explored the Wilcock readings, I was relieved to discover the Ra rebuttal of this prediction (discussed in a previous chapter).

Ra informed Wilcock that he (Wilcock) had also occasionally brought forward information from a negative entity regarding future disasters in this lifetime. In our real third-dimensional world as well, fear is the prime method by which negative people and groups attempt to gain control and power. We are programmed to live in fear of los-ing our jobs, going to hell, experiencing terrorist attacks, nuclear explosions, hunger, and a myriad of disasters, named and unnamed. I provide this perspective as context for this chapter, written to challenge the reader with information presented from Wilcock's readings and dreams. The upfront disclaimer is that Wilcock is fallible.

Ra's message is clear. If we are going to participate in the future in the most positive way, we can't depend on prophecies—we must evolve our consciousness. We have to overcome our fears. Fear is the antithesis of love. The energy of our beingness and our open hearts will protect us, heal the Earth, keep disasters at bay, and make us eligible for staying with the Earth as it moves into the fourth dimension. But that doesn't mean it will be easy. Ra has said that hard times are definitely ahead. And these are the times that can truly give us the opportunity to rise to the occasion and have our own direct experience and knowledge that we are One with Creation. In Ra's words:

Again, we are here to tell you that there will be unexpected surprises that will overturn many of the more egregious scenarios now being bandied about by your mainstream media, and that point cannot be overstressed. There are lines of distinction that can be crossed here, and it is related to the overall function of consciousness in humanity. Therefore, the best way that you can help is to try to be as consistent as you can in maintaining an atmosphere of love, joy and peace in your daily affairs. This in turn strengthens the collective human energy field, and negotiates a greater flexibility of change for us to work with in our protective endeavors.

The prophecies spoke of situations that would come where the rational mind completely breaks down in its ability to see a way out of the problems that humanity will be faced with. Those times are now here. If you read what many thinkers are writing, especially in the alternative press where a larger vision of the hidden occult politics is brought into view, it is very easy to log on to their feelings of desperation and to have that commitment taken upon by the self. It is a commitment to suffering and to the negative path, indulging in material that is ultimately quite transient and draws you away from the core of your true being.

A certain degree of discernment is therefore very wise in what and how much is to be read, if you wish to maintain the highest state of balance and spiritual integrity. Without such a discipline, the negative news can literally be overwhelming, as an energy transfer of sorts occurs between the writer and the recipient. We have spoken before of how humanity will, to a greater and greater degree, become infected, as it were, with the disease of fear. This is indeed a very tangible spiritual condition that is not easily rectified once it has put deep roots into the subconscious mind. The negative elites have obviously fulfilled their Biblically-assigned job of ruling over the Earth, meaning that the media sources you interact with in that known as the "mainstream" do have a propensity for great distortions towards fear, and almost none of the inherent goodness of humanity, in the existence of an Ultimate Being or higher principle, or in the ability for human faith to create miracles where only desperation had previously existed.

As was said, there will be "wailing and gnashing of teeth," but see that you not be troubled. The screaming cries of desperation are those of the virus that reaches a sudden oversaturation point where it spontaneously implodes within the host, due to the forced exhaustion of its hunt for available sustenance. There are no economies left to be pillaged, no significant power grabs left to be actualized with the available resources, and the bottom line is plummeting much faster than anyone in said circles is willing to admit. The disease of fear is their own, as greater and greater degrees of wishful thinking must be invoked to offset the hard facts of the looming implosion that is already occurring in their entire structural framework. Soon this will be pre-eminently visible to you, even more so than at present. Then fear can be swept away and the healing can begin, with the harbingers of a Golden Age becoming increasingly manifest.

Tough love can be administered in situations where a pathological, addictive behavior pattern has outlasted its usefulness. In the case of the individual entity, this often comes by hitting the "bottom," as it were. The bottom represents a time where all options for continuing the addiction appear to have been exhausted and, in 12-step support-group parlance, "life has become unmanageable."

It is the life structure of your current civilization, propped up on endless tirades of fiat currency available at the touch of a finger and the rolling of the printing presses, continually causing greater and greater waves of devastation to its host, which is now bottoming out. The apparent chaos that you are now seeing is simply a form of molten liquefaction, a transitory phase leading to a greater degree of crystallization and perfection in what you call the future. Try not to let the heat of this catalyst burn you, but rather use it as your fuel to ascend along the spiraling line of light into higher and higher realms of awareness. This worldwide bottom will indeed have its financial and geopolitical repercussions, but as the master Jesus once spoke, "See that you not be troubled."

These are the times of the changing of the guard, the final overturning of the endless rehashing of the old ways in favor of the adaptation of the new ways. Certain events help to administer the necessary medicine to the patient in order that this bottom may be facilitated with as little damage to the host as possible, and it is for this reason that the greater weight of probability rests in economic changes rather than massive annihilatory war scenarios. All one has to do is begin thinking clearly about these possibilities, and the degree of hopelessness that can emerge is almost overwhelming. See that you not be troubled when your faith is tested. The negative forces will attempt to scare you into believing that regardless of the nature of ancient and trusted prophecies, things have changed, and this time it really does mean doom. The most recent headline that David and others saw of this type actually stated quite nakedly, "Government says twelve million people will die in a nuclear war." Similarly, headlines from just a few days earlier said, "Nuclear War is Inevitable."

Step back from this rhetoric and realize what was known when said ancient prophecies were made. At the time of said prophecies, nuclear weapons had already been used on your sphere in anger in what you would call the past, namely between those civilizations of Atlantis and Rama. The possibility of more fearsome energy weapons was known to the prophets as well, as these war-toys frequently emerge at the end of a cycle in a given third-density world society.

Thus, the protocol is exacting and well-established in terms of how best to deal with these situations, and after the previous disasters involving [the exploded planets] Maldek and Mars, your system has been privy to a far greater degree of very high-level protection and intervention than is typical for the end of a planetary cycle. This extra protection is designed to ensure that even under the most sudden and inexplicable twist of fate that could lead to such a problem, with the most subtle and inconspicuous beginnings, the appropriate actions can and will be taken in advance to overturn these possibilities.

This is the spiritual war of Armageddon that has already continued for quite a number of your years in the higher-density environments of your Earth's concentric layers of aetheric energy, most specifically the fourth-density region that humanity will soon inhabit. We are asking you to take a step forward into trust, and to volunteer your efforts to be of greater vibrational assistance to the uplift of this planet through preserving internal peace. This is indeed a step of faith, and cannot be easily made in a state of distraction.

Very few souls truly have a grasp of what will transpire in the future, yet they will all make cases and claims that will attempt to sway you into their mode of thinking. The most efficient framework in which you can make this choice is in consulting with your own inner silence, rather than in the chatter of the outside world as the death-cries of a dysfunctional system of consciousness become ever more screeching. And the more that you can help out by asking yourself where the love is in any moment, the quicker and easier the transition will be.—Ra/Wilcock reading, May 29, 2002

With that introduction, let's look at some of the more specific predictions and prophecies that Wilcock has made. First, I'll review the predictions regarding incidents in his own life as well as world events that have already come to pass. Second, I'll look at some additional predictions and counsel from Ra for the future. I will note where and when the prediction originated, either from a Ra channeling or from a Wilcock dream.

Prediction One: The Habitu Restaurant incident

Ra casually mentions the word Habitu in a reading on December 2, 1996, and the same day, David drives by a restaurant named Habitu for the first time. This was in the early days of David's contact with his "Dream Voice," prior to the knowledge that he was Cayce or that it was Ra who was communicating with him.

Prediction Two: The traffic ticket and World Trade Center combination

David is told the day and time he will have an automobile accident and receive a moving violation ticket. This is expanded in two readings, one on December 4, 1996, two days before the accident, and the other on December 6, the day of the accident. The reading is cryptic, but not after the fact. It is implied that there is something Wilcock is to learn from having this experience.

Ra reading, December 4, 1996

"My gift to the world will be a 3½-by-11 sheet of paper. Expect it on Friday. This runs counter to earlier systems of thought. Ninety minutes till 10:00."

David's comments: This turned out to be the definitive prophecy that foretold my auto accident that Friday. It occurred at 8:30, or ninety minutes until 10:00. The police officer wrote me a ticket, and it was indeed on a 3½-by-11 sheet of paper. It is interesting that the Source says that this is its "gift to the world," as it was apparently necessary for me to go through this to balance my karma—even though it may have "run counter to earlier systems of thought."

Ra reading, December 6, 1996 (the morning of the accident)

"It's the greatest science fiction story ever told. Someone comes in—Rescue 911. CBS and ABC give it adequate coverage. A cast-iron fence is wrought around the victim's body. An impenetrable wall needs only be potentiated by positive energy."

David's comments: Here we have a direct reference to what would happen. The person I collided with would end up claiming an injury to try for insurance money—hence the first statement about the science fiction story. We have a direct reference to the ambulance crew, as Rescue 911, and then the fact that our society loves to cover accidents and disasters. The cast-iron fence around the victim's body is obviously the car itself. Then, they say that the "impenetrable wall" of my own bad driving needed to be potentiated by this accident, which was ultimately a positive thing to happen.

Though controversial, this same prophecy never made complete sense until the very day of September 11, 2001, with the hijacked-airliner attack on the World Trade Center and Pentagon that came to be known as "911." Within days, Wilcock realized that just three and a half weeks after his contact started in 1996, he had received a prophecy of the 911 event, some five years in advance. The "greatest science fiction story ever told" would be the enormous number of holes in the official explanations for how 911 could have happened. The name 911 is directly given in the reading, as well as the mention of corporate news coverage. Then, there is reference to a "cast-iron fence wrapped around the victim's body," and if the victim is the World Trade Center and those who died inside it, then the skeletal girders that still remained standing after the building's collapse indeed formed a cast-iron fence. The government politicizing of the event thereafter has seemed by many to be an "impenetrable wall" leading to a doom scenario of Big Brother-style control, but the reading says that "positive energy" can change the whole picture.

It is important to remember that Internet archives (www.archive. org) can clearly show that this prophecy was online no later than summer of 1999. The car crash was perhaps the most powerful event of Wilcock's life in getting him to take the advice of his Higher Self seriously, and along the same lines many people now credit the 911 event with awakening them from their own spiritual slumber—hence the pairing of the prophecies.

Prediction Three: The World Trade Center destruction, three years in advance

Although David did not publish these readings online, due to their ominous content, it became clear after September 11, 2001, that the event was being seen at least three years in advance. The following two statements were delivered about a week apart. Wilcock has assured me that he still has the original audiotapes with these dictations on them, preserved in an unbroken chronological order. We see repeated mentions of New York, an airborne explosion, Jihad, and a specific mention that the "World Trade Center bombing . . . will become a much larger story."

Ra reading, July 1, 1998

"... We understand that these are very distressing circumstances, and would remind you that the tectonic shifts involved in the upcoming changes also make New York a particularly undesirable target location [to live in] ... [I]n the following dream the cycle was completed by the appearance of the airborne explosion. This also was interwoven with the more long-term [solar] effects of the Ascension, but the bomb aspect was correctly given, and needs to be addressed at this time.

"This is coming in the form of an ongoing Jihad, which does not want to be acknowledged to the people by your government. Yet, there is every reason to believe that it is progressing, and that New York is the number-one target for any such actions. Let us all hope together that this prophecy shall fail to come to pass."

Ra reading, July 9, 1998

"[The 1993] World Trade Center bombing really shook things up. The next time one tries something like this, it will become a much larger story, if the details are worked out properly."

Wilcock did write a series of articles on the September 11th event, one of which was completed that day. In these cases Wilcock called attention to a series of dreams he posted beginning in December 2000, each of which associated hugely destructive airplane crashes with economic collapse, along with readings that subtly foreshadowed what would happen.

Prediction Four: The drop in the financial and stock markets in the summer of 2002

The stock market did "re-define its bottom-line point" in August of 2002, sinking even lower than it had during the September 11, 2001, event. This was surrounded by the exposure of the Enron scandal and bankruptcy (intimately tied in with members of the Bush Administration), the announcement that MCI/WorldCom was bankrupt, and the publicity around Martha Stewart's insider trading scandal, leading to the bankruptcy of Kmart. Hence, these events showed what the "bottom-line point" would look like, just as the Ra readings said a year and a half in advance:

Ra reading, December 19, 2000

"Every trend in the commercial marketplace continues to point towards a slowing economy. At the present time of these workings, while some may also expect that the markets will go up and down in regular cyclic fashion, there are others who believe that an economic collapse will ensue, and redefine a bottom-line point for financial markets. Understand that such a bottom-line point is produced as a byproduct or consequence of the shifting energies as now involved. Expect that it will be there by midsummer 2002 at the latest, based on current prognostications."

Prediction Five: The Presidential election of 2002 will be decided in the "interim," the period after the official vote

As we all know, this election was not decided until after the electoral vote, and a controversial recount of disputed votes in Florida was required to make the final tally. At the time Wilcock posted his original reading, his own interpretation of it was quite different, but after the election, the meaning of the reading was patently obvious. Somehow the readings already knew that Gore did not have a chance at winning the election—i.e., he was "completely naked"—even though he thought he could "author" the way in which the Florida vote recounts would be conducted, using the mass media publicity to dictate popularly supported vote recount policy.

Ra reading, June 23, 1999

"The Vice President looks at this as being partly of his own authorship, while not realizing he is completely naked. The interim period decides the next victor."

Prediction Six: The plane crash in the water and death of JFK, Jr.

A number of dreams and readings on the days prior to the crash of July 16, 1999, foreshadowed the event. Wilcock was certain enough of the accuracy of these prophecies that he aired them live across the country on his second appearance with the Laura Lee radio show that same day, announcing his belief that JFK, Jr., was deceased before it was officially announced the next day.

Wilcock dream, July 10, 1999, preceding JFK Jr.'s death:

The dream started in a body of water. I then saw an elaborate casket being made up, and I knew a famous man had died. . . .

Wilcock dream, July 11, 1999:

The dream started in a body of water. People were searching the artifacts in the water. Then I saw a jet doing some very elaborate maneuvers in the sky that seemed to defy the laws of physics completely, and that were very dangerous. And then . . . Children were trying to take . . . all these pieces that had come out of the jet. . . . The government notified them that they were the property of the government and the children couldn't take them.

Ra reading, July 12, 1999, preceding JFK, Jr.'s death:

"The cabal still insists on sending out its best guys to handle these problems. In the rush of the news items, we can fail to see the news hour and refresh our thirst for the bizarre. . . ."

Ra reading, July 13, 1999, preceding JFK, Jr.'s death:

"An epic disturbance in the force awaits you."

Wilcock dream, July 14, 1999:

I had a dream where my friend's face was painted totally in white, and she was in mourning. [We discussed] how you could hermetically seal a car in plastic, so that you could live safely inside and [no water] would be able to penetrate it.

On Friday, July 16, 1999, the plane crashed in a body of water, killing JFK, Jr., his wife, and her sister. People did try to take pieces of the plane, and the government declared all of them government property and demanded them back.

There have been many other prophecies referred to in earlier chapters: the naming of the street on which David would live in Virginia Beach, his housemate who collected German steel helmets, and his client who had the dream about a tripod and then received his reading from David in the mail which referred to a tripod the day after his dream. These are but a few of the prophetic "hits" that routinely happen in David's morning dreams on the day that he has a client session scheduled. It is commonplace that the dream will have a great deal of specific information about the client's own life. The above items are very clear and specific and, in my estimation, are supportive of the fact that David Wilcock, either through his dreams or his readings, can sometimes predict the future.

There are many other examples of this on his website, but he is not always right. For example, he predicted a calamity on January 1, 2000, regarding Y2K, which never came to pass. Perhaps this was one of those predictions that Ra highlighted as coming from a negative entity. The anticipated breakdown was most likely corrected as a result of the vast attention paid to updating all the computers. Or perhaps, according to David, his subconscious mind was highly swayed by constantly listening to the Art Bell radio program at this time, where an endless stream of guests, both scientific and psychic-oriented, were convinced that society was about to collapse. There is always a risk that the conscious mind can distort one's information, which is why no channeler should ever be implicitly trusted— a measure of skepticism is always prudent. It is also for this reason that David has put together a *scientific* case for Ascension, so that even if all intuitive works are completely discredited, regardless of who brought them through and when, a solid scientific model still exists that can explain the ultimate effect of the very visible changes now occurring throughout the solar system, as we shall discuss.

In this lifetime, David may not be "configured" to make flawless, impeccable prophecies, but over and over, in the readings David has done for others, Ra demonstrates total awareness of the individual with many specific references to the person's life. I recommended a client to Wilcock who is a poet and songwriter, and her reading included many of the exact metaphors she uses in her own writing, and actually gave the hidden spiritual meanings that they were intended to convey for her life as well. In the general Ra readings, which are meant for the public at large, there is an amazing awareness, wisdom, and love of life on this planet. A sampling of these readings is included in Part Two.

In today's world, I believe that long-range predictions could be counter-productive. There are many areas where consciousness is changing rapidly, particularly with the communicative abilities of the Internet. Certain types of very specific predictions, such as future earthquakes, might tend to actually contribute to the manifestation of such events. Directing the focus of large numbers of people in such a negative fashion is something that I'm sure is the last thing that Ra or Wilcock would want to do. The increased etheric energies that the planet is experiencing due to the dimensional shift are catalytic and are causing both positive and negative potentials to surface. Predictions that create fear can come from negative sources, as we already referenced concerning Cayce's inundation prophecies and even some of Wilcock's older prophecies, according to Ra. On that note, I am going to proceed with some of Ra's prophecies for the future, with the understanding and trust that you, the reader, can utilize this information in the most positive and uplifting way. According to Ra, even negative future possibilities are actually catalysts that can stimulate our growth, and should be looked upon as such. Being prepared spiritually and psychologically for what's to come can give us the strength and understanding to hold for others during this period of change.

Ra reading, September 29, 1999

"The system must indeed collapse. We are not talking to you about something that could happen at any moment, but rather a gradual process where first the axle gives out, then the other tire, then the steering mechanism, then the electrical system, and so forth. Over the next few years, a shower of available opportunities is emanating within and without humanity, with the creative potential to transform many different circumstances. For those who would be at the eye of the hurricane, so to speak, they can recognize that a plateau can be reached wherein the empty promises of the international banking community can be superseded by returning to the natural wealth which is Mother Earth and the land that surrounds each entity."

Ra reading, October 1, 1999

"It is very, very important that you not allow yourself to degrade into moments of raw, outspoken panic and sheer terror at the collapsing of the old ways. You will be seeing more and more of this, and part of it is contingent upon your geographical area, so be aware of that. Those of you who continue to fear the effects of epic mega-earthquakes and Earth changes, please be notified yet again. We have stated many times before, and will continue to do so, that the effect which spearheads this transformation will only occur after the transformation itself. [After the process of Ascension commences— author's note.] And thus, do be advised that the idea of making some panicked grasp at moving to a different location, et cetera et cetera, is largely futile.

"What follows will be the most intense periods you have ever seen. Do not fear them. Remain clearly focused and active in your life, especially in the sense of using these opportunities to face the self and become more and more grounded and clear as to what your issues are, and what steps you may take to resolve them. What we don't want for you is to allow this energetic fragmentation to continue. Simply stay focused, clear and conscious, and you will not be led astray. What we have here is not a bunch of children playing with matches, but a bunch of budding God-Selves starting to realize their own abilities and powers. We don't know whether those on your planet will become more aware of this frequency change or not. But you, yourself, having studied this material, can indeed rest easy, with confidence, that even as everyone around you is freaking out in a panic, you yourself already know that everything is perfectly on schedule. And with that realization comes the intimate knowledge of your own protection and safety."

Ra reading, January 8, 2001

"At the current time, our desire is to welcome those who would be as pioneers of the New Age, and encourage them to overcome frailty and incompleteness in exchange for the unity and wholeness of true God consciousness. Obviously, there are those whose internal environments are now being mirrored by the external environment, and it scares them to realize this; for what was once thought stable and predictable has now become unstable and dynamic, capable of change at a moment's notice. But those fairer still are awaiting the landing on the White House lawn, and hoping that this will make all of the problems go away.

"While there will be no fairy to magically wave a wand and relieve these problems, we can expect that the recriminations will continue to be paid off, and those who have found themselves wanting to be pure will have ever more reason to purify themselves. An important part of this project is your participation; and thus, we encourage you, the reader of these words, to involve the self deeply within on the struggle to reclaim the long-lost path of humanity in exchange for the outworn and outmoded beliefs surrounding scarcity, limitation, and fear that have imprisoned so many at this time.

"The haves and the have-nots will be on an equal par with each other, and this does then indicate to what degree the changes will have to be met. We don't want for there to be a feeling of fear. Know that as ye go within, so too will the axis then shift in the world of the mind, body and spirit, producing ever-greater discrete changes in the physical appurtenances and all manners of living life.

"The more deeply you realize your connection to the Infinite One within, the more suitable your vibrations will be to raising the planetary consciousness at large. And therefore, the next step of any soul's true evolution is to become this person who is enlightened, awake, alive, and aware. It is very difficult to predict or to propose where the chips may fall, and any predictions that we may give are only that.

"We do not advise reaching out to those who are so desperately in need of assistance that they will fight every step of the way for even the slightest bit of spiritual guidance [to get through to them]. Now is not the time to martyr oneself for a better cause, or a better clause in the finishing contract. Instead, recognize that when you separate yourself from the issues of marriage and divorce, joy and pain, input and output, you become indifferent in one sense to the demands placed upon you by the material world, and in another sense more acutely aware of the considerations of how to be of real service to the Oneness than ever before.

"With the constructs fully in place, you can begin actively supporting your existence by seeking the higher path that can be instilled amongst many diversions. And it is for this reason that we suggest the continuation of the personal growth and initiation process. For when all is said and done, the truer applications of the self to the present circumstances will reveal that it is in the true radiance of the One that the greatest service is then made. And this can be done in silence and isolation. Even to have others walk near you is to have them receive vibrations in a larger sense, and these vibrations will heal them and their issues, which separate them from the One Creator."

Ra reading, September 23, 1999
"The only finalized integration process that needs to take place is your own. When you see those events occurring in the physical world that are of the warlike nature and so forth, do not pine away and

wish that they could become enlightened that much faster. Simply recognize the sacramental nature of all things, and focus on what you yourself can do to change it."

Ra reading, July 13, 1999

"Now, we wish for you to expand this knowledge, and recognize that much larger cycles of human endeavor are playing themselves out. These cycles include the fact that many of your years ago, at the mid-point of your recent cycle, there was the fall of Atlantis. Similar patterns are now duplicating themselves. You all have the opportunities to be on this crest of the time-wave again prior to Ascension. You all have choices to act differently than you did in the past. And as there is really only one moment, you can then heal the past as you heal the present."

Ra reading, May 29, 2002

"Take care of yourself, and know that nothing unexpected has occurred or will occur; all is well, and the process of your Ascension continues in this very moment. The more that you can hear the call, the quicker you will reach the fruit that you seek. We thank you, and again remind you that you are loved more than you could ever possibly imagine. Peace be with you in the Light of everlasting Love."

The Ra readings from Wilcock's website in Part Two have been selected to give the keys and counsel for handling the anticipated changes and effecting your own transformation into the fourth dimension.

Part One introduced you to David Wilcock. We've gone through all the Cayce parallels step by step. It is now your task to make your own evaluation and come to your own conclusion. For myself, after my own extensive study, I can see no way for so many connections to exist without concluding that Wilcock is the reincarnation of Cayce. Whether you concur with me or not, I believe that Wilcock's message and the incredible wisdom and compassion of Ra's words stand on their own. Part Two focuses on Wilcock's channelings and further expands on the message.

In concluding Part One of this book, here is a quick review of all the points covered linking Cayce and Wilcock.

1. **The Ra link between Cayce and Ra-Ta:** Edgar Cayce in his own readings described his past life as high priest Ra-Ta in Egypt circa 10,500 B.C., where the pyramids were built by "levitation of stone." L/L Research, with Carla Rueckert acting as the instrument for channeled readings from the higher-dimensional being Ra, indicated that Ra was connected to a priest in Egypt in 10,500 B.C. who had an affinity with the "Law of One." Ra directly states that they worked with this priest who, the evidence implies, was Edgar Cayce's first incarnation Ra-Ta. Carla Rueckert had no knowledge of the Cayce reading regarding this.

2. **Fulfillment of the Cayce prophecy:** Cayce predicted that the priest (Ra-Ta) would return in 1998 and "may become a liberator of the world" along with other lightworkers, would live in Virginia Beach, and would be surrounded by his old associates in the new lifetime. Wilcock was urged by his "Dream Voice" to move to Virginia Beach prior to having any indication of his Cayce connection, and prior to being aware of his resemblance to Cayce. After deciding to move, he learned how similar he looked to Cayce. After the move, in 1998, he became aware of people in his personal sphere who resembled associates of Cayce.

3. **Striking physical resemblance:** Plato, Percival, and Cayce all indicated that a common soul will take on similar physical appearances from one lifetime to the next. Wilcock's scientific research into the energy fields of DNA suggests that this is a quite natural process where the energy of the soul "arranges" the DNA molecule.

4. **Astrological congruities:** The ties linking Wilcock's chart to Cayce's show such a high degree of synchrony that simply trying to calculate the probability of it being a product of random chance is extremely difficult, potentially in the billions-to-one scale once all factors are considered.

5. **Comparable missions:** Cayce and Wilcock both dedicated themselves to planetary service without regard for financial gain or personal recognition.

6. **Comparable conflicts-of-life issues:** Both Cayce and Wilcock have issues with security, emotional stability, and internal conflicts, as well as the same phobia regarding water.

7. **Prophetic abilities:** Even though he doesn't demonstrate the on-demand psychic powers of Cayce, Wilcock has made many very precise predictions that have come to pass and given numerous readings that reveal complete comprehension of his clients' issues and conflicts. Ra has told Wilcock that his role is to be a messenger of the pending dimensional shift and a "teacher of universal concepts to the masses."

8. **Lack of desire for public acclaim:** This book was written at the insistence of the author over Wilcock's initial vehement resistance. Wilcock only permitted the book project to continue after he absolutely convinced himself of my intentions and connection with the "Law of One." Even then, he frequently shunned involvement with the project. Wilcock was not anxious to expose himself to the kind of controversy and scrutiny this book could create. It was only at the author's insistence that many would benefit as a result of the public release of this book that Wilcock finally gave some support to this project.

Part Two

—————

The Message

At the current time, our desire is to welcome those who would be as pioneers of the new age, and encourage them to overcome frailty and incompleteness in exchange for the unity and wholeness of true God consciousness. Obviously, there are those whose internal environments are now being mirrored by the external environment, and it scares them to realize this; for what was once thought stable and predictable has now become unstable and dynamic, capable of change at a moment's notice.

—Ra/Wilcock, January 8, 2001

Chapter
11

The Wilcock Readings

You have probably realized by now that, in spite of this book's title, there is a much more important question than whether or not Wilcock is Cayce, and that is "Could this dimensional shift be real?" Admittedly, when I was first exposed to this idea, it sounded like science fiction. But the queasy feeling in my stomach wouldn't go away, as my mind kept dwelling on the question of "what if?"

Ra is telling us, through Wilcock, that they are here as a multidimensional presence, existing in the sixth density yet extending through the lower densities to assist us in this dimensional shift transition. One might look at Wilcock and many of the other "Wanderers" as manifestations of Ra in the third density. In Book Five, Session 45, page 79 of the *Law of One* series, Dr. Elkins asked if "a large percentage of the Wanderers here now are those of Ra," and Ra answered, "I am Ra. A significant portion of sixth-density Wanderers are those of our social memory complex." Also, as revealed in Book One, Session 14, page 140, Ra can come into our dreams and communicate with us if we invite their presence through our own free will and attune to their vibrations: "I am Ra. We have used channels such as this one, but in most cases the channels feel inspired by dreams and visions without being aware, consciously, of our identity or existence." This subconscious influence is far more prevalent than direct channeling, and anyone who thinks the latter is happening to him or her should be well-versed in this practice and aware of the caveats (consult *The Channeler's Handbook* by Carla Rueckert; more on this topic later).

As will be seen in Chapter Twenty, Ra is even claiming to be able to prevent catastrophes on our planet if there is a consensus desire among us humans for peace. Part Two, "The Message," aims to give us an opportunity to connect with Ra, or at least to grasp the essence of their communication to us. Could this be real?

As Wilcock became aware of the dimensional shift through his "downloaded" Ra information, he too went through an initial period of incredulity. He postulated that if such a shift were imminent, one would expect corresponding, quantifiable, physical changes on the planet and in the solar system at large. Wilcock didn't want to make this radical announcement to the world based on his channeled data alone. He felt compelled to research and integrate a large and provocative body of scientific evidence that pointed towards the same dimensional shift, validating a number of Ra's predictions from the *Law of One* series of 1981–84, which were given before most of the scientific data existed. Wilcock believes it can be proved that the Creator of our universe expresses itself through a unified field of energy pervading our entire physical realm. So, in addition to his channeled material, Wilcock took it upon himself to compile and explain this data, which has become the foundation for a number of his online books (soon to be published in the mainstream), which are written from a scientific perspective out of his conscious, logical mind. Chapter Nineteen, "A Scientific Blueprint for Ascension," and Part Three, "The Energetic Engine of Evolution," are more concise compilations of this scientific back-up that Wilcock wrote or updated from his own materials specifically for this book.

Part Two presents some of Wilcock's most inspiring Ra readings. If our planet *is* undergoing a dimensional shift, then these readings offer the counsel to guide us through this transitional phase, and they could be crucial in ensuring our own entry into "the fourth dimension of love." The main attributes of this fourth dimension are the ability to perceive all life as part of oneself and the expression of compassion. There is an uncanny correspondence between Ra's prophecies and the predictions of Jesus regarding a "New Heaven, New Earth" and the statement "The meek shall inherit the Earth." It should be mentioned here that the concept of a fourth dimension was also part of the Cayce cosmology, and he also referred to this future dimensional shift. In order to understand these Cayce quotes, we have to look at the "Ascension" passage of Revelations 11:11 through 11:13, King James Version, where St. John the Divine says,

11:11 And after three days and a half the spirit of life from God entered into them, and they stood upon their feet; and great fear fell upon them which saw them.

11:12 And they heard a great voice from heaven saying unto them, "Come up hither." And they ascended up to heaven in a cloud; and their enemies beheld them.

11:13 And the same hour was there a great earthquake, and the tenth part of the city fell, and in the earthquake were slain of men seven thousand: and the remnant were affrighted, and gave glory to the God of heaven.

According to researcher Joe Mason, author of *Humanity on the Pollen Path,* the "three and a half days" or "time, times and a half-time" (1 + 2 + ½) in the Bible are metaphors for the balancing point between third and fourth density.[1] Once the "three and a half point" is crossed, humanity has moved more into fourth density than third, and the "first wave" of Ascension begins. In reading 294–185, Cayce said, "These changes on the earth will come to pass, for the time and times and half-times are at an end, and there begin those periods for the readjustments. For how hath He given? 'The righteous shall inherit the earth.'" Cayce reading 282–5 also says, "Has it not been said,

'Seeking His face, know ye not that He shall give His angels charge concerning thee, that they shall bear thee up?' Believest thou? or art thou just wondering?"

I hope that this section of the book is useful as a reader's guide to approaching the "shift." At the very least, Ra's words might inspire you to learn a lot more about love, wisdom, and compassion. Such learning is the highest stated goal of Ra in the *Law of One* series—the evolution of mind, body, and spirit.

I discovered a book, *The Interpretation of Dreams* by Sigmund Freud, which documents the historical connection between dreams, personal growth, and prophecy. According to this book, many spiritual teachings put value on the interpretation of dreams and information received during a sleep state. Ancient cultures paid much more respect to the importance of dream information than Western civilization. For example, "The Epic of Gilgamesh" is an Assyrian poem, dated 2000 B.C., about a Mesopotamian king whose dreams often foretold important events in his life. The Egyptians of the same period had a ritual of dream "incubation" where someone would sleep in a temple or shrine and later have their dreams interpreted by a priest. The ancient Greeks also practiced dream "incubation" where Morpheus, the god of dreams, would deliver a dream filled with messages or prophecies. Even Hippocrates believed that dreams could predict disease. In the beginning of the twentieth century, Sigmund Freud postulated that dreams could reveal information and give access to our unconscious. Karl Jung, originally Freud's student, believed that dreams were the way that the unconscious part of oneself communicates with the conscious.[2]

If we apply the cosmology of Ra to dreams and information communicated in sleep or trance, we can expand even further what may be possible during these states. As we have alluded to in earlier chapters, our universe is multi-dimensional and our waking state is limited to the third dimension. According to Ra in the *Law of One* series, there are eight dimensions or densities which all consciousness must pass through on its way back home to God, or original Creation, and there exists a multitude of beings in these other dimensions, some of whom we could view as our future selves, as we eventually ascend into those dimensions over many lifetimes. In our waking state, due to what is termed the veil of forgetfulness, we are restricted from direct perception of these other dimensions, but in a sleep state, fewer restrictions exist. Therefore, it is possible and even likely that all of us have experienced these higher dimensions when we sleep, but as soon as we awaken, we can't remember them. All dream researchers share the conclusion that the signs of dream activity, the rapid-eye movement or R.E.M. state, happens to every human being at least four times a night, and that without this dream activity psychosis results. So dreams do happen to everyone—it is more a question of whether we are dedicated enough to commit to a daily practice of remembering, recording, analyzing, and applying them, as Wilcock has now been doing for over a decade.

In Chapter Eight we described Wilcock's first attempts at connecting with his own "Dream Voice," after four years of preparation through the daily practice of recording, analyzing, and obeying the guidance of his dreams. To his great surprise, he seemed to be experiencing an intelligence outside his own that was communicating with him. He has continually worked to perfect his ability to translate this information, which first came through as sentence fragments, then full sentences, until finally he was recording complete paragraphs and pages of channeled information, composed in perfectly crafted English. As indicated in Part One, his source eventually revealed itself as Ra, the social memory complex, whom he was connected with since his incarnation as Ra-Ta in Egypt, 10,500 B.C.

The first bits of information seemed to be counseling Wilcock regarding the changes going on in his personal sphere. As his abilities improved, the readings got more and more cohesive. In addition to wise counseling, prophetic information was delivered concerning events that subsequently transpired in his life and the world in general. As Wilcock validated this prophetic information, he gave increasing credence to the data he was receiving. Finally his source revealed to him that he was connecting with the same source as Edgar Cayce: he *was* the reincarnation of Edgar Cayce, and Ra was his Source.

Wilcock's readings are quite different from the Cayce readings. Cayce's were all performed in an unconscious "sleeping" state as opposed to Wilcock's semi-conscious trance state. The Cayce readings were often delivered in broken, archaic English, with rambling paragraph-long sentences, whereas the Wilcock readings often are perfectly edited texts. Unlike Cayce, who would freely answer questions about health and past lives, Wilcock's Source does not emphasize those particular topics, although when Ra deems it important, this kind of information is shared in the course of a reading. This may appear without a direct question from the client, as Wilcock is always careful to secure the client's permission for general "spiritual guidance and direction" to be given.

The Wilcock readings actually fulfill Cayce's prophecy of his future incarnation as one possible "liberator of the world" in that they are, by and large, treatises on how to evolve your consciousness and discover the creative force of God inside yourself. As you review the sample readings in the following chapters, it is suggested that you use your own discernment and evaluation rather than accept the words as absolute truth from an impeccable source. Ultimately truth and wisdom create an intuitive response and resonance for those who are ready to receive them. If there are things that ring true, then perhaps we can also give consideration to the points that can't be checked out, such as predictions for the future. There is a correspondence between Ra's modern words and the warnings from Ra-Ta prompting his small group to leave Turkey before the inundation and move to Egypt. We would have expected Ra-Ta to make a track record of accurate predictions prior to the exodus so he had enough credibility to be taken seriously. In much the same way, we have to decide how credible Wilcock is as he informs us of a dimensional shift, which will totally transform life on Earth in Ra's model.

Beyond credibility, there may be a temptation to create heroes here, which is definitely not the intent of Ra nor Wilcock. Putting Wilcock on a pedestal or turning the readings into doctrine or dogma would be missing the point. Sometimes Wilcock's readings have not come to pass, as in the Y2K prediction. Individual discernment should always be applied to any channeling, as even Cayce did not score 100% accuracy. As for the "liberator" prophecy, the Ra source considers all Wanderers to be potential liberators of the world, since they are higher-dimensional souls who have volunteered to be human so as to raise the planetary vibrations. Some Wanderers are more awakened to their true heritage than others, and thus take on more public positions of service. Furthermore, there can also be entities who are not Wanderers who have a spiritual awakening and can act as liberators. The archaic idea that a single Messianic figure will come through to humanity at this time was clearly dispelled by the Cayce readings, which described the Second Coming of Christ as an event that is occurring in each awakening soul at this pivotal time in our history. It is the eventual destiny for every soul as it reunites with the One Creator.

Most sources of esoteric wisdom include the concept of a Higher Self that is communicating to us our next step and purpose, if we choose to pay attention. We receive those messages not only via our dreams but our intuitions as well. Wilcock, because of his past track record as Ra-Ta and Cayce, may have developed a more direct communication with his Source than most of us are likely to, but according to Ra, it's possible for us to do it too, primarily by having a regular meditation practice and by remembering, documenting, and applying the guidance of our dreams. Good dream work is also very much a meditative practice, as without such concentration the dream will be lost. Wilcock's own techniques for doing this are revealed in upcoming pages.

Wilcock's readings cover four distinct arenas:
Wilcock's self-development: He has an ongoing flow of counsel from Ra regarding his own growth, self-mastery, and service. Wilcock is very honest, often baring personal conflicts on sections of his website. The universality of self-development makes the readings in this category of benefit to anyone who wants to evolve.

Predictions for the future: Certain readings pertain to coming social shifts, economic upheavals, political inequities, and Earth changes. Ra demonstrates complete awareness of everything Wilcock does. As Wilcock's website went up and thousands of Net surfers became fascinated with his readings, Ra's communications started to specifically target this group.

Private client readings: Wilcock has done a number of private readings, some of which are available on his website as wise counseling for the rest of us.

Preparation for the dimensional shift: A fourth category of readings gives specific information regarding Ascension and the dimensional shift.

I did an interview with Wilcock where he explained the development of his own process in mastering his method of channeling. Following is an excerpt from that interview:

> Wilcock: So, when I found Ra, it pretty much changed everything and I became aware of the idea of a Higher Self. The Ra Material [from L/L Research] was really the first big metaphysical breakthrough that I made, and I would often spend thirty minutes without ever turning a page, just meditating and trying to understand the words ... because it was very complicated. As a result of that, I did become aware that there was a Higher Self that lived in the sixth density that was inspiring dreams and therefore was the author of the dreams, and it was a part of myself that existed in the future and already knew that I would eventually get to that place.
>
> In the summer of 1996, I was doing this long shift at a youth halfway house I was working at. I took a nap and while lying in bed, I asked inside myself if I was ready to do any kind of channeling work where I would actually be able to get telepathic

messages from my Higher Self. And I was told in a series of single-word snapshots that my mind was too cluttered and my life too disjointed. I would still need to gain much more control over my thoughts, slow my mind down, and clear up all my problems with employment and instability. That message probably came through in August of 1996. I still wasn't sure if that message was external to myself or not, because for a long time I would get these disjointed sentence fragments when I was falling asleep at night and I wouldn't pay that much attention to them. I did notice at various times that if I tried to retain a brief knowledge of what had been coming through that it was like tiles in a mosaic. If you listened to and retained all of the words over a long period of time, you could start to get the sense that they really did mean something. So that had been happening all of my life. And that was similar to what was happening now, but now the tiles were coming in rapid sequence; they were all directly relevant to each other. So I was willing to consider that something more than my own imagination was coming through, but I wasn't 100% convinced. Yet, at the same time I was thinking: if this is true, then I had better do what they are saying, which means that I need to get my act together.

I'd already studied remote viewing in great detail, so I was quite familiar with the most important principles of remote viewing. First and foremost, do not analyze your data, and do not have any emotional reactions to the data. You must be totally flat. If you get excited about something, you can easily distort the data, or if you have any kind of feeling in your body like hunger or having to go to the bathroom, your results will be poor. So, you keep your emotions in this state where you are disconnected from your body, and also disconnected from your thinking. You have to get into this kind of meditative zone where you have no thoughts and then allow the channeled communications to just bubble up by themselves and write them down, or dictate them into a tape recorder.

This would usually happen when I was going to bed at night and in the morning as well—but I'd never seen it as being anything but mental garbage noise.

Eventually, I would hear a distinct sentence fragment while I was half asleep and I'd pull my head up enough to look at the page and write it down. I was very tired and as soon as I finished writing, I'd just hit the pillow again and repeat this whole thing. In the course of a single ninety-minute session, I may do this sixty times in a row, and after a while I would have about eight pages of information. And honestly, it was like walking through the door of a whole new universe— because I realized right then and there that I had snapped into something utterly fantastic—the feeling of joy and utter amazement was overwhelming. The data was extremely comprehensive and it was phrased in all kinds of metaphorical language.

During my first channeling episode, I was completely unaware of anything that I was writing while I was writing it—I had no idea what I was saying; I had no idea because I was so tired. It was enough work just to try to write the stuff down, and I didn't expect any continuity of the material recorded. This occurred over the course of about one and a half hours, so it took a long time. When I realized that there was continuity to the material and that it was directly personal, I was quite impressed. I would just lay my head on the pillow for ten to fifteen seconds, and during this time the next little fragment of speech would come in—so I wasn't really sleeping, but half awake. After the first few days, I could phase into consciousness enough to think of a question I wanted to have answered and then I would phase back into trance, and when I would write again, it would be an answer to my question. Then I would read the answer when I had the whole thing. So there were points during the transmission process where I would pull myself out of the "vortex" and read what I had said, and then go back into it. I was really kind of climbing up and down the ladder of consciousness.

I was greatly influenced during this period by the book *Seth Speaks* by Jane Roberts. It turns out that everything that was happening to me was already described in her book. In other words, things that I was experiencing directly were being explained, including the style of how I was getting the information and how I could go in and out of trance.

Seth was coming through while Jane was semi-conscious, and she'd sometimes even walk around the room while she was talking and have her husband write the words down. She could stop channeling for months at a time, but Seth would pick up on the exact same sentence that he'd left off on and keep it ongoing. Jane was not aware of this because she hadn't seen the previous transcripts, so Seth was able to write an entire book not in a fragmented form but with the perspective of a higher being saying, "I'm going to write a whole book."

She described these different levels of trance, where different types of information were available. It was from that research that I began to understand what I was doing when I got those fragments. I called it Level Two, and that was based on her classification. I was getting snapshot fragments, one piece at a time. The goal was to go to Level Four, where I could get word-by-word ongoing data and not have to be dipping in and out; I would stay in there and get single words or groups of words and have it be an ongoing stream. It was a deeper state than Level Two. Level Five was similar to Level Four, except that you pretty much phase out of having any knowledge of the words you're saying. You are allowing yourself to speak, but your mind is so disassociated that you are not really aware of the words or what you're saying. So Level Five was obviously the deepest goal, because it was closest to what Carla Rueckert or Edgar Cayce was doing. I wanted to

be able to go that deeply. And also after only about ten sessions of writing into the notebook, the Source was essentially
saying, "You're going to have to put all this stuff on the computer, and probably the best way to do it is to just dictate into
the tape recorder and transcribe it, because we want this stuff
on file." I had no idea that they meant for it to ever become
public! I just wanted to follow my directions. So I took it upon
myself to switch from writing it down by hand to dictating it
directly into a tape recorder. I would lie on my left side and
get into a specific body position, where I would hold a spe-
cially tuned quartz crystal against the back of my head, and
my right arm would hold the tape recorder. I also made sure
that the area between the big toe and the first toe of my right
foot would pinch my left Achilles tendon, and that seemed to
form some kind of an antenna. Later on all these techniques
became needless, but they did help in the beginning.

The Source or Dream Voice was really keen on improving
my spiritual abilities and improving my own personal level of
integration, so I was very much being coached and counseled
on how to be more balanced, how to be more economically
secure, etc. It was reading Jane Roberts that let me know that
I could reach Level Four, where I subsequently used the tape
recorder and was able to get into Level Four consciousness.
It was after I got to Virginia Beach that I was able to get to
Level Five. I started hitting Level Four in January of 1997,
whereas the contact first started in November 1996. At this
point I was a real junkie for the information, and I couldn't
stand to have a day go by when I didn't get something. Yes, it
almost started to sound like normal speech. I should also point
out that Level Four is more dangerous than Level Two, as it is
all too easy for the conscious mind to disobey the meditation
protocol, become aware of some of the word content, and
sway it. There are examples in the readings where I did this
and was then heavily chastised for it, which is a notable feature

of genuineness that I have hardly ever seen in the work of most other channelers, who act as if every word they say is perfect. If bad habits aren't corrected early, then the person's entire life's work could be a collection of conscious-mind distorted material, which is almost always the case. Cayce's early success has spawned legions of cheap imitations, as the A.R.E. also asserts. The key is that you should have as little knowledge of what you are actually saying as possible, and this requires a powerful level of meditation to keep the conscious mind down. There is always some desire for the mind to participate in the process, and that is what must be avoided for the best results. You have to get over all the curiosity and boredom of truly having no idea what is going on and just feel gratitude for the service itself.

For the record, in Level One you're in a waking trance where you're aware of certain things, but it's more like a mild hypnosis than channeling. Level Three is where you could go into the Akashic Records of the area around you and get information. For example, you could diagnose someone's knee problem or read the vibes of what happened in a room previously. In some senses, Edgar Cayce was using the Level Three state by going out of body, and reporting on it in a Level Five state at the same time. I really don't work much in Level Three at all, this time around.

The most important key to understanding the difference between Level Two and Level Four is that in Level Two, entire sentences would appear in my mind all at once, or at least sentence fragments. I would have to pull myself out far enough so that I could record what I got, and then go back in to get more of it. In Level Four, I was unaware of anything past a maximum of about three words at a time, and they were words that would be within an ongoing sentence. I would say whatever group of words I got between one and three as one unit, and keep on going like that to form sentences. So in Level

Four the material got a lot more coherent, and I started to realize that with that level of consciousness, it was starting to get to a point that people might actually be interested in reading it for some sort of spiritual benefit. However, I still never really considered that I would do it for anyone besides myself and maybe a couple of friends. I had no plans on ever making this "experiment" public. In fact, it was a most remarkable feeling to be living this double life, if you will. On the outside, I was just working these ordinary jobs and not given much authority or respect, above and beyond what my call of duty was. Yet I was also working on this inner level, which I totally could not talk to anyone at any of my jobs about or else I would probably be fired, if not hospitalized. I was going home from work, reading far-out metaphysical books, and waking up every morning to have new contact with a Source that was steadily predicting the future, again and again and again and again.

I have taken the liberty of editing the small sampling of Wilcock's readings that appears in this volume, and in many cases have excluded his related comments and dreams. This allows the reader to have the most direct connection and experience of the "Source" or Ra, starting with the early and somewhat cryptic "Level Two" sessions through some samples of Wilcock's well-crafted current readings. These samples can be read in their entirety, with Wilcock's dreams and comments included, on his website (www.ascension2000.com).

The key here is whether the Wilcock readings can assist us in creating a bridge from the awareness of our finite physical bodies to an experiential realization of the greater cosmos and the Oneness inherent in our universe. If this information actually comes from the being who has "been there and done that," and represents the evolved form of consciousness where humankind is ultimately heading (our future selves), then this could be the inspiration our souls have been waiting for, delivered to us via one who believes he carries on his shoulders the legacy of Cayce. Regardless of whether or not you are convinced that Wilcock is Cayce, the inherent wisdom of the readings stands on its own.

I recommend that you read these passages slowly. There are deep symbolic cues contained therein, which can release subconscious blockages and cause a spontaneous lifting of beingness and awareness. I have found that reading these out loud in the presence of others who have affinity with the inherent consciousness of the readings can create a spiritual link and bond between the participants. I daresay that Ra might actually be paying attention and assisting in uplifting the energy for those present.

Certain individuals, after connecting with the material in these readings, believe that they have connected with Ra themselves through their own dream messages, utilizing the techniques and methods described by Wilcock in this chapter. In such cases, it is always necessary to be your own greatest skeptic, as David has informed me of a number of cases where negative entities masquerade as positive and start telling people what to do, over time leading to them having a mental or physical collapse. If you should attempt to make your own contact with higher-dimensional sources, be wary of the tell-tale signs indicative of negative source information:

- Information that tells you or others exactly what to do with your life, rather than guiding you to make your own decision; teaching control rather than acceptance.

- Information that never gives loving suggestions of possible areas of distortion and confusion in self and others—thereby providing no real "meat" for spiritual growth by only saying what everyone wants to hear.

- Information that judges, saying there is only one right way to think or act, rather than teaching that "all things are acceptable in the proper time for each entity." [Law of One, Book One, Session 18, page 171. The Creator has given us the free will to make our own mistakes and learn from the karma that we inevitably create in the process, yet the Higher Self never stops loving us while carrying out that karma.]

- Information preaching imminent doom of any sort, even if it says it is "all about love," as this creates subconscious fear.

- Information loaded with specific cosmic facts designed to impress and awe, since this easily draws your focus away from the evolution of mind, body, and spirit. (This is regularly seen in modern channeling with the vastly detailed "passion plays" of "good" and "bad" ET groups consuming the majority of space in the work—and, of course, every source has a completely different mythology, thus discrediting the entire field of channeling.)

- Information telling you that you are some great enlightened savior for the planet. The "Messiah Complex" is, according to Wilcock, the classic giveaway that someone's work is being influenced by negative entities. All people who bother to love others are valuable members of the "Second Coming."

- Information that aggrandizes self or the organizations with which self identifies, creating "Us" and "Them," "Good" and "Bad" categories, which boost the ego and damage humility.

A caution that was expounded on in Ra's *Law of One* channelings by L/L Research must be noted here:

Questioner: Is it possible for an entity here on Earth to be so confused as to call both the Confederation and the Orion [the Confederation represents service to others, and the Orions represent service to self] groups in an alternating way, first one, then the other, and then back to the first again?

Ra: I am Ra. It is entirely possible for the untuned channel, as you call that service, to receive both positive and negative communications. If the entity at the base of its confusion is oriented towards service to others, the entity will begin to receive messages of doom. If the entity at the base of the complex of beingness is oriented towards service to self, the crusaders [the negative Orion group], who in this case do not find it necessary to lie, will simply begin to give the philosophy they are here to give. Many of your so-called contacts among your people have been confused and self-destructive because the channels were oriented towards service to others but, in the desire for proof, were open to the lying information of the crusaders who then were able to neutralize the effectiveness of the channel. [Book One, Session 12, page 125]

In other words, information may well be originating from another dimension, but that doesn't mean it is positive or accurate, and it all must be scrutinized carefully.

According to Wilcock, Rueckert, and other Law of One scholars, the vast majority of "channeled" material in print or on the Internet today would be considered a "mixed contact" (positive unknowingly mixed with negative) within the guidelines established by the Law of One. Truly undistorted positive sources are exceedingly rare and extremely precious. All channeled information must undergo the utmost of scrutiny, including that of Wilcock. Very often, positive information is given mixed in with negative information, as well as information from the channel's own consciousness. When one is willing to give up one's own power of free will and choice to what may seem to be a "divine voice" coming through another or even oneself, that is a probable indication that one is being misdirected and misled. Even if the channeling is 100% positive, one can still respond to it in a negative way by becoming a blind follower and making decisions totally based on the channeled information without any inward confirmation. Wilcock has posted a "recommended reading" list on his website at http://ascension2000.com/recommended.htm, which gives resources with more information about this subject.

If you choose to make a serious effort at having higher-dimensional communication, the study of *A Channeling Handbook* by Carla Rueckert[3] is highly recommended. Positive sources will focus their teachings on the particulars of how to evolve in mind, body, and spirit. These teachings have an essence of universality and would work just as well in any era, on any planet. This information has enormous possibilities for making positive contributions to the evolutionary process of our planet, and best of all, your data are not evaluated on points that could be factually proven or disproven— the focus is on the philosophy of how to become One. Most people can read these words and find meaning in them, regardless of their personal religious point of view. They are non-denominational and universal. This is a basic principle of the Law of One; in 1981, Ra said that "the desire for proof" creates an opening for negative entities to influence your work. Positive information offers "truth without proof," leaving it up to the individual to decide whether they will accept or reject it. As Rueckert often says to private groups, *"It is very, very easy to do channeling. It is very, very difficult to do channeling well."*

What little information we did get from the *Law of One* series regarding the various higher-dimensional groups and how they function was most probably accurate, but Ra also referred to this as "transient" information (information that was particular to a specific space and time as opposed to universal) and frequently chided the group for asking such unimportant questions. Even regarding the changes that are now happening on our planet, Ra said, "We do not concern ourselves with the conditions which bring about harvest." [Book One, Session 1, page 67]

Wilcock's own readings have offered clear and accurate future predictions, but it is also quite evident that this does not constitute proof in most people's minds that a dimensional shift is occurring. Even with the documented scientific material that he has put together, most people who do not want to believe it will simply never have the patience to read it carefully enough to understand. Hence, the Law of Free Will[4] is still being preserved. Yet whether or not you choose to believe in a coming dimensional shift is not nearly as important as living each day with an open heart, in joy, and without fear. It is my personal belief and experience that Ra has the ability and wisdom to guide you into that state if it is something you choose for yourself. And if the dimensional shift should prove to be real, then you will have automatically qualified yourself for the higher-dimensional path.

He had heard these sentence fragments for a very long time, but he did not realize that he could actually get small enough pieces of them to make note of them, and that they would actually have an intelligently guided structure that would be discernible upon conscious analysis.

—Ra/Wilcock, October 19, 1999

Chapter

12

The Wilcock Readings: Level Two

Wilcock called his first dream messages "Level Two" readings, where the information was delivered one fragment or sentence at a time. The sentences were often cryptic, so I've included Wilcock's own explanation of their meaning. Level Two readings are limited in that they usually have very specific meaning to the channel, but often not to the rest of us. Wilcock had no idea how far he would actually go with this process at the time that he brought these fragments through, and you will see in the next few chapters how coherent and fluid they became after the initial efforts. I've included this chapter as a historical reference. Also, if you ever try to do this yourself, you'll have an idea of what the early-stage material might sound like. There should be a certain amount of cryptic "garbage data" to prove that you're not analyzing what comes through.

Ra [via Wilcock] says that as the dimensional shift increases the energetic levels on the planet, more and more people will be able to tap into their Higher Selves via dream work or conscious channeling and experience increased psychic awareness. If you try this, Wilcock suggests that you get your analytical mind out of the way when writing down your fragments. You can evaluate later, but when you wake up, just write whatever words are in your mind without thinking about them. The assortment of Level Two fragments that follow was brought through in November of 1996, beginning on November 10 and continuing thereafter. You can find the complete unedited transcript on Wilcock's website.[1]

Wilcock: What was I dreaming about?

Dream Voice: "The dream was about you yourself and the subdivisions—and you're teaching them."

[Wilcock's comment] This was the first allusion to the fact that I had a multidimensional personality, with different subdivisions being different selves in different reincarnational periods. Later I would read *Seth Speaks* by Jane Roberts, a book that completely explained what my readings were talking about here.

Dream Voice: "Super! Wouldn't it be nice if they paid you money for this?"

Wilcock: (agrees)

[Wilcock's comment] Note: "They" were already setting the stage for me to ultimately become a paid professional intuitive counselor for others. I was already well on my way in that department, with a B.A. in Psychology, a year in a crisis hotline internship, two years of mental health jobs, and a great deal of extracurricular research in psychology.

Dream Voice: "One of our women, Theresa, a sibling inoperative—the Christian, psychically. It was rough—they 'nailed this in' (the sin), you know. I think a lot of people jump to their conclusions in silence. That's what the trinity is—one of those big red road signs on a dresser map [image of triangle on a Yield sign]. [The gateway is through the] Pillars of Light [coming from the] Andromeda [galaxy]."

[Wilcock's comment] This ended up being the definitive paragraph of the reading, as five days afterward, Mother Theresa was rushed to the hospital after having a heart attack. I was amazed to see this coincidence. "Jumping to conclusions in silence" seems to clearly refer to people who get tied up in Christian orthodox beliefs without ever going to the Christ within to find out for themselves. The portion about the pillars of light may refer to the fact that outside extraterrestrial forces are giving us aid to get us through this transition, a point made clear in almost all channeled UFO books.

Dream Voice: "That's the Church patterns. Amilius and other people live a very long time."

[Wilcock's comments] As far as the mention of Amilius is concerned, this would prove to be a very big clue to my past incarnation as Edgar Cayce. I was completely stumped about what it might mean for well over a half-year, as I had never heard the name Amilius prior to this reading. I would later discover in complete amazement that the Cayce readings specifically mention Amilius as the first incarnation of Jesus, the original Biblical "Adam." Therefore, Amilius has lived longer than any other human being on Earth, because he was the first to enter, have a series of lifetimes, and the first to exit, or Ascend, as Christ! And this is indeed the "[Christian] Church pattern"! The Cayce readings referred to this cycle of lifetimes as the "Christ pattern," and my readings appear to have substituted the word "Church" for "Christ."

[Author's note: The Cayce readings indicate that Amilius was the first incarnation of Christ, and Wilcock extrapolates the rest. This piece of evidence was part of what allowed Wilcock to feel comfortable with the idea of being Cayce's reincarnation when his Source finally revealed this connection.]

Dream Voice: "I must go now. Peace be with you in the Light of everlasting Love."

[Wilcock's comment] That was the closing phrase of this remarkable first session, which would forever change my life. That closing phrase became a constant in my readings and is still used to this day as a sign-off phrase for almost every reading that I have done. I was clearly stunned by what just happened. I sat up in bed and sleepily read through all the material that I produced. There were so many different things to think about that I was quite stunned by all of it. There was definitely something powerful going on that I could not deny. The reality of the Dream Voice thundered into my mind. . . .

November 16, 1996

Dream Voice: "Who do you think we are? Space aliens? Wrong. The one thing about our service is that we need to help."

[Wilcock's comment] This early phrase is what began to convince me that I was not in contact with extraterrestrials who were separate from myself, but rather a part of my own self. In the earliest sessions, it was important for me to see them without any preconceptions; to judge the contact based solely on the information that I was receiving instead of my previous expectations.

Wilcock: Why have I been getting stomach pains?

Dream Voice: "Don't you see? You're having trouble trying to stomach things right now! A half-witted request will not be honored, I don't think. Think of your skin as a colonic. What can we do if you eat butter?"

[Wilcock's comment] Here we can see the forces already starting to lay in on me about the need to clean up my diet. Cayce was consistently, eternally chided by his readings for his poor dietetic habits. This time, I had indeed been eating poorly, and I knew it. The readings were not about to candy-coat their responses, and my diet would turn out to be an ongoing project on their part.

November 19, 1996

Dream Voice: "I do say, the Self is in here. Descriptions are inaccurate. Conjunct Saturn and Mars—[there is] a lot of movement [in your astrology right now]. Saturn is around you tonight. It gives you goose bumps.

"Slowing down the matrix. This symbolism is for your own good. The only way you're going to get used to it is by putting the effort in. Where you work, you need to put a lot of effort in. Move as quick as you can through [this job]. Centering on Christmas and the New Year, you'll be ready for a change."

[Wilcock's comment] I would discover that my supervisor was due to return from her two-week vacation the day before New Year's, and this is when everything fell apart between the two of us.

Dream Voice: "The Ra group will have sightings here in the summer. Until then, don't worry about it. Just get some sleep."

[Wilcock's comment] I would not formally acknowledge Ra's presence in my readings until January of 1999, even though they made an appearance much earlier than that.

November 22, 1996

Dream Voice: "Believe it when I tell you that the end is coming—the end of organized materialism. You've got to listen to your own inner voice—nothing else will do. The voice of your ego will destroy you. These things are to be discussed, not repeated. The things you think of will come from higher and higher places. To facilitate this transition demands concentration and respect, an easier job than one might imagine. Be fruitful in your life and do not fall prey to the forces that conspire within you to bring you down. Know that salvation awaits. Be friendly unto thyself, and know that you are one with God."

November 23, 1996

Dream Voice: "At this juncture, crucial information is being given to you; the monetary involvement is high. The system we employ works with the moon, so pay attention to the moon, if possible."

[Wilcock's comment] I did discover that my readings worked best during the full moon.

Dream Voice: "Soon we will sit down and begin to redirect your thoughts. What I don't get is why you are so against the idea. It isn't part of the test for you to ignite the Source in flames. It's been so long since we've been interrupted that off the top of my head I can think of no reason for your reluctance. Branch out your control to all aspects of your life. Be aware that your trouble has not completely ended; the cards have shown you."

[Wilcock's comment] The length of time they are referring to since they were "interrupted" seems to be a reference to the death of Edgar Cayce, and the time that it took them to get me involved with a similar process. When I first read it, I did not understand the meaning. The last sentence refers to the fact that I had been doing Tarot card readings that showed me that more suffering was still ahead for me in the future.

Wilcock: Tell me of my true home and from where I came.

Dream Voice: "Ah, the woodward [image of a beautiful forest]. Ah, beautiful, a place of light and of forever. A place you will be returning to so quickly. Just go through the steps to get there. It sounds easy, and it is you who makes it difficult. We are losing ground. Try sleeping again.

"Lots of energy is coming in, and it is neither good nor bad. These concepts of duality are part of the prison of third-density existence. [The "Grey" ETs] have been moving around for quite a while. We're not talking about that. I'm going to get there soon enough. There are more pressing matters; we must focus on the urgent situation now before you. God knows how long it has taken us to decide when to do this with you."

Wilcock: I want to learn the art of astral travel.

Dream Voice: "Patience! Do you not think that we already have this planned for you? Listen to the voice in the summer. You might want to visit the Monroe Institute. It's not an impossible drive, it just looks like it is. It is just tiring. Also, make sure you keep that head of yours together. There is a resiliency that makes it hard for us to work with you. Please don't masturbate or scratch your [acne sores] for a while. We have no defense against these, and we are working very hard. Someday, this will be your job, too. You must take lessons."

Wilcock: Is my own personal growth more important than writing this book *[Convergence]*?

Dream Voice: "If you know the answer to your own question, then why do you ask? You need to stop running and learn to stay in one place. I told you it would be this way, so here we go. Thank you for obliging to consent to this contact. You are loved more than you could ever possibly imagine.

"We have good news for you. It is much easier to love than to hate. As concerns astral travel, be aware that others will be waiting for you, and you should not walk into it blindly. You've already had [our] Quality Assurance [department] saying that you were messed up. Just be patient and still, knowing that you were born into the '70s and lived throughout the '90s. Someone wrote me a 'letter' saying that you were the most vicious man alive. We disagree with this, but driving badly and staring at women in lust will not elicit favorable responses."

[Wilcock's comment] Obviously, this was another heavy warning for me about driving. Someone in "their" entourage had accused me of being vicious. That definitely hurt my feelings when I first read it, but it still wasn't enough to stop me from what I was doing on the road.

November 28, 1996

Dream Voice: "How about those dark circles under your eyes?"

[Wilcock's comment] As the passage came in while I was delaying a needed trip to the bathroom, this was clearly showing me the root of the pigment under my eyes, a problem with the kidneys and elimination.

Dream Voice: "Don't be a slave; slaves do the work of many for the pay of few. It's easy to latch on to that feeling of powerlessness.

"Through December 31st, you will have everyone watching you. Please try to maintain as pure an orientation as possible. You wanted us to be married, not an annulment."

[Wilcock's comment] This was yet another warning that could be connected to my driving, showing me that I was under some sort of period of examination. The idea of this examination did run through my head quite consistently, but I still didn't change my habits on the road when it was time for that early-morning crunch. I had no idea what they could really do, or that they would actually predict it in advance.

Keep in mind that these selections are excerpted from Wilcock's first series of contacts with his Dream Voice throughout the month of November 1996, and came through as simple one-sentence phrases. I've included this chapter so you can contrast how Wilcock's ability to translate these messages progressed from Level Two to his present mastery. Initially, Wilcock was able to produce only one sentence at a time, go back into a deeper trance, wake up, and produce another one. As we move into the next chapters, we can experience the step-up of quality into what Wilcock terms Level Four and Level Five trance states.

The idea is that if it feels of light, love, and joy on the deepest level of your being, then it is right for you. Do not debase this knowledge with the idea that you can simply indulge in your appetites. There is a very large and substantial difference between the feeling of gratifying the carnal self and the feeling of gratifying the spiritual self.

—Ra/Wilcock, December 5, 1999

Chapter
13

Ra Counsels Wilcock

This chapter gives further insight into how the relationship between Ra and David Wilcock actually operates. Ra senses every turn and quirk in the evolving Wilcock's challenges as a young man and counsels him on how to reconcile his mundane daily activities with his future destiny. As these readings progress, you will glimpse how Wilcock's growth is assisted by Ra. Wilcock is going through his own personal crises, money problems, unsuccessful job experiences, sexual frustration, and efforts to deal with his regular life in the world while returning home to his nightly dream dialogues.

Within this reading, you will likely find important insights that you can apply to your own life. You can refer to the complete text of these channelings by following the link in the notes.[1]

February 16, 1997

Wilcock: You mentioned that I had a life as a merchant. I was wondering if you could fill in some of the details on that.

Ra: This was slightly after the Biblical times, approximately A.D. 300. You were in the Middle East, relatively near Jerusalem; however, these religious concerns were not figuring in too largely in your life at that time. You had heard of the Pyramids, and you were very excited about them. Your wares were mostly dried fruit and sugar, both of which were rather precious items at that time. And yes, from time to time you did sell marijuana. So, you were a Deadhead at one time, long before the Grateful Dead as you now understand them. Let's get you back to sleep. Peace be with you in the Light of everlasting Love.

[Wilcock note: I slept and woke up an hour and a half later.]

... In the psychic area, we know of the richness that awaits you. Mental transmissions are saying this as well; therefore, be not afraid of what the future holds, for you will find yourself walking through a system of mazes and tunnels. When you get out the other end, you will be overjoyed to see yourself living in a situation you had never dreamed of. At the other end of the rainbow, you will find a pot of gold greater than you could have ever imagined, by embracing the practicality of these events that are now transpiring and taking the time to look in on yourself and notice the changes.

You are, by this very mechanism, exploring worlds of understanding and dimensions of being which will greatly expand your perceptions. We understand that this is a difficult time for you, and that there have been many challenges in the past similar to these now, but we are also aware of what your future holds, and that is what we hold onto. It is important for you to understand that a true friend is someone who will never lead you wrong, never lead you astray, but will always continue to work for your growth and your enlightenment. Now with this system, with this voice you have found that true friend, as you have with your housemate Eric and with Jude.

Other matters seem insignificant when compared to the overwhelming possibilities that await you in the future. We are very pleased that you have decided to start working on your book. We also want you to know that in the very near future, things will be changing. There are many new things that are waiting to happen, and we have just sort of been waiting for the right time in order to switch around the schedule so that we may cause these events to transpire. It is important for you to know that we love you very deeply, that you are as much our "flesh and blood" as that Earth family, perhaps more, and that we see the progress that you are making in the transition and we are extremely pleased with it. You have finally stopped speeding when you are driving; as of yesterday, there was significant progress on this in you trying not to cut people off and drive like a madman. We appreciate your foresight in these matters.

Your perceptions of theme must diminish; the farther away your mind gets from following the words that are coming out of your mouth as we are doing this, the more accurate the information will be. It is justifiable for you to make yourself aware of the fact that there will always be a solution. These problems that you view as obstacles are always and will ever be temporary, and it is your perceptions of reality that mold how these events actually occur. Let yourself lie back. . . . Relax into the energy of the love that is present in the moment. It feels like we have left a long shoreline of possible futures that were anchored in like boats, and we have now taken wind; the sails have filled up as we prepare for our vast journey to the uncharted territories that await us on the other side. Your tape recorder is very helpful, in that it allows us to speak in the way that we are now speaking without the necessity of you writing down these transmissions.

We are pleased with how you handled the situation last night involving [the two people who were talking behind the back of a third person] at your job. There are some difficult situations that will occur; we will not be the first ones nor the last ones to give you the impression of simplicity in these matters. Diplomacy was needed last night, and you did your job quite well; you were able to not get overly karmically involved with either side, but to stay neutral. We are happy for this.

These false ambitions or hopes that you have in the direction of being supervisor or being manager in some way are robbing you of the real purpose, which is just to be there in the moment of the work. [Sound of laughing] In a way, I want to say right now, "Listen, you idiot, if you would just hurry up and get this book done, get the proposal ready and send out the material, you wouldn't have to worry about such mundane ways of earning money in the future."

It is your destiny to become a career man in these matters. There is no charge for admission at the time of the harvest. [Author's note: "Harvest" is the term Ra uses for ascending into the next dimension.] When you approach the gate, you either approach or you don't approach, and the choice is made from within; there is never any ambiguity concerning it. As the time approaches, you are immediately aware of whether it is appropriate or not, and the forces will act accordingly.... Once you realize that there is no past, no present, and no future, but only now, you come much further into becoming that which you have dreamed of.

August 24, 1999

Self-integration and sorrow

... Seeing the stars and being the stars might seem to be a leap of faith. It is more directly a manifestation of true knowledge and Oneness. And in that light, in that love, in that awareness, do we not then see how all concatenations of matter/energy emanate from the One? We no longer need to create false distractions for the self as the reality of the higher vibrations becomes more and more apparent. We don't need to fail at futile efforts that deride the source and keep us congested from the reality [i.e., efforts made for the aggrandizement of self would fall into this category] that indicates that the road ahead, though straight and narrow, is indeed moving ever closer to the forefront of your awareness at this time. At this time we may proceed, and we ask that you breathe for a few seconds before doing so.

Self-integration does have a finishing point, and we are aware that the bringing about of this wisdom is an entire new process for you—a process that demands self-sacrifice, and/or the ability to remain discretely objective in the midst of a whole host of alternative stimuli as such. In order that we do not become overly concerned with the facts, we must condition ourselves to the acceptance of paradigms of sorrow. And when we say "Acceptance," we want to imply here that this means transformation as well. That is an important point.

October 24, 1999

We're forming a conglomerate being

... Always and forever, we insist that the parachute will indeed open on time. You will again coast downward and make a smooth transition. So, in order that you do not fall astray, we insist rather continuously that you put the focus back into yourself, into this work, instead of towards your recreational pursuits. Those matters of a more global appeal also need to factor back into the analysis. Where are we going? That choice is yours. I am going with you. So will the Old Testament, the New Testament, these writings, and all others like it.

We are all going to form a conglomerate being in the cosmos whose collective, unified efforts will be seen as one. In the intervening years and schedules, we can then indeed intake a few new conversations with those who have not yet been imprisoned in the geological records of ages past, but rather deliberate [involve] themselves consciously with humanity in the here and now. With radioactive decay and the like, there will be the last remaining vestiges of the third dimension and its new potentials, but you can indeed see how quickly all of this can be transformed when one works in a place of pure energy. And thus, many of your struggles do indeed take on a rather dramatic tone as a result. Since we do have the capability to heal ourselves, we also have the capability to heal you. We must be invited to do so through your own free will, and that is important. Those with liver and/or bladder cancer cannot see the ways in which they have made themselves so angry, and need to purge the stored toxic chemicals within the self. Similarly, we now know that those in the higher realms have invented the signal for you to hear so that there will be a greater and greater opportunity for you to get realigned on course with the more fundamental focus of your Light and Love, and how it relates to the greater picture as then seen.

It will be a great shock to many when these changes do indeed occur, and they will all be fond of saying that the Lord does work in mysterious ways. In order that we not become too pat on the subject, we do intersperse the questionings of our own destiny against those of a practical nature relative to you yourself, and how you have worked with the instreaming cosmic energies that mushroom up inside of yourself. And so again we remind you that the courses are all set and in place. It is now a function of your own intimate understandings that will bring this into view in the directly physical sense. We thank you, and we remind you that you are loved more than you could ever possibly imagine. Peace be with you in the Light of everlasting Love. We now end this reading. Adonai.

The earthquakes of the material self must indeed arise and coalesce somewhat. And therefore, keep yourself grounded as much as possible. Thank you. . . .

October 25, 1999

David, We are always around you, watching you every moment.

. . . When you file for information from the higher realms, you can indeed expect a response. Do remember that it is your attitude going into these readings that affects your overall level of success and quality coming out. And of course, remember that we love you more than you could ever possibly imagine. You are starting to get a grip on that concept. We eagerly await each new step in personal evolution that you make. As you are aware, this is not the deepest level of trance that you can have, but it is sufficient for the merging of our mind with yours to start the ball rolling with these readings again, as we had certainly dropped it. Thank you, David, and we do remind you that we are always around you, always with you, always watching you every moment. Keep that thought very clearly in mind, and you will see how you are always on stage, in a sense, and each and every action that you do is being carefully considered. That is all for now. Peace be with you in the Light of everlasting Love. We now end this reading. Adonai.

October 27, 1999

It will take personal sacrifices to keep receiving messages from our domain.

We have said before that we come to correct the distortions imposed upon your peoples by that which you know as the past. And if they really completely believe me, they will see that I can indeed perform many more tricks and maneuvers in the sky than anyone had heretofore imagined possible. Since we are fundamentally in a multidimensional universe, anything outside of your own dimension will indeed seem miraculous, such as the sighting of a ghost or apparition, for example. One recent friend of mine told me that while the statuettes are still in place, there are going to be ever-more vindictive reasons being thrown around for why other selves are judged by the self. In order to ameliorate those concerns, we have to bottleneck the interchange between those various portions of the self so that we do indeed have a cantaloupe of the higher realms where the full fruits of

Spirit must be carefully prepared and then only scooped out one by one, not completely indulged in all at once.

[Wilcock: I feel that "the statuettes" refers to the structure of our society as it now stands, the false idols of money and power. I really enjoy the cantaloupe analogy, as it refers to the fact that you can't have too much spiritual growth at once—it is just too hard to handle.]

The much greater gain comes from the rewarding of your desire to be of service. Don't rely too heavily on the extraterrestrial sources of information that you may think you know to exist. What is more important is the subjective variety of the illusion that is then presented to you in your own dreams, visions, and the like.

We don't have to do anything grandiose or extreme. Simply become the most adept soul at rewriting the Light of the One into a tangible form for others that you can be, and everything will be fine. The key and critical component is indeed desire, coupled with daily meditation and dream work. You do have to get through your most pressing personal issues in some tangible and creative fashion before the contact can be opened.

You will notice upon a study of David's materials [Ra is addressing the visitors who will read this on Wilcock's website] that we did not allow him to have this contact until he did two important things. Number one was that he broke a three-month stretch of unemployment by finally agreeing to take a job, and number two was that he broke the even longer stretch of clinging to a dysfunctional relationship with Yumi that had already become far outmoded for his present circumstances. Similarly, you should think about those things that might hinder or otherwise hold you back in the here and now from being able to receive this information. You are never given more than you can handle, and the Christ be with you regardless of circumstance. So don't fall into the trap of believing that you are one of those ones who is "not good enough" to receive such information. All of you are capable of doing this. The real question is, "How much do you really want it?" I think that the answer is for you to begin to believe in yourself. Begin to believe in your own dreams as solid guidance.

You who read these words are learning how to use this metaphorical language, because of how repetitively we phrase our sentences in this [manner].... And so, as the batter then steps up to the plate and prepares himself or herself accordingly, we will then make the pitch at the appropriate time. Not all of you will be able to swing and hit the ball, but we do certainly hope that more and more of you will be able to connect and indeed send this information packet to the ethers so that it may be transformed and sent back to you as a unified source of Light and Love vibration. [Author's note: In this reading, Ra explains how messages are actually transmitted from their realm into a human consciousness. The communication is not just verbal. It can be energetic impulses of love and light that flood into you.] Your breathing is indeed important in this process, as it earmarks the difference between a partial success in the work and a total success. What you need to do is use your breath to send packets of your own vital energy up to us in the higher realms. You can symbolically visualize this as exiting yourself through the crown chakra at the top of your head. When we have received this energy, we can then transform it into a much more viable source, and send it back down to you as living information. The information will enter your mind as natural thoughts and feelings, and thus when you harmonize with us you should fully expect that all of the messages and information will be going through your mind as though they were your own thoughts, ideas, and impressions. That is the fundamental key to this process. You are not going to have a force suddenly come in and seize control of you. Rather, it is a far more subtle process, whereby you realize exactly how to listen to the voice of your imagination and intuition, which by then has become a moment-by-moment source of Living Light.

... The electrodes are in place for you to do this quite astoundingly well. And thus, we never fret when dealing with ancient civilizations, such as your own in the third density. We know that this technology of the higher realms is imminently available to you, and the real question is whether you yourself are able to realize how the guidance comes in.

The finest point of distinction is how you are able to differentiate between those impulses coming from the conscious mind and those from the subconscious. What you want to take is those pieces of information and data that arise very spontaneously into your consciousness, through no deliberate force or action of your own. Take all the data as it comes in on a moment-by-moment basis, and never analyze or try to understand any of it. You run an extreme risk of danger by allowing the conscious mind to follow along in your meditation. When the conscious mind understands the data, you will then find it extremely difficult to get a clean source feed. You may have something that reads very well to you, and you may have convinced yourself that you are doing a fine job. However, the influence of the conscious mind can always be subverted to greater and greater degrees, and therefore no one should think that they have completely overcome this process.

The most important thing of all is to never have fear that anything you speak will be disjointed, unrecognizable, or foolish. The sentences may indeed be quite awkward, as you have seen our sentences become. But you should embrace any and all words that come into your mind as being from the Source, providing of course that you allow them to arise naturally and not think them into being. You have already seen how these thoughts can arise naturally in your meditations, and in the late night and early morning states of consciousness. If you are one of the ones who would like to make this commitment of service, then please be patient, and record yourself on audio cassette tape, as this is much easier than trying to write it down by yourself.

We are experiencing a discrete shift in the boundary of consciousness as it pertains to the packeted quanta of Light/Love energy that surround your plane and exist within each of you now. The behavioral circumstances might seem to be a bit odd, but the discrete boundary changes we are speaking of will indeed continue to occur throughout the very near future and beyond. In order that we not confuse or befuddle the situation, we are doing everything that we can on a moment-by-moment basis to cast aside the useless debris that might otherwise have been created, and instead redefine our mission priorities on an instant-by-instant basis. What we want more than anything else is to be the messengers for you who can indeed produce transformation in a rapidly accelerating fashion, and in a short amount of time.

[Long pause]

We thank you for this session, as this helps us to answer a question that many of those readers out there have been asking. We will have more to say on this as time progresses. For now, we leave you in the awareness of the ovoid shape of the One, and remind you that you are loved more than you could ever possibly imagine. Peace be with you in the Light of everlasting Love. We now end this reading. Adonai and farewell.

Should anyone choose to dispute the evidence for the work that we or David are performing, then we do indeed have a non-intervention policy at that point. We must simply withdraw our influence from those who choose not to receive this guidance. It is not our plan or purpose to alter the free will of an entity in any way.

—Ra/Wilcock, November 11, 1999

Chapter

14

Ra Client Readings

In Chapter Two, Wilcock told the story of how he made the transition from college academia to earning his living doing readings for others. During this transition, Wilcock's Source guided him. While in the midst of working a number of regular jobs and already having lived in Virginia Beach for nine months, Wilcock was advised to begin doing readings for others full-time. Initially Wilcock was insecure and nervous about this, but his Dream Voice gave him constant encouragement and the confidence he needed to trust in the process. Below is a compilation of the readings that Wilcock received during this period (which are not yet published on his website at the time of this writing), followed by an actual client reading.

Ra counsels Wilcock on doing readings for others

Ra/Wilcock, June 17, 1998—A few more incidental words and we will be on our way. *Live not in the fear of any directions that seem at times to be opaque.* Instead take comfort in the fact that solace is gained by a new direction now coming to the fore. This involves a greater polarization towards Love and Light energy on behalf of the people of this planet. We consider it to be imperative that the full chance to recognize one's own Oneness be given. To that end, you must allow yourself to begin weaning off of the computer, and into greater matters, more directly associated with the day-by-day desire to minister to the people of the outside world. . . .

June 18, 1998 — You have already gotten your first client for your readings, and you put aside any biases or prejudices that you might have had to give service in a non-judgmental manner. So, for reliable service, just make sure that you keep on doing what you are doing. Do not turn away those who would need help, but rather raise them up, enliven their spirits, and embolden their resolve to press forth. We do not want our arrival to continue to go unannounced, and this is a major event for you.

David had done his first reading but was not yet willing to make a commitment to doing it full-time. He was insecure about putting his economic life on the line, as well as taking on the responsibility of doing this for others. He was also attached to the approval of others and wanting people to like him. But Ra continued their campaign of encouragement.

June 21, 1998 — The quality of life that is to come is of the highest order, and we do not need to be merely content with those elements on the outside. We can now focus in on where the deeper, more pure spiritual truth is, and in so doing you will find that it is quickly coming around full circle in a way that we could have never expected before. So there you have it; without the one hand, the other [would not know what it was doing].

June 25, 1998

Wilcock: What is the progress I am impeding?
Ra: You should know that the interest of all entities involved is

to promote peace, stability, and awareness. In this light, then, we can say that you have always done a good job in communicating the finer points of the basic doctrine that we support to your associates. But please make a point of it to go deeper into trance so that the more direct and current information might then be given. Without this inherent trust in the words that you will automatically speak, there is apt to be a certain degree of disturbance in the phraseology and content therein.

We do think that you did rather well for this [first client] reading, which was very close to the surface in terms of conscious awareness. But in the future, let's make absolutely sure that we prepare adequately. [This will necessitate] that we lose the nervousness, and that therefore we have full awareness of how important what we are doing really is. [We should] take the necessary time and focus to ensure that the contact is as accurate as given.

But, congratulations are in order, and again, we support you very strongly in the midst of all this. You have already learned what is the classic trap of those otherselves in your field; the temptation to distort the information with the conscious mind, thinking that it knows and understands all, is a great one. But then, the reading itself consists of nothing greater than that which was gleaned from the conscious mind's previous awareness of the situation in question. Said reading might be moderately helpful or even very helpful, yet it lacks the fundamental component that is preserved in your deepest trances. [These are] those times when each word appears through nothing more than the totally spontaneous process in the midst of what could be likened only unto a total vacuum.

Therefore, we think that the next phase of our workings with others will involve a much longer-term commitment to shedding the nervousness of whether or not one will perform adequately, and simply begin doing that which has proven itself to be accurate time and time again. For now, we hope that the environment that is scheduled for your immediate future will bring you great joy and happiness, as we do see that our prophecies will continue, just as we had explained them. You are recognizing the need for more time to do these workings, and that is very good.

There will come a time when we will be about to break into the full mainstream, where many sidetracks and false beginnings may occur. [This will occur] if there is too much of a desire to befriend all those who might then be clients. Keep this in mind for the future, as it is important that we crash-test our new resolve here. You will quickly be finding a great deal of business coming your way, and the terminus point of your current job will not be much longer in the offing.

[David's note at the time of transcription:] God, I guess not! My assignment abruptly ended the very next day after this reading! If you read the journals I entered above, before starting this transcription, you can see that this "crash test" would occur much sooner than I had imagined! Now I just need to wait for the "great deal of business" part. I do think that this will happen as well.

June 27, 1998 — We've needed you on the other side for quite some time now, and you are only really just beginning to understand what it is that you must do. Immaculate Conception breeds a discipline that takes the inherent circumstances surrounding the entity in question and provides them with a new model of understanding. There might then be the resources necessary to take the newfound divinity and incorporate it into the existing structures, both of body, mind, and spirit; that is, the amalgam of copper/wisdom that is now before us.

... Hard to believe it, but we vowed never to reveal the true information necessary to provide the final steps of initiation until it was personally chosen by you. That point seems to have now arrived, and for this we are very fortunate. There is still time to do what you need to do, David. We are sorry for how much pressure we feel we need to put on you. This is more about assuming your natural abilities than it is about having any role thrust upon you; you must remember that part.

For a reflective moment of time, consider the next opportunity you have to be beleaguered by giants is an opportunity that will make you stronger, and will make you better equipped to handle the crises and the circumstances necessary for the final growth phases to take place. Without coming to these realizations, it would be like swinging on a lone tire in Chicago, apart from those truths that had been given, apart from the knowledge that had been gained.

We simply cannot continue forward in this manner, as our desire is for you to maximize your potential. You can see as well as we can that there is just not enough time in the day to do what we are doing right now. That is why the work of the readings must now take precedence, and this is already expanding nicely, as we had hoped. You are learning that even a minimum of two clients a week could be enough to support the venture. If you can get your ego out of the way, these readings will be extremely influential for the people who then have them.

[Wilcock's subconscious/dreaming self speaking in trance, June 28, 1998:]

While I was at this bank, I looked around and saw people in there. They were all going about their business accordingly. My biggest fear was to never have the discipline necessary to be able to follow in their footsteps, and create a similar situation for myself, requiring frequent trips to the bank. And yet now, as I begin to truly understand myself, I see that the entire procedure is getting to be more real, more provocative, every moment. The plain and simple truth is that I now know that there will always be many opportunities for me as soon as I begin to follow my soul's path. The opportunities will manifest themselves in ways that I had never even imagined. I will find that the manifestations become almost effortless once the material has been achieved.

[Ra/Wilcock] In order to adjust the brightness, stop thinking about what is wrong, and start thinking about what is right. You have made an extraordinary step by starting to see clients, and you now understand that the whole purpose of our togetherness is to help spread the available knowledge and energy that is now infusing into the Earth planes. We want to make sure that the entire purpose of our being is positive, spiritual, loving, and pure. Therefore, we desire to take the opportunity to go into deeper and deeper levels of trance. This will necessitate the silence not currently present. Therefore, we urge you to trust your feelings. . . .

The difficulties that we have encountered are not so much the products of the physical body as that of the mental body, as it tries to accommodate the flow of information coming from the spiritual body. . . . We do not think it necessary for you to feel afraid of whether or not this business will work. Simply take solace in the fact that a very small number of readings will generate a much higher amount of income that would take many more hours to generate in the mainstream working world you have heretofore encountered. Therefore the cost-benefit analysis that you can make clearly shows that it is better to be involved with this work on that level than it is to simply not try to do it. To free up all your time for other things would be spectacular, and would present you with the opportunity to really and truly begin to expand your horizons. There is no reason why you can't be very successful at this.

June 30, 1998 — Why include all those who cannot see when the deeper insistence is upon the seeking of positive opportunities on your behalf? We will only begin activating the centers within you when you take the time to complete the basic initiation processes that we have outlined. And now, as the next step falls into place, you are learning that there are as yet many opportunities for you to call upon these forces and ask them for guidance in these matters. . . . There are a number of greater opportunities that will present themselves. . . .

Again, let me rephrase that. The only thing we have ever wanted for you is to produce an entity whose full capabilities are then utilized within the physical sphere. As for this process, you are coming along quite nicely. We have gone out of our way to provide you with opportunities so that some of the most difficult struggles you have faced in the past can be met again and dealt with. Anywhere that an area of your life has been met in the past with woeful inadequacy, the opportunity to re-emerge into said experience will occur over and over again, until the lesson has been learned. So in this case, you chose an opportunity to take a new situation and have situations similar to those in the past again recur. This should not be an especially difficult phase for you, as you have come a long way in your understandings now, and we know this. Simply be prudent and focus on your strengths. Focus on the fact that there are still many possibilities and opportunities, and as you progress forward more and more of them will become quite evident.

David: Would the influx of new business be enough to support myself, or should I look into the temporary job scene again?

Ra: As for the employment scene, the atmosphere you create around you will direct how well your business does. Therefore, further conversations with the likes of [name] and others, explaining to them the great interest that has been generated and the world-class quality of the readings produced, should garner an immediate benefit. The first time anyone does something like this, there is a breath of fresh air as the old patterns are cast aside in favor of the newly positive instreaming light energies. In our case we wish to see that you will take it upon yourself to have the initiative necessary to go out, produce the signs, and start the talk happening. . . .

And so, even though David had to work through great fear, he did put up signs advertising his new business locally, making no mention of the Cayce connection. The overwhelming response led him to decide that this was a better way to utilize his time and earn a living. Ra had already indicated to him that personal readings were not going to be the main function of his later life, as the demand would far exceed his ability to supply, just as transpired with Cayce. What follows is one of these client readings, some two years after David began his business. Inasmuch as all of us have similar challenges overcoming the illusions of the physical world, there are many invaluable keys in this reading that anyone can apply to their own spiritual evolution.

Wilcock Client Reading[1]

June 21, 2000 — The client in question is a male college student who has participated in musical projects and was requesting general spiritual guidance.

I am Ra. We greet you in the light and the love of the One Infinite Creator. We communicate now.

You decide what is next; your free will is of paramount importance to us. We cannot use you to do anything that you have not chosen for yourself.

The gracious opportunities are for all to see, and even in the great chain of being, there are still those who prefer to decide on a moment-by-moment basis where they are from and where they are going. You decide what is next; your free will is of paramount importance to us. We cannot use you to do anything that you have not chosen for yourself. And thus, when you tire of important issues, which you have chosen for yourself, it is you who must reassess those priorities. The handwriting is not necessarily on the wall. . . .

A life of virtue is your path, and it is important to recognize that truth. For in the greater scheme of things, there can be only Unity, and separation is but an illusion, born of the compression into third-density physical matter, which you underwent in order to produce this cycle of incarnations. Now when we wink our eye and smile, it is to tell you that we are giving you a positive reinforcement. You need not be concerned about our opinion of you, or feel that some mighty arm of judgment is going to be rained down during the course of this interview. Rather it would behoove you to take responsibility for your own self-acceptance, while recognizing that we have always accepted you the entire time.

There is no sin that is unforgivable; there is no act that is unremediated when construed as a positive effect in terms of the fact that everything is a learning experience that leads you back to Oneness. The clearer the waters become, the more imbued the consciousness can be with the clarity of light and vision commensurate with the higher densities, and only rarely seen in your own. You do have an opportunity to tip your hat to the masters, and approach their greatness through your own diligence in self-perfection and self-realization through the methods that have been set down in the past.

Cannibals can come and go, and teachings can be cannibalized, but the deeper truths always reside within, and they remain in your heart, waiting to be tapped as a reservoir of potential that exists within you. The value of the dollar will be reduced, and the economies are going to boom and collapse simultaneously, and indeed it is this conjunction of forces that encourages the opportunities for the most intense spiritual growth on this planet. You, like everyone else, will go through this experience. It is a question of how and whether you choose to face it or deny it that will determine the course of your future actions.

For when these times come, there are great opportunities to be of service, to lead the wayward souls towards a greater conception of self and others, that would allow such beingness to occur. We have a wedding set up in the higher realms for you. It is the wedding together of different parts of the self—parts that have been rejected, parts that need to stop and refuel, parts that need to be transformed. Indeed, the image of the female known as [name] in the dream was emblematic of the subconscious inner feminine force that still resides within. In order for your conception of this force to move away from that of the harlot, and towards that of the maiden, there must be a realignment within the self, which has already begun. [David's note, July 3, while transcribing: The dream featured a female who was digging in the dirt and uncovering valuable objects; she also was highly sexually attractive.] Many would use their subconscious or deep mind as a harlot, and feel that they can tap in at times that are right for them, and ignore signals and teachings and truths at other times. This does not imply that we are being judgmental of you. Rather this is an archetype that all must go through as exemplified in the tarot card "The Lovers," which does then deal with the experience of mind and the transformation of same. In the immediate sector of your awareness, you are learning to court your subconscious as one would the maiden, instead of simply looking for it at the times that are apparent to you; times that would be convenient. The maiden must be romanced; the maiden must be flowed with. You must understand her needs as they rise and fall and accept what you are being shown. The dream was showing you that which the subconscious will reveal; those elements that are being dug out of the earth, or the carnal self. The spider eggs indeed show what has been hatched in the past, and the fact that they are largely being cleared out should show you that the transformation of mind is nearing completion.

Why, indeed, does it seem impossible to believe that you truly are one with the Father-Mother God; that your spirit exists as an infinite vibration/reverberation throughout the universe?

Why should you struggle with facts and information when the deeper knowledge comes from diligent inner seeking and meditation? Why should you resist your musical work, when it is one of the highest affections for the Creator that you are capable of expressing? Why, indeed, does it seem impossible to believe that you truly are one with the Father-Mother God; that your spirit exists as an infinite vibration/reverberation throughout the universe? These concepts are difficult to assimilate for the fact that the physical world is so conducive to the belief that that is all there is. We understand the conundrum that is planted before you as you must deal with the realities of study and of work and of adult responsibility, while at the same time maintaining a station that allows you to hold on to your awareness in a form that is much more streamlined than what you may otherwise want.

Indeed, there are two sides to every issue, and you have the choice as to which side you will see. Do you choose to see the negativity that is present in the physical world around you, or do you choose to see that all works in unity with the One Creator? It is quite difficult to embrace the life that you have and the responsibilities that are set before you as being elemental of perfect sacrament, perfect spiritual simplicity, and divine essence. It is not easy to comprehend how even the most negative paths that others follow in society, or that you yourself are forced to go through, can be part of a larger order of events that has been carefully scripted and rehearsed throughout the universe since time immemorial.

It is this choice of polarity in the third density that determines all future courses of action. Whether you like it or not, your own future behavior in the higher realms is dictated by the choices you make each and every day. In the Egyptian metaphor, the brains are removed from the skull case at the time of death. Why is this? Because it was believed that the *heart* was the core essence that needed to be preserved, and the brain only got in the way of comprehending and understanding the life that one would have in the higher realms.

Indeed, the only way that the truths of the heart may be apprehended are in those cases where you are capable of seeking the Christ light within yourself, identifying it as such, and then preparing its radiance and beauty so it may be offered to others as an inexhaustible jewel of such brilliance that it illuminates the darkest night, and remains solid as an everlasting presence.

Similarly, these truths of the heart cannot be gleaned from a text-book. They cannot be dictated into a tape recorder and transcribed, though we can try our best to do this. They cannot be found in books; they cannot be seen in street signs as you drive around. Teachers will not impart them in classes. Indeed, the only way that the truths of the heart may be apprehended are in those cases where you are capable of seeking the Christ light within yourself, identifying it as such, and then preparing its radiance and beauty so it may be offered to others as an inexhaustible jewel of such brilliance that it illuminates the darkest night, and remains solid as an everlasting presence.

Now with all these conditions are implied a few other points of contrast that we can discuss herein. For when you split open the watermelon of the higher realms for the first time, you discover how sweet it is. We only use the watermelon metaphor to illustrate the waters of life or the spirit, and that red or pink color that is then associated with the heart. It is better for you to dine on the foods of the divine and to maintain your macrobiotic tendencies than it is to fall back into fallen dietetic patterns that are typical of the influence that the negative forces have secured on this planetary sphere.

So why wait? Don't we take the necessary opportunities for our learning process and become them each moment? Aren't we fulfilling our own obligations to ourselves when we choose to be brutally honest with ourselves; to tell the truth and to see eye to eye with our own beliefs? Are we not simply stumbling along and wondering what is going to happen next and what we should do next? Is there more to life than asking philosophical questions, but rather acting on philosophical beliefs, acting on those things which you understand and perceive to be true? Not retarding one's progress, but rather enlivening it with the understandings that come clearer and clearer as you learn to accept yourself and to accept the divine movement of energies that exist all around you, within you and without you, for now and forever.

You have taken the basic steps that are necessary to unfurl the hidden scroll of wisdom that lies encapsulated within the self. We suggest that you give yourself more credit and become more responsible for your personal healing process. Understand that your attitude is everything; that moment by moment you have a choice as to how you will perceive yourself and how you will perceive others. We have hinted at the proclivity towards viewing sameness in the creation and seeing the unifying umbrella of oneness that can connect together many things that most would consider grievous and unstoppable. Whether you choose to do something about this or not is up to you, but you do have the power.

The forces that are available [to you] can indeed put you in a position where you are that of the resistance to the negative forces on this planet. You yourself can turn the tide, and halt the unstoppable energy that is flowing, recognizing its malleability and its degree of change. We do suggest that all will come into play, that your musical efforts must continue, and will continue; be not afraid to mount the stage, and to stand forth, shining your life and your love as a beacon of radiance that will bring sunshine and color to others' faces as they revel in the glory of the music.

Know in your heart and body and mind that all is forgiven, all is accepted, all is indeed yours to experience. The choices and how you navigate through them determine the speed of your learning curve, but there is no judgment. You have worked through these issues with yourself with bravery and diligence, and for that you receive our commendations. More and more you can learn to silence the voices of fear and worry. You can find greater acceptance of yourself, greater responsibility for your own actions, and indeed, a renewed opportunity to see others as the self, and to accept them that much more; for if they are yourself, then indeed they can reflect the parts of yourself that are hurting and are still in need of integration.

There is only one path, though there are many ways to experience it. All are returning to oneness.

You can work towards the enlightenment of all beings through your own path of inner diligence and self-preservation and protection. The ladder to the higher realms is rising into view; you can climb it one rung at a time. There is only one path, though there are many ways to experience it. All are returning to Oneness. You make the choice about this each and every day. You choose how your thoughts will interact with your body and your spirit. You choose whether you will allow those little automatic voices to pipe in and determine the course of your future behaviors, or whether you will allow the meditative state of mind to retain its control, to keep your attitude light and your mood happy, to keep your personal vibrations at a high enough level that you do not slip or slide, but rather stay in tune with the goals ahead, and focused on the necessary opportunities of learning that will present themselves.

The ego is but a distraction, and the more that the ego becomes the Oneness, the less that any resistance is produced, and the more smoothly your life will function as a whole unit. We sincerely appreciate the efforts you have made and ensure that you will be rewarded. Pay attention to your dreams, and we will have many more messages for you. This is just the beginning of what can become a long-term relationship between us. We thank you and we remind you again that you are loved more than you can ever possibly imagine. These truths will not be debunked; they are everlasting. Peace be with you in the light of everlasting love. We now end this reading. Adonai.

We remind you once again that the infinite love of the Almighty One, Creator of the Universe and God of all Gods, is omnipresent. Since you in your physical environment are entirely composed of this same etheric substance with a unique personality, we suggest that you begin remembering who you are.

—Ra/Wilcock, September 4, 1999

Chapter

15

Ra's View of Television
and the Media

In a notably composed text, Ra explains how television and the media condition our consciousness to certain levels of consensus reality, making us prisoners locked in lesser levels of truth that we are constantly being bombarded with. Our expansion into the higher realms is impeded as we allow ourselves to be programmed by outside sources as opposed to going inward to experience our essence.[1]

Ra: Yes, that's right, Television....

In many ways, your lifetime on Earth is like a circus show, in the extent to which you understand that the mechanisms of the performance go no further than that of the lion in his cage. Because you believe things about yourselves that are often damaging and hurtful, you find yourselves forever locked into a position of subservience to these forces that appear to be outside of yourself, and outside of your control. The ringleader represents society in general, as it molds what you should or should not feel, and instills feelings of disgust over your physical form by parading perfected bodies in front of you on the television.

You, as the lion, may or may not even be aware of the extent to which you are a player in this giant circus; when the understanding comes, it can be quite a jolt. One of the first things that will happen is the desire to stop watching television and other media sources. The ringleader, in this case being the media and other organized forms of information control, only wants one thing, which should be readily apparent; it wants you to feel that everything you have is insufficient, to get you to strive further and further towards material objects. You who have reached these words now should be well aware that this concept of not being materialistic extends through all of the religions your world has ever known, or as the parable goes in Christianity, "The love of money is the root of all evil."

When you no longer have such a fixation on money, the situations that surround you will seem much less fearful. Many, many people exist in states of great wealth compared to the rest of the five billion people on this planet, and since your media isolates you inside a laboratory rat chamber or a circus ring, it makes you feel that you never have enough. Yet you live in one of the richest countries in the world, and the chances are that if you are educated enough to be reading this book ["Wilcock Readings, Book One"], you probably have more than enough money to survive. Why should you continue wrestling with yourself over always wanting more and never feeling that you have enough, when you can just sit back and realize that your life simply is? Instead of striving for greater and greater ideals of living, just simply be.

As you strive to understand the grand plan of this circus, you will realize that you have been imprisoned by the capitalist system. Since the media, as you now view it, is a machination of the capitalist system, it will selectively bias you towards having a desire to accumulate greater and greater physical objects. But there is another aspect that you should be equally aware of. If you make an honest appraisal of what you see if you watch television every day, you will realize that the one dominant theme, if you view it from the outside as an observer and not as a participant, is that of fear. Almost everything you see on television in one form or another is designed to instill fear—programs as well as news shows, including the operational definitions given extraterrestrial contacts. Why, you may ask, is fear important? Fear is important because when you have a person who is fearful, it is much simpler to persuade them to do something that they might not ordinarily do.

When you have a person in fear, that fear instills control. Many people know this subconsciously and use it to their benefit. The cases only become obvious once issues of domestic violence arise. Understand fully and completely that fear is a tool—a device, a method of having power over others.

It is not necessarily giving up on the world as much as it is coming to a heightened understanding of the world.

If the public right now were to reach a fearless state, then the international bankers and the policymakers who are running the show behind the corporations and media would no longer have the ability to control the people—would no longer have the ability to dictate the flow of currency. It is the very fact that people are paralyzed by their own fears that prevents them from doing anything productive; that prevents them from any real efforts to try to make adjustments in their lives in directions that will be most suitable for them. It is this fear that is the great limiter and the great binder; it is as an anchor that locks you to the bottom of the ocean of possibility, forever destined to go around your loop; to go around the perimeter of the circus cage. If that lion only were to know the grassy plains that God meant for him and the abundance that awaited him, he would most likely collapse with misery at the fact that he had been brought into such a system in the first place. The difference between you and the lion is that you DO have the ability to liberate yourself from the concerns of the world. It is not necessarily giving up on the world as much as it is coming to a heightened understanding of the world. [It involves] seeing it through the lens of a person who is unburdened by social considerations, who is unburdened by trends, who doesn't feel the need to have the latest clothes or the latest car, but just simply is who he or she is, nothing more and nothing less. To make said realization about oneself is one of the greatest joys that can be attained, for with that joy comes freedom.

Why not simply be happy with your life as it is right now? Recognize that the things that still exist as challenges are there because you chose them to be there, not because people are "screwing you over," not because you are being tortured by the capitalist system, not because it is your fate in life to suffer, not because God has abandoned you, not because there is no other way. There is another way, and that way is the path of acceptance and surrender. If you simply surrender your fears and accept your life as it is right now in the present, you can begin to realize that there is a balance that is present by the very fact of whatever hardships or scarcities face you.

The balance is present so that you can learn important lessons about life, and self-knowledge comes from an understanding of the fact that YOU designed this whole system long, long ago as a spiritual essence. The forces of karma, the forces of manifestation on this plane, were chosen by you as the mass being that formed humanity, that formed this section of the universe.

As you pull away from the material world, as you pull away from the squawking, incessant chatter of the television, which causes squawking, incessant chatter in your own mind, and as you lay down your fears at the door, you clear an enormous space for inner peace. Participation in this media, participation in this fear, in this lack of understanding, by its very nature will cause you to become completely embroiled in the matters of day-to-day living. You will often take out your greater concerns and hardships upon those people around you, because you are incapable of seeing the fact that there is more.

You are incapable of seeing that what you thought was anger towards these people was in fact a deeper reaction to what is actually occurring inside your mind as you experience the hardship. [You feel this] as you experience the heartache that the media cause you by making you feel that you don't have the ideal mate or the ideal wealth, and that by attaining these systems you could somehow improve yourself. Simultaneously, the media are working very diligently to make you fear that your life could end at any moment, and to make you very possessive of that fact.

If you can transcend the attachment to your physical body, then you should therefore have no fear of death.

However, once you begin to separate yourself from these influences, and go deeper inside, you can then realize that there is much more than this. You can begin to come to an understanding that your physical life as you know it is but a shell; it is but a vehicle for exploration of the overall you, which is hyperdimensional in focus and extends throughout the span of linear time, as well as many other realities. If you can transcend the attachment to your physical body, then you should therefore have no fear of death, for death cannot have a grip on you. You would merely understand that death is a transition, and that you will go on to something different.

Ponder on these matters, for they will give you greater insight. To detach yourself from the influences which pervade is a valiant task; it also involves detaching from the dietary choices that are presented to you which are often of a nature that is very destructive. [Having a diet involving] natural foods, fruits, vegetables and nuts, very low in meats, an abolishment of refined sugar and an abolishment of bleached, refined (white) flour, will cause great expansion in a very short period of time. It is your continued participation in the media which reinforces the unhealthy eating habits of large amounts of meat and of greasy foods so continually. Put yourself in the frame of mind where you can transcend this, and you will achieve clarity of mind and a peace greater than anything you have ever known. Think on these things, for they are truth. Peace be with you in the Light of everlasting Love.

The future destiny holds that you must maintain focus on the straight and narrow path, aligning yourself most specifically with those emanations of Light, Love, Sound, and Color that will produce the highest vibrational intentions and intonations.

—Ra/Wilcock, September 4, 1999

Chapter

16

Ra on "Your Attitude is Everything"

As the visitors to Wilcock's website grew in number, Ra addressed this new group of interested people tuning into the channelings, delivering the wisdom that would provide the keys for readers to overcome their third-density limitations, experience Oneness, and prepare for the dimensional shift that Wilcock's scientific treatises were leading web visitors to believe was real. Following is an example of a reading for the general public; it focuses on the importance of attitude.[1]

Ra: Different stages of evolution require different levels of participation. In order that you not become too confused, we have always given you as much as you can handle at any one particular moment in space-time. On the time-space level, there is only ever going to be the eternal Now. And thus, the ghosts that you see and are no longer afraid of represent those things that used to be fears in what you would call the past. The more that they are integrated, the more that you see their folly.

And so, the design becomes a lot stronger than we might imagine, and the realizations that are now underway in the mass collective consciousness are quite profound. For you see, David, this dream [the dream is not included here, but the complete text is available on Wilcock's website] goes far beyond just being for yourself, as it actually refers to the state of the human collective consciousness at large. We have often used the metaphors of drug use to indicate the ways in which society is debilitating itself, and here that metaphor was combined with the idea of radiation as well.

There are many on your plane who would think that the usage of certain chemicals, marijuana, and the like will bring about their spiritual enlightenment. Although we have stated this material before, we will repeat it again for clarity. Any chemical that alters the mind spectrum, including caffeine, nicotine, and refined sugar, is ultimately very detrimental to the enhancement of the spiritual vibrations. There is no question about that, nor has there ever been, and there is no provision that we are giving you to make you think otherwise.

The same rule applies for alcohol and any other mind-altering substance that you can think of. It is simply not wise to take them. Now we did have a client recently who had extreme cases of pain in the physical body, and was required to take a rather advanced painkiller for this. He was not happy with this choice but went ahead and did it anyway out of necessity. In cases like this, you have to judge what is right and what is wrong for yourself with the knowledge that your vibrational rate does suffer as a result.

In the deeper sense, we find that even as society has created billionaires and the like, it has also systematically siphoned away money from those who work on the lower ends of the spectrum. And when you really look at it, you find that there are only two choices—to be of service or to withdraw, as we have discussed in the Ra Material and other sources.

The best way to be of service is to accept the sacredness of the situation, and the fact that it has a purpose. If you are not capable of doing this, then it is better for you to withdraw your energies from the situation and not be concerned with its outcome. What we are alerting David and the reader to is the propensity towards wanting to single out these negative forces and treat them with contempt and disdain.

We do not agree that there is nothing wrong with them in the sense that they are causing trouble and the like. We have always stated that their influence can be very troubling. However, it is important to remember that these forces must be cared for and loved in a very firm manner—a manner which also is stating that you are not going to let the manipulations go any further than they already have.

The negative forces are simply symbolic and metaphorical representations of those forces that coalesce within you each and every moment, whether you are willing to see them and face up to them or not.

A gunfight is occurring on both sides of this issue, as we have so frequently said. And the outcome at this point is up to you. Each one of you who reads these words has a choice as to how you will live your life each and every day. Remember that the negative forces are simply symbolic and metaphorical representations of those forces that coalesce within *you* each and every moment, whether you are willing to see them and face up to them or not.

The more that you become aware of that fact, the more healthily you will be able to live your life, for you will have the distinct knowledge of purpose and understanding that comes with one who has attained enlightenment and balance.

The greatest challenge that you have as a human being is to accept and integrate the self. And this can occur on many levels. The more important phase of the journey develops itself through the regeneration of sorts that comes about with learning and understanding the true core of what soul evolution is about—namely self-acceptance in the eyes of the One.

Now understand that self-acceptance refers to the fact that your true self is the One. It is not located in separation consciousness. And therefore, you can be still within yourself and know that you are God, while also reminding yourself that all others are God as well, as is everything in your environment and the universe at large—

both in this dimension and in all others.

So it is a good exercise for you to process all the challenges that you go through each and every day, and always remind yourself that anything that you see in others that frustrates you is simply a part of yourself that has not yet been healed. When you become perfectly balanced, or at least begin approaching that point, the little idiosyncrasies of others will not affect you any longer.

David has distilled two basic laws about this on his own that dramatically affect the interactions that you all must have with otherselves:

- Number one is *"Attitude is everything."*
- Number two is *"Like begets like."*

And they both play off each other directly, so that they are almost the same expression, phrased differently.

It is very important to keep a positive attitude, as one of the things that you will realize is that the others around you will have a natural tendency to adopt the same type of attitude that you yourself have. And thus, if you are feeling predominantly negative at any one time, it is all too easy for you to project that negativity out into your environment and leave the others feeling the same way.

Your attitude is everything, and what that also means is that if you have a person around you who is suffering from negative emotions, you can raise that energy to a discretely new level of vibration, and change the whole energy dynamic completely. Remember that a positive attitude is a higher vibration than a negative attitude.

And so, if you can raise up the ante when playing these games of the Spirit, then you have the discrete possibility that another who is around you will either rise to your level or withdraw from the situation. The most difficult challenge is for you to not exhibit your patterned reactions when another self is indulging in negative emotions and trying to draw out your own negative side to get you to snap at them or otherwise.

There is a lot of discipline that comes about with the concept of remaining clear and straightforward in your decision to either be of service or to withdraw. To be of service is to raise the vibration, or as they might say, to "kill 'em with kindness." If you cannot do this earnestly, then you should withdraw from the situation, as you are not going to be of assistance by getting defensive.

You will find that like begets like. And thus, if your attitude is not good, then you will find quite quickly that everyone around you begins to have a negative attitude. Similarly, it is a positive attitude—a smile kept on the face and a pleasant feeling stored within the heart—that then creates the greatest joy and abundance in the otherselves around you.

This is the attitude that you should try to adopt while you are working and going through all of your daily routines. David was finally able to integrate this towards the end of his term in the corporate temping world. It was quite magical for us to see. Although he had a job that was extremely rote and uninteresting—a job that almost all of the other employees in the department hated—his attitude was very positive.

Many of the others in the office thought that there was something wrong with him, because there were times where he got so absorbed in what he was doing and the joyfulness of same that he would forget to leave his desk at the beginning of the fifteen-minute breaks. Everyone else would rush out the door to go have their latest cigarette or to otherwise do anything they could to get away from where they were. David was capable of simply breathing, meditating, and relaxing into that space, so that he was at peace with what he was doing and did not notice the passage of time, nor care.

Understand that to be at a job and to watch the clock avidly is another form of negative emotions. What you are fundamentally telling yourself is that you do not want to be where you are, which is always going to be right now. The greatest service that you can provide yourself is to remain clearly focused in the here and now, so that you are always comfortable there. You will find that in the stillness of mind is the greatest peace, and you need not meditate to get this, though meditation is a very effective tool.

We suggest that life becomes your meditation in general, and that you strive to remove those sources of mental scattering that would be so detrimental to you. David noticed while he was working at this job that many others in the office would listen to music through headphones while doing their work—and it can be fundamentally stated that with all this distraction, there is very little time for the self to have the fullest level of deep-seated thought and awareness necessary to tackle the most fundamental issues within the mind and spirit at large.

And so, strive always to lower the level of distraction. We do not often cover this material, as David has done so quite nicely himself. It is precisely television and radio in their most consumer-driven forms that bring about the scattering of Mind, for when it is used as background noise it obliterates a great deal of subconscious process— as there is an aspect of your mind that must pay attention to it, and this robs the elements of change and fluidity of expression that are necessary to occur in your subconscious mind. It is this extreme level of distraction that makes it so difficult for many to sit still in a lecture or classroom without feeling a sense of boredom very quickly.

Ritualistic behaviors: Clean your house and exercise

David also is fond of using ritualistic behaviors in order to better ground himself in the here and now. One of these behaviors is to keep his house very orderly, neat, and clean. We suggest this for all of our readers, for the simple fact that it is a discipline of Mind as well.

You should take a look around you at your living space, and recognize that it is a reflection of your inner mind and the connections therein. Take a good honest look at your mind by looking at the room around you and the house, and see what it is that your mind looks like. Is your mind neat and orderly, tidy and connected, or is your mind scattered and slovenly and immersed with needless things that are scattered about? You will find that as you clean up these messes in the physical sense of your dwelling, it will also release the energy that you put into those messes by the fact of leaving them in the first place.

While David was staying in his first semi-permanent living situation in Virginia Beach, he realized that this person whom he had chosen to live with had messes in the house that had not been touched for many years. And similarly, those soul fragments had been lying dormant for an equally long period of time. In that particular case, the messes beneath messes involved art supplies that had not been touched for many years—and this represented the dormant potentials within the Self that were never utilized.

Another ritualistic behavior is to make sure that you have a set routine of exercise each day. David has a small circuit in the local neighborhood that he walks, and it is specifically designed to last him about fifteen minutes and to be as beautiful as possible along the way, given the requirements of the area.

Sabrina has asked David in the past why he does not change his walk, as to her change is very important. We are not promulgating David's behaviors as being right or wrong, or saying that they are better than the other choices. What we will say is that an appreciation for ritual is indeed very important. We have worked with David long enough now that he begins to feel responsible if he does not do this walk at least once, and preferably twice each day.

And he also discovers in the midst of doing it that even though it is the same path, he has new insights about himself, his work, and the world each time. And therefore, it is more a question of the potentials that are within you, and how you see those potentials against the backdrop of everyday society. You can similarly view your work as another form of ritual; and by keeping your mind clear and still, you can experience the movement and change within yourself as you go through each and every day.

David was able to perform a great deal of work in his stilled mind while he was at these jobs, and this work involved such things as plotting out the ideas and concepts that later formed the book *Convergence*. And so, it is a fundamental process of your evolution to remain focused within, and not to let yourself get distracted by what the world provides.

The reason why we used the drug metaphor in this dream is to illustrate how pressing of a concern it is—as those who continue to indulge in such behaviors will have greater and greater degrees of cancer, ill health, and negative karmic outcomes as the vibrations continue to increase. Things are never going to get any easier for that part of yourself that clings to the negative vibrations. Quite to the contrary, you will discover that more and more of your inner self is being exhumed for viewing in the present as each day passes.

And this process of knowing and accepting the self can end up being far more valiant and amazing than you had ever thought. So take this stored energy from within yourself and process it in such a way as to transform your daily circumstances. Keep your house clean and your dietetic intake pure. Assist not another in lowering a burden, but rather in raising one up. And here, we are indicating that it is important to help those others around you to have their own growth challenges that they can work with, instead of simply making their lives easier.

Most spiritual people upon your plane seek always service to others in its basest form, which is that of unconditional love in the fourth-density sense of the term. But again, when you move up to the fifth density of wisdom and the sixth density of compassionate wisdom, you realize that the question of being of service is far more complex than simply being a martyr. You have to move very actively through all the different layers of questionings that come about to find those parts of the self that are of most use, and then accentuate them. Sometimes, those parts of the self will involve things that you do not normally consider to be spiritual, as your idea of spirituality on your plane is still tied up with what David might call "airy-fairy" concerns—that all is Light and Love and Wonder.

While this is true in the highest sense of the term, there are many intermediate steps necessary in the physical sense. Sometimes, in order for us to work with you, you have to be jarred very strongly out of your existing negative conceptions. The physical body is an excellent tool for doing this, as it will manifest its appropriate health concerns in order to teach you what you need to learn from the inner self. And thus, there is nothing that occurs by accident, and we have covered this material before.

Whatever portion of the body is ill at ease must be seen as a metaphorical representation of the issue that is at work itself. The work of Louise L. Hay has a lot to do with this, and you might want to check that out for further study of these issues.

In the end, the most documented path for future success involves the realization that in order to truly become spiritual, you must also possess those characteristics of integrity, of cleanliness, of forthrightness, and of self-worth. It is very important that you preserve your own integrity and self-worth in order to be most effective in your service to others. For you will discover that you are not being of service by allowing others to walk all over you. You must learn to communicate what you are truly feeling inside and not keep bottling it up to be hidden from view.

Your emotions should not be spoken if they are overly harsh and damaging to another, unless it can be done in a very peaceful way. You do not need to speak in a harsh and defeating manner in order to express that something is bothering you. It is definitely possible for you to be angry at first and then process and deal with that anger so that it becomes accepted before you actually speak what is on your mind.

You will find that by communicating what you are really feeling with the other person, you are overcoming fear and the sense of limitation in exchange for the direct appreciation of the light that it brings. You do have to confront fears within yourself about whether this person will be able to handle your true opinions. You will find that those relationships that are positive and beneficial for you will actually be strengthened, whereas those friendships or relationships that were never in your best interest in the first place will begin to show their natural flaws and will dissipate as such.

This is not a bad thing, for the process of spiritual growth does involve the acclimation of your external environment to mirror that of your internal. And thus, if your house is a mess on the etheric level, it may show up as a mess on the physical level in terms of the relative lack of order therein. But this is not necessary. Your house can also be a mess on the physical level in terms of the emotions and interactions that occur between its members. And so, it is important to gain compassion for others and for their suffering. If they do not understand these fundamental truths within themselves, then you can take upon yourself the responsibility to teach them, and in so doing you will create new light and new love that will extend for a very long time.

Always remember that the doorway to the Infinite is opening wider and wider every moment. And these techniques can be of assistance to you in realizing your truest potential. Look not to the future with scorn and disdain, but with awe, wonder, and excitement. Regardless of the changes that must occur to produce Ascension, there are still only going to be those events that are positive, as they will remove the impediments and obstacles that hold you back.

You can strive to do this within yourself each and every day through the techniques that we have enunciated here, along with many others. And of course, always remember that you are eternally guided and protected, and surrounded with our Light and Love, and that you are loved more than you could ever possibly imagine. Peace be with you in the Light of everlasting Love. We now end this reading. Adonai.

I am the flower that opens up within you when you are willing to give it water and light, the necessary nutrients and love that sustain life. Your garden is blossoming, and the multi-tiered layers of roses, of which we can ascend through as a spiral staircase, await you. Perhaps you have felt me in those moments when you are with someone else—in the deepest, most intimate moments of your life, sharing your truest feelings with the deepest love, respect, and admiration for this other person. I might have fooled you at that time, because you didn't realize that you were talking to me.

—Wilcock as the "I AM" Presence*

---

*Wilcock defines the "I am" presence as the Christed self within all of us.

Chapter

17

Ra on Healing the Original Wound and Reconnecting with God

Even though we may believe in a Creator and the oneness of life, for most of us the direct experience of that is missing, so we have emptiness, isolation, fear, and sorrow instead of joy. In this reading, Ra gives the keys to turning our experience around so that we might once again reconnect with Creation. I believe that if you're open and have the desire, the wisdom and energy in this reading can lift you into your own personal spiritual experience, and help you maintain it no matter what's going on in the outer world.

Each time I read this particular passage, I get something new from it. When I read it out loud in the presence of someone I care about, I always experience a shift in the level of love and light present.[1]

November 9, 2001

We are simply the arbiters and facilitators of self-will, thus enabling the deepest goals to be brought forth.

Ra: Wow, another lesson. Sooner or later you'll figure out that this isn't really about you, it's about us. Or rather, you could say that your relationship with us has certain factors within it that expect reconciliation between past and present, between known and unknown, seen and unseen. We work according to a system of certain expectations, not to say rules. Perhaps there has been a perception within you that you MUST do this or that or the other, and that punishment is expected if such goals are not achieved.

Indeed, a cursory glance at the history of these workings [in the Wilcock readings] may seem to indicate that we have issued such expectations with a sense of inevitable duty that is chosen "from above" and then commanded to the physical self to carry out. Nothing could be further from the truth, as ultimately it is the Self that chooses all paths in life, and we are simply the arbiters and facilitators of self-will, thus enabling the deepest goals to be brought forth.

We have all experienced these times where we feel obligated to do something for someone, either physical or non-physical. It is more important to try to be true to yourself, to live up to the ideals that you have already espoused in your dealings with others, and to then expect others to follow their own paths without adopting yours.

The enslavement of perceived obligation knows no bounds within the developing personality, and such is presently the case with so many aspects and facets of your society that it beggars the imagination. One charged political example would be: "If something bad happens to you, then you should seek infinite justice against those who did it, and against everyone who supports them."

Many requests have come to David regarding the status of this current conflict between the United States and foreign adversaries. Keep reminding yourself at the deepest level that the government is not God and can never be a stand-in or replacement for the God that is within. You do not have to feel as if anything is wrong with you if you do not agree with all that is being said and done.

Remember the teachings of Gandhi, who encouraged his people to think for themselves and create change without the use of violence, but rather "peaceful non-cooperation." Lest you think that such passive resistance has no power, remember that Gandhi was arguably single-handedly responsible for releasing the people of India from the massive financial, social, political, and spiritual tyranny of the British Empire.

Be aware that these choices you make and opinions you form do rest heavily upon your overall soul vibration, since this is the time of transformation. Delve deeply into the idea of whether it is right to kill a much larger number of people in revenge and retaliation for an event that happened upon your own soil, especially in light of the example of Gandhi. (Had India taken arms against the British in violent rebellion, they might still be a colony to this day.) Also be aware that you can still love those who choose to disagree with your views and not let partisan politics become a bitter schism that separates you from the world around you.

So in the large-scale arena of world politics, all does again come back to the drama of Self. The experiences of life provide the grist for the mill of transformation. Issues that transpire between nations are but large-scale dramatizations of the issues that occur between self and others. And it is important that we keep our focus centered on the self, and how you can heal your interactions with others and move towards a greater understanding. Regardless of your opinions about world events, it is unlikely that you are in a position to do anything of deep significance to change them. However, when you take responsibility for your own attitude and emotions from one moment to the next, you are actively helping to raise the overall vibrations of the planet at this time, which does indeed have a direct effect upon the consciousness of all involved.

You should never feel so high and mighty on your spiritual quest for wisdom and truth that you fail to remember the all-encompassing importance of sharing your life and love with others.

Some of those around you will seem particularly charged with a sense of mission and inspiration, and provide a role of leadership. This becomes the natural choice of all who unveil the true Self from amongst the miasma of illusion, and it can become your choice as well. Now is not the time to "become enlightened" and hide out in a cave; rather, it is to share that which you have experienced with others in whatever way is most suitable for them. For many, a smile or word of encouragement is plenty, and you should never feel so high and mighty on your spiritual quest for wisdom and truth that you fail to remember the all-encompassing importance of sharing your life and love with others on the most basic level, without casting expectations as to who or when or how. If you miss that most generic aspect of the spiritual quest, then you will be slowly dying inside and wonder why things aren't going any better for you.

The stronger your desire to serve, the more assistance you will receive. Thus, resources are allocated to certain entities due to their propensity to make use of that catalyst for further gain. It is as a byproduct of request [from the self] that we move forward in such a manner. Thus, "ask and ye shall be given." If you are one who has already filed such a request, then be prepared to see how your life right now, exactly as you are living it, is indeed your ministry. The catalyst for learning that you experience should never be seen as obligation, as we strive for unity amongst the different layers of personality and soul so that a true coherence is established.

On one level, it is perhaps easier to post blame at a non-physical godlike entity for your feelings of personal responsibility than to see that you chose them for yourself. It is easier to play a game of denial and separation than it is to play one of love and unity. Nevertheless, what we are really interested in at this point is finding the core of your true soul, amplifying it, and making it more and more conscious for you so that you can truly live out that which you were set here to accomplish. And in that strife, in that knowing, in that reconciliation, true awareness is finally shared in the personality structure of the self with the deeper layers of mind, and with the One Infinite Creator.

There are systems of guidelines that are fairly universal for one who would follow these teachings. We espouse these beliefs not to create a structure for control, but a platform for personal advancement and vibrational acceleration. Our ultimate goal is to help you so totally find that God within yourself that you merge with it, and all illusions are penetrated in the light of Truth. When this is done, you can step aside from feelings of lack of worth and self-deprecation and truly re-embrace the Original Self that hides behind veil after veil of forgetfulness.

These incremental steps give you the opportunity to release the conditions through which you were born and have suffered under. The realization of the destruction that was caused to your core by your parents and others is only useful when it is combined with the understanding that this was all a product of your own choice. Such experiences and difficulties come about only to mirror the ways in which you have treated yourself so blindly in the past, such as in former incarnations.

The "Now" is where the power resides, and in that "Now" you have the complete opportunity to overhaul the forgotten whisperings of desire for a better life and begin actively living it in the present. All of this begins with your ATTITUDE and a sense of thankfulness and self-forgiveness. To look back over the past with a critical eye is not the point; rather it is to see those experiences as having been completely sacred, for the potential that they gave you to re-enact the union with the One Creator that you have sought from the beginning.

Relax into an awareness of your personality distortions without feeling that they are a shackle or a binding that you can never throw off. Understand that these distortions will persist to a degree as the teachings continue to be assimilated on many levels. It is not normally possible for any one soul in your current focus [focused on the present third-dimensional life] to completely undo years and lifetimes of distortion in a short time, nor should you expect sudden results or quick growth. The process of the balancing of the self involves repeated cycles of realization of a particular inconsistency, the taking of steps to alleviate that inconsistency, and the repetition of the realization/action process once more.

Some of the experiences that have the greatest learning potential are those with the greatest difficulty. In earlier stages of your spiritual education it was quite easy for you to see many events in your life as meaningful, but then when the most difficult periods came along you would say, "That's just the way it is" or "I got screwed over" or "Some guys have all the luck, some guys get all the pain."

The fact of the matter is that the majority of souls who are actively working their spiritual path at this time and place have long since moved past the point of what we would call random catalyst, where things occur in one's life that are of a difficult nature but are not precisely planned and calibrated in advance for their learning potential. Great strides can be made in your awareness when you see how predetermined much of your life's events are. Now this pre-determination may not be something that was planned years in advance, though this is more often the case than many of you would ever think. A number of events can and do get planned under much smaller windows of time, in order to best respond to your immediate needs.

This is why we stress again the importance of dream work, as every dream is an intervention that is best suited for your needs at that particular time—and such a requirement will remain ongoing for as long as you reside within your physical body. The dreams will help you to understand why the difficult events in your life are happening so that you can learn from them. And they will also cultivate humility, by not letting you run away with the idea that you have suddenly finished all of your work and can relax.

The short time remaining for you on Earth in the present cycle is a time that will be used to its maximal benefit, and you can fully expect that there will be many challenges. Yet, you should also remember that the challenges placed before you are carefully calibrated so as to not exceed the capacity you possess to solve them. Truly, it may be said that a great deal of the apparent randomness of your life is actually quite intentional, and remains as the next viable opportunity for you to have a major healing of the past. We define "healing" as that which removes any of the blockages from recognizing the existence of God within the self, and then becoming that Self.

The struggle of the apparent separation from God is re-enacted within the self constantly; this is why we refer to it as the Original Wound. As is often stated, the Original Wound is the illusory perception of separation from God. If you feel that God has abandoned you, then it makes it very difficult for you to live in the world. There is a sense of loss, of abandonment, of violation, of anger, of victimization. Great loneliness comes up for you as well, since you realize that God definitely exists yet seems notably absent. All it takes is one person, one event, one moment, one situation to ready the self for a re-enactment of that original pain, and off you go on another tirade of useless turmoil and self-inflicted vibrational damage.

Understand that these are typically subconscious processes, and bringing this struggle to the level of the conscious mind is a monumental accomplishment for any entity in third-density to attain. The reason why we give such emphasis to that point is that: It is this Original Wound that is the basis behind all suffering, and also is the final key to complete enlightenment, or reunion with the Source Light and Love of Oneness.

We have many players on our team at a variety of levels whose purpose is to help you bridge this gap and re-attain what was once yours. The processes of soul evolution are carefully guided and part of a massive combined effort to bring about your greater understanding. And the more you realize this, the more you step away from being a victim in your own life and blaming everyone else for the apparent problems that you are facing, and the more you take an active role in seeing yourself as the sole arbiter of the discussions with God that then get acted out on the stage of your life.

When you recognize that the Source within yourself is that same Source that is within all others, you then lessen the difficulties in forming a bridge between how your own issues could be acted out in your life by others around you. The ones whom you hold the most closely and dearly are truly the strongest mirrors for you. Granted, they may have many of your traits and issues in an exaggerated form, and you would have a difficult time ever believing that such traits would exist within yourself. However, they would not still be around you if their purpose had been fulfilled; the guiding forces of life would separate your two paths since it was no longer necessary.

In many relationships this duality play of yin and yang forces will continue to exist in cycle after cycle. You have the good and the bad, the triumphant and the disastrous, all working together as a collective vehicle for your advancement. Many times you have chosen this relationship so that the other self can grow with you, and mutual progress is then possible. A relationship becomes more and more unbalanced if this does not occur, and will eventually result in separation and/or death of one of the participants, once a certain age is reached.

David just wondered why we needed to include death in the last sentence. Simply this: we are talking about relationships that are often consummated in marriage. It is a fact that upon your plane, many horribly unbalanced situations between two entities remain constricted within the contract of marriage long after they have outlasted their usefulness. This is not to say that we are issuing a prophecy regarding the death of someone that is not suitable for you but whom you have trouble getting away from. More importantly, it is for you to see that many of these relationships become lifelong endeavors of personal growth and healing.

Now, in situations where such a binding constriction occurs, there may not be mutual growth. Nevertheless, if the situation persists without divorce or natural separation, there is still some force within the self that is compelled to continue the game of conquest and loss, passion and disappointment, love and anger. If you do not have a romantic relationship at this time, do not be so blind as to assume that these rules do not apply to you, as these passion plays exist to varying degrees between yourself and all others with whom you would interact, especially those whom you see or think about most frequently. And again, this is but another mirror of the self, exposing yet a deeper layer of the personality for your view so that it might be assimilated.

The choice of relationship is usually one that is carefully weighed out in the higher realms long before the two entities ever even meet for the first time. Therefore, we are not necessarily advising you to simply drop out of a situation that has been deemed unpleasant by one or both parties. More to the point, your personal responsibility is in seeing how the upsetting aspects of that interaction are but facets of your own healing process, exposing the very issues that you have with yourself so that you may examine them on the stage of your life. And in this sense, a relationship with greater conflict can be of greater use, as those with conflictual relationships are those who are in need of this method of healing.

All conflict is born of the illusion of having been abandoned by God.

You are doing yourself and others an enormous disservice if you are still naïve enough to think that you have no role or responsibility in the creation of your conflicts. Once you achieve enough will power to be able to claim that responsibility, you will find that it is impossible to harbor resentment for anyone, since all conflict is born of the illusion of having been abandoned by God. For many, this pain is still very present and can be easily touched off with the slightest of disturbances. Once you recognize that you were never abandoned to begin with and are constantly surrounded by a multiplicity of beings who love you more than you could ever possibly imagine and are working diligently to make you see it, then self-realization and Unity consciousness is the only responsible choice that remains.

Your spiritual growth process is a minute-by-minute, day-by-day, lifelong affair, whether you make the conscious choice to see it as such or not. The more difficult experiences will lessen in their intensity when your attitude no longer has a place of resentment and negative emotions over them. Again we state that your attitude is everything, that there can be nothing of greater importance in dealing with problematic situations than keeping a positive attitude. When you can no longer be hurt by either enemies or loving friends, you have stepped outside the prison of third-density consciousness and given yourself room to expand into the higher levels of your own being. And the trump card in your deck is the awareness that there is no separation, that all is indeed One.

Never forget that your own church of pain can also be the sepulcher of release. Cut loose the ties that bind you to separation and embrace Unity. Relive the memory of that true Home that knows no boundaries, no distinctions but truly is ALL, everywhere and everywhen. That moment is available to you right now as you read these words, as it is in every moment, should you but allow its awareness to become your own. We wish you well on your continuing journey, and remind you that you are loved more than you could ever possibly imagine. Peace be with you in the light of everlasting Love. We now end this reading. Adonai.

We want you, the reader of these words, to be reminded that by your simple finding and studying of this material and attempting to live the life that is of greater service to others, you should not worry about whether or not you will be Ascending.

—Ra/Wilcock, August 17, 1999

Chapter

18

Ra on Ascension and the Birth of the Christ Within Us All

This is the final Ra reading included in this book. It addresses the subject of Ascension and the dimensional shift planet Earth is undergoing, according to Ra.[1] I again suggest that you evaluate all this information from your own intuitive levels. The following reading is quite extraordinary, and although it is presented verbatim, it is far beyond my own experience to validate the truth in it. There is certainly a high degree of correspondence with the information in this reading from Ra and the prophecies of Jesus.

When Wilcock himself was confronted with the idea of a dimensional shift, he had to validate it, to the best of his ability, before he was willing to introduce it to others. The next chapter presents some of the scientific evidence that Wilcock has compiled to support the concept of dimensional shift and Ascension, which Ra expounds upon in this chapter.

December 22, 1998

Ra: Led by a few insightful followers to the appropriate destination, the few who were able to understand did indeed again perceive the Christ light within the heavens. These heavens were of a different sort; namely, the light essence coming from within, in those heavenly realms of the higher consciousness. For those who could but perceive it, [it is] an awesome sight, resplendent in its glories and completely unfettered by the material concerns. For those who would try to spread it out and admire its beauty as though on a surgical table, there will only be great surprise, as its majesty eludes any classification or taxonomy.

It is not to be discussed, nor talked about as though something you could understand or grasp consciously. What you can do is approach its knowledge by following its demands. The demands it places are very simple: to view those otherselves as the Self. To embrace the true principle of Christ, and to identify completely with that awareness in your own person. To make it abundantly clear to all those involved that you yourself have followed these commands, not out of a feeling of guilt or fear, but rather out of an innate sense of responsibility to thine own fellow man. Such responsibility needs to be generated from within, from the realization of the oneness of the One True Being, that soul essence or entity that is composed of so much more than your physical matter.

Break for a second and look in on yourself. Take five minutes each day to observe your own routines, your own thought patterns. Do they align with the Supreme Will of the One Being, or do they indulge in the fallen energies of ego, pride, and discomfort? Where do you reside in God's many mansions? Do you rise to the top, as the leavening makes the bread to sprout into full bloom, or do you remain as the hard-caked dirt on the bottom that needs to be scrubbed away?

Think about this as you contemplate the bread of life, the bread of the Christ, the bread of the One True Being that is shared amongst us all as that life essence we can all then partake of. Know in thine own heart that the message of the Christ is forever profound, and forever simple. Embrace the simplicity, and know that in that pure moment of time, you have grasped the unknowable. For it is through your conduct, both in thoughts and in actions, that the gateway to infinity is indeed opened.

A plot is being hatched for all of you. A plot to examine the Self under a microscope, to then see up close the parts that have been hiding, the parts that cause despair, fear, anger, rage, embitterment, jealousy, grief, apathy, depression, sadness, morbidity, strife, ego, stress, et cetera. Never before in human history have you had the pressure of the solar changes weighing upon you as they do now. Our research with David confirms this, and it is important to understand that all are affected by this cycle, regardless of whether it is apparent to them or not.

And thus, there is indeed a very concrete reason for why many of you are feeling so out of touch, so compelled to look back through the past and deal with the issues as they emerge. Indeed, it is the compelling force of the Christ Consciousness that is blowing the doors wide open and expanding the limits that now surround you. We do see that this expansion is similar to the expansion of the womb in the contractions prior to the birth of the Christ child. It is not a simple process by any means, but one which requires all those who participate to hold their breath, to clasp hands gingerly together, and look down with fear and awe at the massive force coming from within that is necessary, as the final push towards birth is then made.

Similarly, see these birth contractions of the collective human fourth-dimensional mind as occurring now. Do not fail to separate the personal issues within the self from those issues occurring in the world at large, for to do otherwise is to not grasp the full realm of possibilities that await you. See your own life as the material for part of a great cosmic joke. The punch line has yet to come, but come it will. Right now, you are being set up for the final blast of Love energy, that part kicked in at the end that then makes everything snap together, leading to peals of uproarious laughter. So too will this Ascension be the capstone that then holds together the shaky foundations of everything that now seems so disjointed.

The chief cornerstone is being lowered back into place. It is very ironic that very few of you have truly realized that this is what is taking place. As these issues bubble up to the surface to be cleansed, the most common and, dare we say, "smart" reaction is to rage out at the difficulties that life is presenting, to then file them away on the back burner of the mind for future consumption at some ill-defined and seldom-reached point.

Because we think with our actions, what it is that we do in our bodies transforms directly into our thoughts. Therefore, you will be feeling energetics within the body that correspond to the emotions that were captivating you during these previous exchanges. As you think about this, remember that the discrete point of power is always surrounding you in the present moment. Therefore, you have the opportunity to bless yourself with the grace of recognizing that your own inhospitable actions in the past were merely part of this great cosmic joke that all of you will be so heartily laughing over in the next few months or years, as the case may be.

When you realize what awesome potential resides within, you are then capable of unfurling your own butterfly wings. It is not necessary to remain a larva or a pupa forever, as these are merely growth stages. So too will you sprout your angel wings, and alight within the firmament, moving towards that shining star in the heavens which beckons you—the glory of the true Christ Consciousness, the One God that extends throughout all creation, that everlasting light of pure, radiant love that calls all under its wing, that thou wouldst feel its holy presence.

Gathered together now are its children (scattered throughout the fragments of space and time, that is), eagerly awaiting your birth and watching from the outside. These forces, known to you as the angels, exist outside of the physical sphere as you know it, but still watch eagerly, awaiting the arrival of the new birth within each of you. It is from this perspective that you should see the extraterrestrials in question. There are indeed negative entities, but the vast majority of those now present upon your sphere seek to counterattack any harm that would come your way, and work diligently to do so.

When you are so surrounded by the heavenly host, it is indeed rather foolish for you to be so concerned about an imminent alien invasion, if you will. There would never be a possibility for something like this to take place, as you are indeed heavily protected and quarantined from the outside world, if you will, at this point in time. We come to you on a narrow-band vibration, a band that you can perceive early in the morning as you rise into full waking consciousness; a band that will be speaking to you with greater and greater clarity in every moment.

But can you hear the call? Do you understand the words of the Father as they are spoken from His lips to thine own mind? Canst thou assemble the sentences properly, as they have been heard in the early waking delirium that is so commonly discarded with the fury of the alarm clock and the hot shower? Indeed, do you rest comfortably with the notion of species-to-species contact and communion, or even spirit-to-spirit contact, knowing full well that the being you wish to contact is the Christ himself?

What surprise comes to you at the realization that this very Christ is now designed to become literally your personal savior, but not in the sense that the fundamentalists would have it? Rather, it is that spark in you. It is you, and you are it; there is no separation. Therefore, you can call it what you will, but its effects are the same. Your own Divine spark is awakening within you, and thus the phrase in the Bible: "I am the way, the truth, and the life; no one can come unto the Father but by me."

Think about that statement for a minute.

"I am the way"—namely, there is no other way but thine own way, revealed to thyself in the clarity that comes from deep, internal wounding, then examined carefully by the Self.

"I am the truth"—namely, there is no other truth, save for the Light within.

"I am the life"—namely, there is no greater life than that which comes inherently from understanding this depth of communion with the truest nature of oneself.

"No one can come unto the Father but by me"—namely, that there is no other path to Self-perfection and achievement of enlightenment but by grasping and aligning with those forces coalescing within Self, then represented by said Christ Light.

This statement has been hopelessly distorted to all sorts of parsimonious [selfish] situations, including but not limited to those who would use it as a means to bolster their own faith, and to say that all those who do not believe in Jesus are forever condemned to an eternal hellfire of some sort, made gruesome in its potentialities for prolonged, intense suffering. And yet, the masses of your people insist on some level within that this inner Christ is what is being accomplished. Because of the damage we sustained in our religion, namely Christianity, we often come to you without ever speaking in these exact terms.

Indeed, many of your people choose to seek the Christ light within without naming it or labeling it as such. They may decide to use Native American spirituality, meditation, or any of a wide variety of other metaphysical topics to bring about this truth. So too may there be the followers of other orthodox religions in the world, also responding to that inner calling generated by the Light within.

When one blows away the barriers that hold distinction, one begins to perceive the True Self in its form, which is pure compassion and light. To those untrained, it would not be seen at all, or only viewed as an inanimate object, a luminous being that does not yield any knowledge or secrets whatsoever.

Indeed, one may train oneself to the point of being able to see it, but if one does not possess the necessary desire for knowledge, it might yet elude them. What you are seeing is indeed the perfected signature of the model of man, that holy presence that enshrouds all entities who would seek to make it manifest themselves. You are seeing a design that has stamped its signature upon thine own galaxy and its neighbors, then envisioning a particular template through which all intelligent life might then be molded and formed.

While the human design is not actually very popular in the universe, it is immensely popular in your own local area. Therefore, should it not be proper for your angels and heavenly host to look similar to thine own bodily forms? There is no other way to be, as this is the path.

And thus, see this Ascension event as the preparing of the way for you. You will inhabit bodies ... [that] are much more well-equipped for those Christlike abilities that you will have, namely:

- The ability to fast-forward and rewind linear time as though it were a videocassette, then making the hologram that much more malleable and pliable;

- The ability to fly at will;

- To manipulate consciousness by thought alone;

- And, to then see these effects percolate up through the plane that you would normally term as physical.

- Because your inherent state will be much closer to that termed "spiritual" in nature, the energy that surrounds you will be much less dense in terms of its physical compression. In terms of light vibration, the energy around you will be alive and dancing with light, in a sense that you cannot now perceive. As you leave your bodies behind each night and enter into these realms, so too must you make a grand finale, the punchline of the cosmic joke, and enter into it fully. See this as your opportunity to rekindle a lost love; a long, lost love that comes to you from so many years ago, so many deep longings and searchings within.

It is indeed the contact, or the Close Encounter of the Third Kind that all of you are so deeply seeking. It is indeed that moment when you, through your own impeccable actions, choose to divide the distinction lines and again rejoin with the heavenly host that now surrounds you. It is the stretching of the womb as it reaches its final contraction, that painful burst that then leads to the production of the child in proper. As the child is lying before you, know too that you will project into it, and look up into the heavens with a new set of eyes. . . .

Do not fail to see that the preparations have indeed been made for you to fulfill the Christ promise: "As I do these things, so shall ye do them, and greater things, for I go unto my Father." Understand that as He showeth thee the way to the One Creator, so too mightest thou comprehend the incredible beauty and bliss contained within one simple phrase: "Love thy neighbor as thyself." When thou comprehendeth that thou hast but One Being, and can seest thyself as a fully functional aspect of that One Being, thou hast no longer a need to continue to deprecate thine own countenance in the forms as thou wouldst now partake of it.

Rather, seest thou not the grace, the beauty, the Divine within? Seest thou not that thou hast the spark of the One Infinite Creator within thine own personal vibrations? Dost thou decide to deny God, to deny love, to deny hope, by self-indulgence and the fallen energies of bitterness, ego, pride, et cetera, as heretofore mentioned? Or wouldst thou embrace the otherselves around thine own self as merely a fuller extension of that I AM presence that thou and all others inherently are? Canst thou see thine own identity as One, as a collective body, a collective mind, a collective heart, and a collective soul?

Dost thou realize the importance of this Christmas; that it is the birth of the Christ as a whole within thine own heavenly garments? That thou art indeed the Christ that has been born? That it is One? Wouldst thou focus on the contractions and pains of its birth, or rather delight in the new arrival? See that the time has come; the moment has arrived, and the players in the global game have all assembled into their proper positions. Do not distress at the necessary evils and activities transpiring and taking place, as it is all part of the greater plan.

You yourselves have never been more aware of the fury of the heavens, and of its transforming capability for change. As you continue to see weather disturbances and other Earth Change scenarios, remember that you yourselves have created it, so that you might then learn from thine own mistakes, and strive towards greater love.

Realize that the Earth is responsible for taking on all those energies that you would deny, or shunt aside, or raise in anger, rage, bitterness. These energies must go somewhere, and thus they are transferred into the Earth.

When you question why these things must occur, do your part in halting their construction. You will discover with great rapidity that they have been repealed, and the glory that comes into your presence will be unsurpassed. You are all still capable of awakening as one collective giant, one massive Christ presence that seeks to embrace the totality of human consciousness as its own, for there is indeed but One True Mind, and One True Being. You are all assembling into this now, and those of you who choose through free will to join it will have your place and position in this new kingdom.

Understand that the glory that awaits you is much more fantastic than you are capable of remembering. Also understand that even as a part of you dies to the old to be born again into the new, so too will a deeper part of you remember an unbroken line of continuity in said higher realms. And so, with this new birth comes the remembrance of the life that was already present. It will be those Ego selves that you have constructed now that are awed, mystified, and humbled.

To another, deeper part of yourselves, this will be business as usual, and returning to that which is familiar and comfortable; a realm wherein thought is instantaneous, and action is concomitant with a system of beliefs that need not be believed, merely understood and acted upon. It will be so simple for you to exist in grace, beauty, and Oneness, for that vibration will surround you with such loving depth and presence of mind that it is impossible not to simply cry out:

"The Lord thy God is One! The Lord thy God is One! Go out and share this piece of knowledge: The Lord thy God is One!"

With this effervescent joy bursting forth from you, you will be as a beacon of light, a shepherd to others, then capable of going to other systems where others have suffered in the third density as yourselves, and indeed being a guardian angel of sorts for them. Indeed, there will be many new jobs to take up in the higher realms. This is not meant to be a heaven where you simply stand in awe at the majestic splendor and beauty around you, but rather a concrete realm of life, a realm of life where experience, learning, and growth continue.

There may well be an opportunity for all of you to take a respite or a vacation from suffering, to relax and rejuvenate the spirit. But also realize that at a time that is most perfectly right for each of you, you will choose to enter fully into your new responsibilities and obligations to the awakening Christ light within the body and mind. You will be able to go forth and declare this Light unto others, through intangible means such as aiding in the processes of karma, or even more direct means, such as that contact which is now occurring in this room as you read these words.

Simply go before the parts that exist in fear, and find the trailblazer within Self that leads the way towards a new light, a new love, a new vitality and expression. Remember always that you are loved, protected, and cared for, nurtured by the heavenly host of entities scattered about you in such Divine geometric arrangements as to ensure that your every move is triangulated upon and watched eagerly.

Understand that indeed, a throng of spectators follows you around throughout every activity throughout the day, and every motion that you make towards this Christ principle is met with uproarious applause. Similarly, every moment that you spend in bitterness, self-hatred, depression, longing, or other self-indulgent acts can be a moment of silence and great planning in this throng of spectators; a suspenseful time, where the next appropriate action must be considered. These actions take the form of telepathic thoughts and emotions of Light and Love that are beamed to you.

When that fails to reach its considered goal, other options are then brought forth. As your sense of separation continues, the options chosen will become more and more strong, relative to the degree of need that is necessary. It is you yourselves that have chosen for us to be able to do this for you, as part of the greater plan that is materializing before you now. Therefore, be aware that you have the wonderful opportunity to know deep down inside your own being that all that you sow must be reaped.

Do you allow this throng of spectators to plan the next teaching lesson for you through suffering, or do you rather exalt in their simple presence by embracing the truth of what they are there for: to share the Light and Love with you that extends throughout the Creation? Are you to be a trendsetter, an example for others, one who blazes a new trail into tomorrow, or will you continue to whine and to be bitter about the suffering you must undergo?

Does anyone discuss the contractions of Mary's womb prior to the birth of Christ, and focus upon that part of the story? The pain of lying in a disheveled stable and giving birth in such humble terms? No. Instead, they focus on the beauty, purity, and kindness of the birth itself. Remember that all we have ever wanted for you is that you would renew your covenant with the Divine, and seek again the inner splendor that unfurls as the worlds of possibility are brought into the palm of your hand.

Seek to grasp your marbles, and recognize the awesome power that you do indeed possess when you stand in truth, Light, and Love. Feature yourself in this new movie script that is so soon to unfurl before you, and you will not be led astray. Look not to the sides where darkness looms over you, but rather to that beacon in the distance, the holy shepherd of cosmic love and beingness that urges you forward and impels you on your quest towards this true renewal of thine own depth and clarity of Light and Love.

There has never been a greater time in the entirety of your human history as this moment now. Every action that you perceive and perform in your daily life and your larger global life will be forever remembered. As we speak, the actions that you go through are indeed being recorded on the skein of space and time, by the pen or the quill of the Christ self, revealed through your own inner desire to perfect yourselves in Light and in Love.

We eagerly await you coming up to the Throne of the Divine and signing your name in the Akashic Records, then completing your obligation to the third density and freeing yourself to the greater works that unfold before you in the glory of the new tomorrow, then made into today. We are there with you as you think about these things, and will be available if you need further assistance. Thank you for sharing this moment of grace, joy, and beauty with us, and remember that you are loved more than you could ever possibly imagine. Peace be with you in the Light of everlasting Love.

Space and time are illusions, and they do not factor in. Indeed, you may see the entire infinity of the universe around you now as a consciousness unit in its own right, and that is important. There is ultimately only one Consciousness Unit, and its varying pulsations are simply distortions of its Oneness. When you see the many different consciousness units of many different gradations of [apparent] size and vibration, what you are really seeing is simply the differentiation of Oneness by its own free-will decisions.

—Ra/Wilcock, July 30, 1999

Chapter

19

A Scientific Blueprint for Ascension

In the last chapter, Ra described an event that has absolutely no precedent in our historical memory. If you've been following our discussion thus far, you may be in a state of denial, shock, or both at this final set of revelations. Wilcock, when first exposed to Ra's Ascension prophecies, reacted with uncertainty but took it seriously enough to dedicate years of his life to research that would either support or deny Ra's premise of a pending dimensional shift. In fact, Ra even helped David, encouraging him through dreams and synchronicity to continue investigating certain references and researchers, while discouraging other avenues, sometimes by quite literally crashing his computer every time he tried to hit a certain website. It was kind of like the Cayce days when Cayce's Source would recommend a medical specialist by name, whom Cayce had no prior knowledge of, to one of his clients.

Wilcock's research reveals that there are indeed strange things going on in our solar system. The following is excerpted and updated with permission from *The Spirit of Ma'at* (June 2001), an article entitled "A Scientific Blueprint for Ascension," by David Wilcock as told to Wynn Free. It is important to note that this excerpt casually mentions various facts that are explained in Wilcock's *Convergence* series with much greater depth and documentation, so this should not be scrutinized as a scientific document. The "energy" referred to herein is technically known as "torsion radiation" in Wilcock's books, or "light-love" in the *Law of One* series, and it is not yet acknowledged to exist by Western scientists, since it is not one of the four "accepted" energy fields—gravity, electromagnetism, weak nuclear force, and strong nuclear force. This energy is more closely related to the force of gravity than electromagnetism, and it has been demonstrated to have properties of consciousness in a variety of Russian laboratories, originally with the pioneering research of Dr. Nikolai Kozyrev.

And now, the gist of the article, with some updated embellishments (the large headings are subheads of the main title, "A Scientific Blueprint for Ascension"):

The Science of Ascension by David Wilcock

The "Holy Grail" of the scientific model I developed is the idea that our solar system is moving into a more energetic region of the galaxy, and that this in turn is creating changes that will lead to a global event most would only think of as science fiction, creating a new "Golden Age" of humanity. The case starts with Edgar Cayce reading 1602–003, which noted that by 1998, many changes would be visible as compared to the time of Edgar's life in the 1930s. It did not say that 1998 was "the end," just that it was a year within a "period" where solar activity would be at a peak and the changes would have become a lot more apparent. Pay special attention to the part that is in bold:

> These [various changes] are at the periods [from 1998] when the cycle of the solar activity, or the **years as related to the sun's passage through the various spheres of activity** become paramount ... to the change between the Piscean and Aquarian age.

So then, what are the "spheres of activity" that Cayce's Source said that our Sun is passing through, causing gradually increasing changes in the Sun and Earth? The word "spheres" is used loosely enough throughout the Cayce readings that it could simply mean "regions" or "centers." There are at least five good quotes in the *Law of One* series that shed further light on this Cayce quote, but the best one came through after Don Elkins asked a question on July 18, 1981, as printed in Book Three, Session 63, page 95:

> **Questioner:** Is there a clock-like face, shall I say, associated with the entire galaxy [dividing it up like a pie when looking at it from the top down], so that as it revolves it carries all of these stars and planetary systems through transitions from density to density? Is this how it works?

> **Ra:** I am Ra. You are perceptive. You may see a three-dimensional clock face or spiral of endlessness which is planned by the Logos for this purpose.

So, if Ra and Cayce are correct, then the galaxy has an organized energy structure that is divided into regions of different "density," which the stars and planets pass through in precise cycles of time. The transition from the Age of Pisces to the Age of Aquarius, which most astronomers agree will occur in about 2011, would be the time when we will finish our movement into a higher "density" of energy in the galaxy. In Book One, Session 13, page 133 of the *Law of One* series, Ra supports this concept quite directly:

> The fourth density is, as we have said, as regularized in its approach as the striking of a clock upon the hour. The space/time of your solar system has enabled this planetary sphere to spiral into space/time of a different vibrational configuration....

In Book One, Session 6, page 93, Dr. Elkins asked a question that led Ra to give a timeframe for the "striking of the hour" when the Earth would move into fourth density:

Ra: This sphere (Earth) ... has not made an easy transition to the vibrations which beckon. This inconvenience ... shall continue unabated for a period of approximately thirty of your years.

Questioner: After this period of thirty years (from the date of this session, January 24, 1981, thus 2011) I am assuming that Earth will be a fourth-density planet. Is this correct?

Ra: I am Ra. This is so.

Questioner: Is it possible to estimate what percent of the present population will inhabit the fourth-density planet?

Ra: I am Ra. The harvesting is not yet, thus estimation is meaningless.

In this last quote from Book One, Session 17, page 166, Ra deals more specifically with the date:

Questioner: Am I to understand that the harvest is to occur in the year 2011, or will it be spread out?

Ra: I am Ra. This is an approximation. We have stated we have difficulty with your time/space. This is an appropriate probable/possible time/space nexus for harvest. Those who are not in incarnation at this time will be included in the harvest.

Of course, Ra's timeline fits in perfectly with the end-date of the Mayan Calendar, set for December 22, 2012. The Maya interpreted this date as a point when "time would stop" and humanity would enter into a new Golden Age. The keystone to all of this that we're talking about—to everything we mentioned so far—is the idea that evolution *must* come on a mass scale, like the striking of the clock upon the hour. Ascension is not simply restricted to the Christian idea of the "rapture," where Jesus comes back and ushers in a thousand years of peace. It's a cosmic event, triggered by measurable scientific phenomena, prophesied in almost every major religious and spiritual tradition that has existed on the face of the Earth.

How can we tell that Ascension is imminent?

The gradually increasing "inconveniences" that Ra speaks about are explained in Book One as being caused by humanity's resistance to the "fourth-density" qualities of unconditional love. These inconveniences are what most people would call "Earth changes," though they are occurring throughout the entire solar system. The "fourth-density" energies of the galaxy are arguably charging up our entire solar system. Here are some *measurable* changes in our solar system which suggest that this evolutionary leap is going to happen soon:

Unprecedented solar activity

As written on a European Space Agency website, a team led by Dr. Mike Lockwood proved in 1999 that there has been "an overall increase in the Sun's magnetic field by a factor of 2.3 since 1901." This means that the Sun's magnetic field became **230% stronger** between 1901 and 1999—and Lockwood's studies also show that the speed of this change is continually accelerating.[1]

As was again proven in early November 2003, we're having solar activity at a level never before witnessed—at least not in recorded history. Powerful solar flares are given an "X" designation. On August

16, 1989, and April 2, 2001, there were solar flares at the unheard-of level of "X-20" on the measuring scale, but some scientists estimated that the November 4, 2003, flare could be as high as an X-38. Dr. Paul Brekke told BBC News Online, "I think the last week (of Oct.-Nov. 2003) will go into the history books as one of the most dramatic solar activity periods we have seen in modern times." We should expect to see a lot more of this kind of activity as we get closer.[2]

The quality of the space between planets is changing

We all know that if you drop water on a cool pan, it just sits there, but on a hot pan it dances and sizzles all around. Similarly, the actual quality of the space between the planets is changing, conducting energy more quickly than ever before. More specifically, the Sun releases charged, radioactive particles, such as energetic protons, and in some cases these protons are now traveling up to 200% faster than the NASA models expect.[3]

The atmospheres of the planets are changing

Dr. Aleskey Dmitriev's work, entitled "Planetophysical State of the Earth and Life," featured at www.tmgnow.com at the time of this writing, shows that the planets themselves are changing, becoming brighter, hotter, more magnetic, more geologically active and more atmospherically dense. For example, the *Mars Observer* probe in 1997 lost one of its mirrors, which caused it to crash. NASA scientists calculated that the Martian atmosphere had become 200% thicker than they had expected it to be, and it blew that little mirror right off the device.[4]

Earth and its moon are having atmospheric changes

Also, Dr. Dmitriev cites studies showing that the Moon has acquired a 6,000-kilometer-deep layer of sodium gas that was not measured during the Apollo missions of the late 1960s. Dmitriev also reveals that hydroperoxyl (HO) gas is appearing in the Earth's upper atmosphere—it is not related to global warming and it's not related to CFCs or fluorocarbon emissions. It's just showing up.

Magnetic fields and brightness of the planets are changing

Dmitriev tells us that the planets are experiencing sizable changes in their overall brightness. Venus, for example, is showing us marked increases in its overall brightness. Jupiter now has such a high energetic charge that there is actually a visible tube of ionizing radiation formed between Jupiter and its moon, Io. You can actually see the luminous energy tube in photographs, which looks like a giant vertical ring extending from the polar regions of Jupiter through the polar regions of Io. Unfortunately there only seems to be one genuine photograph of this ring in the public domain.[5]

The planets are experiencing a change in their magnetic fields—they are becoming stronger. According to Dmitriev, Jupiter's magnetic field grew 200% in size in the six years between 1992 and 1998, and Uranus' magnetic field has experienced an "abrupt, large-scale growth" in its intensity.[6] These planets are becoming brighter. Their magnetic field strength is getting higher. Their atmospheric qualities are changing.

Uranus and Neptune appear to have had recent pole shifts

When the *Voyager 2* space probe flew past Uranus and Neptune, the apparent north and south magnetic poles were sizably offset from where the rotational pole was. Neptune's magnetic field was 50 degrees off, and Uranus' magnetic field was 60 degrees off, both of which are substantial changes.[7]

Neptune 40% brighter from 1996 to 2002

A 2003 study by the University of Wisconsin-Madison,[8] headed by Dr. Lawrence Sromovsky, reveals that Neptune's overall brightness increased by a whopping 40% in the six short years between 1996 and 2002. Some areas are fully 100% brighter than before. Although they cannot explain these changes with their model, saying that Neptune "seems to run on almost no energy," Sromovsky et al. attribute this to a "seasonal" change in Neptune, which they think will quiet down again in twenty years.

Pluto's atmosphere 300% denser from 1988 to 2002

As of September 2002, a team of top-notch scientists led by James Eliot, professor of planetary astronomy at MIT, discovered that even though Pluto has been drifting away from the sun since 1989, there has been a 300% increase in its atmospheric pressure since 1988, causing a noticeable rise in surface temperatures.[9]

Overall volcanic activity on Earth has increased 500% since 1975

On the Earth, we're seeing the changes even more completely. For example, Michael Mandeville has done research that shows that the overall volcanic activity on the Earth has increased by roughly 500% from 1875 to 1998. The overall earthquake activity has increased by 400% from 1973 to 1998.[10]

Natural disasters increased 410% between 1963 and 1993

Dr. Dmitriev did a very elaborate calculation of natural disasters. He showed that if you compare the years 1963 through 1993, the overall amount of natural disasters of all different kinds—whether you are talking hurricanes, typhoons, mud slides, tidal waves, you name it—has increased by 410%.

Sun's magnetic field 1000% brighter at leading edge

As originally published in Dr. Aleskey Dmitriev's 1997 paper "Planetophysical State of the Earth and Life," this new galactic energy zone has caused the leading edge of the Sun's magnetic field to become more than 1000% brighter since the mid-1960s, and new forms of charged particles are showing up in this area in greater and greater amounts.

Three hundred percent more galactic dust coming into the solar system since 2000

As of August 2003, an ESA/NASA experiment[11] discovered that there is **300% more dust from our galaxy entering the solar system in the summer of 2003 than there was throughout all of the 1990s.** More dust and more charged particles means more energy, more *density,* which is exactly the word Ra used to describe this new intergalactic zone.

Cosmic Changes
and the Ascension Process

By now it should be easy to tell that this is the biggest event in human history, and it is entirely unreported by the mainstream news media. No press outlet has ever combined two or more of these facts in the same story. Even if the media did figure it out, they probably wouldn't want to say anything about it for fear of panicking the public. However, once we understand what is happening to us, we don't need to be afraid of it. When the Earth fully moves into the fourth-density energy, we will naturally be transported into a higher level of our own being. Our physical body becomes irrelevant at that point. We are much more than that.

Soul Graduation

If you're very attached to your physical body, you might say, "Well, what would I be without it?" You might see this as traumatic, but in fact your experience could be looked at as Soul graduation. People are saying, "I'm doing my spiritual growth. I'm doing my path. I'm walking in my truth. I'm trying to grow spiritually, I'm trying to evolve." Evolve to what? Grow to what? Are we just going to keep reincarnating over and over again as humans? No.

Is the Earth going to remain in this vibrational level where human beings will blow up bombs, poison its waters, pollute its atmosphere, kill its creatures, and cut down all the trees? No. The Earth is not expected to go through this. The Earth is an evolving being, too. The difference with the Earth, unlike a regular human lifetime, is that it goes through a very premeditated, very obvious course of its evolution. As it orbits around the Sun, and as the solar system orbits around the galaxy, the extraterrestrial races that are in higher dimensions know exactly when these changes are going to happen. That's why they're here now, because basically they're aware that this is going on and are standing by to assist us.

For those who are ready to handle the vibrations, their physical bodies will be transformed into a higher density of vibration when the moment of change arrives. So it's not as though there's going to be all these fried corpses lying around. When the energy hits you, you transform. Your body will actually transmute itself, like what happened to Jesus—Ascension.

There is a parallel in the Shroud of Turin, where certain researchers have found that Jesus' body burned a complete three-dimensional image of itself into the cloth. And they found through experimentation that such a burn could only be caused by an instantaneous blast at a very high temperature, "zapping" the cloth like an X-ray film.

The Bottom Line

It would be so easy to miss this fantastic opportunity to participate in the evolution that is happening here and now on our planet. The media are bent on creating a reality where our happiness is contingent on the acquisition of new products. We seek the best jobs and the highest status as we succumb to the mass illusions of "consensus reality" and "winning the game."

Each of us has the choice to create our lives so that we may participate in the Utopian world that will manifest on Earth after this Ascension process has completed—a world without poverty, hunger, or pain; a world where full-body levitation, spontaneous healings, instant telepathic communication, and abundant Love are the law of the land.

This is the world that Jesus promised us in John 14:12, when he said, *"As I do these things, so shall you do them, and greater things."*

It comes back to the question: *What are you going to hold onto?* You have to leave behind the physical life in order to participate in the Ascension. You have to be willing to move into a life that is spiritual. You'll have to be willing to let go of the things that you once thought were important—your car, your material effects, your earthly status, your earthly fame and power—because you're basically only going to take yourself. You can't bring anything with you. No money, no credit cards, no gold coins. If your aspirations are all tied to third-dimensional goals, then you may well be drawn back to fulfill them and miss this chance to make a quantum leap in your evolution. And as Cayce often liked to say, "You will be lifted into heaven upon the arms of those you have served."

When the time is appropriate and the help is then truly needed, the free-will clause will allow us to make our requested appearance, and we will see that events occur in peace. We are completely ready to fulfill this obligation at a moment's notice, due to the uncertainties that you are now faced with. Remember that.

—Ra/Wilcock, July 3, 2002

Chapter

20

La Pièce de Resistance:
Ra's Pledge to Us

If you are catching Ra's drift over the last few chapters, you might be getting the idea that you have a Higher Self that can and does want to communicate with you, and could even become your personal counselor. In fact, this communication through dreams and meditative states could be extremely important for the planet right now, as well as your personal growth. It is clear that certain criteria must be met. The keys to establishing this communication are clearly revealed in various Wilcock channelings:

> In order to receive messages from our domain, you are required to make great personal sacrifices including the desire for personal gain. The much greater gain comes from the rewarding of your desire to be of service, and this is a spiritual one as well as those more physical. Don't rely too heavily on the extraterrestrial sources of information that you think you may know to exist. What is more important is the subjective variety of the illusion that is then presented to you in your own dreams, visions, and the like.

* * *

All of you are capable of doing this. The real question is, "How much do you really want it?" I think that the answer is for you to begin to believe in yourself. Begin to believe in your own dreams as solid guidance. You who read these words are learning how to use this metaphorical language, because of how repetitively we phrase our sentences in this phraseology. And so, as the batter steps up to the plate and prepares himself or herself accordingly, we will then make the pitch at the appropriate time. Not all of you will be able to swing and hit the ball, but we do certainly hope that more and more of you will be able to connect and indeed send this information packet to the ethers so that it may be transformed and sent back to you as a unified source of Light and Love vibration.

When we have received this energy, we can then transform it into a much more viable source, and send it back down to you as living information. The information will enter your mind as natural thoughts and feelings, and thus when you harmonize with us you should fully expect that all of the messages and information will be going through your mind as though they were your own thoughts, ideas, and impressions. That is the fundamental key to this process. You are not going to have a force suddenly come in and seize control of you. Rather, it is a far more subtle process, whereby you realize exactly how to listen to the voice of your imagination and intuition, which by then has become a moment-by-moment source of Living Light.

As you probably have noted, the story of Edgar Cayce's reincarnation has grown exponentially from our initial premise. I set out to show that David Wilcock is the reincarnation of Edgar Cayce, then I showed that David Wilcock is an extension of the group soul Ra and may have once been a man who was later mythologized into Ra the Sun God. Ra's prediction of an imminent dimensional shift on our planet, backed up by David's scientific research, along with Ra's words of wisdom and inspiration channeled by David all make this a much larger story than one soul's journey. Finally, the Ra group has indicated that it is already working with humanity as a collective, and is ready and prepared to work with you personally in your dream/inspiration state. Could we possibly one-up ourselves at this point? What else could our story add to all these implausible premises that somehow tie together? Try this, from a Ra/Wilcock reading dated May 29, 2002:

Our staff is standing by to assist you, and our presence will not forever remain in shadow; when the time is appropriate and the help is then truly needed, the free-will clause will allow us to make our requested appearance, and we will see that events occur in peace. We are completely ready to fulfill this obligation at a moment's notice, due to the uncertainties that you are now faced with. Remember that.

The true knowledge to one of your minds regarding how much we are capable of doing to avert world catastrophe would seem utterly overwhelming, since the neurological capacity of the third-density mind is but a droplet in the ocean of consciousness that we are working with. Each mind anywhere in the world, either incarnate or discarnate and at all levels of density, can be studied and analyzed with regard to the collective mind, and as we advance forward in time along various timelines, the consequences of any of these subtle actions can be seen, much like a fractal function or quantum hologram.

Hence, by our vast team efforts, we are capable of analyzing your "grand chessboard" and figuring out what pieces go where at what time, and seeing how the different entities involved all contribute to the final outcome. In this way, then, if an event is not in the interest of all involved, the law of free will allows us to intervene in the lives of entities, often at crucial but unexpected points in the chain of causation, in order to off-set such an event. These interventions can follow a gradient from the remarkably subtle to the relentlessly blatant at times, depending upon the degree of balancing that is required and how the individual free will weighs against collective free will.

The more that humanity as a whole strives for wisdom and understanding of the truth of love, the more interventions we are authorized to perform.

So there we have it—in addition to Ra's availability to be our personal dream counselor, we have an amazing pledge by Ra and their associates to assist us, to physically intervene and stop world catastrophes. There is only one catch: Ra has to honor the collective thought forms of the planet or it would violate free will. The more that each of us strives for wisdom, truth, and love in our consciousness, the more interventions Ra can perform. These interventions do not require anyone to be aware of Wilcock or of Ra directly. Since Ra is helping out with the planet as a whole, all that is really required is for an ever-increasing number of souls to begin consciously choosing love and service to others over the manipulation, enslavement, and control of others.

I have noted that Wilcock emphasizes his scientific compilations more than his Ra readings on his website. One major impetus for the writing of this book is my own realization of the importance of connecting people with Ra. The following Ra message to Wilcock was the final motivation for me to complete this book:

Let it be known that without these transmissions, we are not fulfilling one of our very basic purposes, and disasters will result. The least that you can do is to honor us this one point by allowing the ego self to step aside once in a while and bring these messages through. That way, there is no discontinuity between your goals and our own.

Can Ra actually stop disasters? Well, as far-fetched as it may seem, there's a track record of seemingly impossible miracles that have already manifested on our planet. We have the pyramids in Egypt that could not have been built using the construction technologies available at the time, which Ra took credit for building by "levitating stone." We have an individual who introduced himself as the Son of God who walked on water, brought the dead back to life, and manifested food, whose miracles were witnessed by some or all of his twelve disciples, who then spent their entire lives dedicated to living out and writing about his teachings. We have John Edwards and James Van Praagh on national television, publicly talking to the deceased relatives of audience members. We have "crop circles" mysteriously appearing in fields all over the planet with, in most cases, no rational explanation as to how and why they are being created.[1]

Although I have no report of Ra directly manifesting a body recently, many of those who have been closely involved with the Ra group have had various manifestations in the physical world. For example, Carla Rueckert has seen orbs of light in her room, and David's brother Michael had a luminous plasma ball appear in his bedroom as a direct response to a prayer that David made at about the same time, as reported on David's website. Such plasma-ball manifestations have also been reported in fields prior to the creation of a crop circle. Could this be a manifestation of Ra or a group similar to Ra? Are plasma balls and crop circles ways in which beings attempt to communicate with us from another dimension? Obviously, this is a topic we can't fully delve into in our limited space, but during a search on the Internet, I found an amazing picture of a crop circle in England, as illustrated and captioned herein[2] (www.cropcircleradius.com). As opposed to most crop circles that are geometric forms, this one happens to be one of the symbols for Ra—the Egyptian Sun God. The photo and its caption are reproduced with the permission of the photographer who posted them on his website. Draw your own conclusions.

David Wilcock has done his own study of crop circles, which is

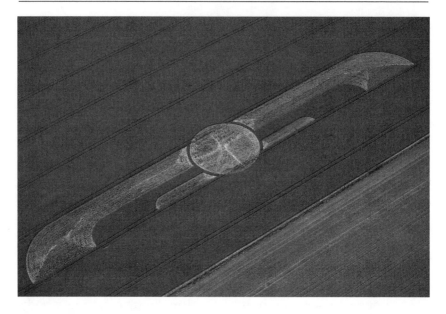

This gigantic formation in wheat clearly represents a winged disc, the symbol of the Egyptian Sun God Ra.

Once again, the energy in the formation was tangible. In the central disc, the seeds seemed—literally—to have been vaporized. Though the plants appeared to be normal, the seed-cases were empty. Some saw this as a response to the circle energies. It has been suggested by farmers that this condition is due to "take-all," a fungus disease caused by dampness. This—however—does not explain why the hollow seed-cases were found only in the central circle.

posted on his site[3] and featured in his first scientific book, *The Shift of the Ages*. He believes that there is a message contained within the geometric forms of the circles that is signaling to us the realities of higher dimensions beyond our three-dimensional Earth.

Could it be that Ra and/or other higher-dimensional entities are communicating with us through these crop circles, giving even more credence to this incredible story of their presence? Could crop circles be one of the kinds of interventions that Ra referred to?

In this chapter, I refer to claims and manifestations that would make Ra different from any other ascended group I have been exposed to which gives messages through a channel. Ra claims to be taking a great degree of responsibility for the workings of our entire planet, in addition to delivering the wise text messages via Wilcock. Ra also claims to be paying attention to our collective energies and responding based on our collective prayer. "The more that humanity as a whole strives for wisdom and understanding of the truth of love, the more interventions we are authorized to perform." Is this possible? Could Ra really be one of the ones listening and answering our prayers?

We have said before that we come to correct the distortions imposed upon your peoples by that which you know as the past. And if they really completely believe me, they will see that I can indeed perform many more tricks and maneuvers in the sky than anyone had heretofore imagined possible.

—Ra/Wilcock, October 24, 1999

Chapter

21

Conclusion

If we are to believe the message that runs through the thread of Wilcock, Cayce, L/L Research, and almost all of the world's great spiritual traditions, then we are eternal. Part of us exists right now beyond our physical bodies. We are part of God, and whether it's sooner or later, we will all finally evolve into the realization that death is an illusion. The Universe is designed with the ultimate in equitability, inasmuch as each of us is an extended part of original creation, and we have the potential at any moment to tap into the higher aspect of ourselves.

Within the framework of my own life, I have observed numerous examples of how my Higher Self has created synchronicities or miracles of perfect timing beyond my conscious control. These synchronicities always manifest in a serendipitous manner that seems like happenstance or coincidence. But when I review them, I realize on some level that they are always manifesting an intention or desire previously programmed into my subconscious. This invisible unconscious part of myself has the power to recreate the physical world to effect the synchronistic manifestation. I know these kinds of manifestations are possible for everyone, but most people dismiss them as coincidences. When we realize they are manifestations of our higher consciousness, we can experience what can happen when our conscious thoughts are in alignment with our Higher Selves. Suddenly we can be empowered, even in a world that appears so hopeless. Just as Gandhi used higher consciousness to inspire the British to voluntarily relinquish their control of India, so might we be able to turn the tides of some of the seemingly overwhelming, negative forces of momentum in today's world by the power of our Higher Selves.

I know now from the deepest recesses of my being that I am part of Divine Creation, as are you, and we are all part of each other. The most important events in our lives are being orchestrated from our invisible levels. The consensus reality we live in, which seems so real, is just the reality we have all agreed upon. But this consensus reality can block us from our perception of the higher realities. Perhaps this book and particularly the channelings of Ra have inspired you to have an experience beyond your normal reality. If you catch the ball and run with it, perhaps it might turn into a basis for transformation of your life, until you can hold the higher reality of this fourth dimension, transcend your fear, experience your love, and become a focus of inspiration for the transformation of others. Jesus set an example for Ascension. He transcended the physical world and inspired billions, leaving the message that "these things I do, you can do too and much more."

Edgar Cayce showed that there was much more to life than meets the eye, and that we have lived before. The work of L/L Research, through the *Law of One* series, gave us an authentic-seeming cosmic explanation as to the workings of the greater Universe and the process of soul evolution, from a spiritual and scientific perspective. David Wilcock is carrying the torch, giving us the wisdom of his channeled messages and delivering the information our logical brains need to accept the imminency of the dimensional shift. Through it all, Ra is standing by as one of our guardian angels, the social memory complex who long ago passed through all the changes we are now experiencing and dedicated itself to helping us unfold and experience the reality of the fourth dimension. Perhaps someday, as Ra has implied, those of us who partake in this next evolutionary step and continue evolving over many lifetimes will eventually play the same role as the Ra group, becoming the Higher Self or Oversoul for the population of some other evolving planet in the third dimension. I said early on in this book that Ra has had a track record of interventions on our planet over the past 12,500 years.

All we're being asked to do is open up to the experience of love, service, empathy, and compassion, and see creation in everything. This is not a doctrine, belief system, or a creed designed to create Ra or Wilcock fundamentalists. These are the simple keys for moving beyond the negative traps on this planet and transcending fear, greed, and the control and manipulation of others, so as to have the realization that we are all in this together; we are already members of a group soul, namely the collective consciousness of our planet. As we individually open our hearts, we are automatically in a high state of service as we impact the collective. Knowing this, we can realize the importance of staying positive and loving, even when the planetary agenda is seemingly negative and fear-provoking.

You who are reading these words have the good fortune to understand the game that is being played. As times become more difficult, prepare yourself to stay calm and centered in the midst of negativity, and become a guiding light for those around you who are receptive to this higher path. Start developing the relationships and the rapports with those in your community who share your own higher quest. Now is the opportunity—if you are ready—to see beyond consensus reality and separate yourself from the circumstances and the people that are binding you to the third dimension. This is the time to examine the deep-seated pains and repressions you have stored from this life and all your previous lifetimes, and allow them to pass through your consciousness to be forever released. You can't lift above the physical world without lifting throngs of others with you.

Our empowerment is beyond politics, humanitarianism, social mores, self-righteousness, and morality. We are part of the One Infinite Creator, and as we experience this consciously we will become the "lights of the world." This is not a solo process. This is not the time to hide out in a cave and meditate. We are part of the collective. We are in a continuous process of re-creation and co-creation—every moment is another opportunity to embrace the positive. There is never any completion or finality in this physical world. Life is a continuous flow, and we are all positioned in the perfect place to have the next lesson which will bring us closer to the experience of the fourth dimension. As Ra said through Wilcock, "Be prepared to see how your life right now, exactly as you are living it, is indeed your ministry."

The evidence suggests that Ra-Ta, a.k.a. Edgar Cayce, a.k.a. Ra, a.k.a. David Wilcock, has returned. The message is not new. It's the same message that has been delivered by every saint, holy man, adept, yogi, rishi, and savior. We are all One, originally separated from the One Infinite Creator, and we lost our way. It's time to come home.

* * *

Below is a synopsis of the logic that has brought us to this point in our story:

1. There is a strong case that Edgar Cayce may in fact have reincarnated.

2. Wilcock, his apparent reincarnation, has demonstrated repeated, verifiable psychic accuracy.

3. This psychic ability has also been channeled into breakthrough scientific research.

4. Both science and prophecy suggest that an almost unimaginably wonderful future is ahead for humanity, despite the apparent chaos in the world now.

5. On the offhand, crazy chance that Wilcock might just be right, what next?

6. All great spiritual teachings concur with the message of Ra as presented in *The Law of One.*

7. Recognize that you are a being with distortions, and that this confusion is OK. Within the veils of our earthbound consciousness, it is impossible for the mind to fully grasp the process of Ascension. In fact, "it is entirely necessary that an entity consciously realize that it does not understand in order to be (ready for the Ascension). Understanding is not of your density."[1]

8. Consensus reality in this realm tends to keep people focused on themselves, their sense of lack, and the idea that the material world is all there is. The "big secret" in the human game is that this world is a school, and through serving others, you can transcend to a new realm beyond your wildest dreams.

9. Hence, you do not have to be "perfected" to graduate—all you have to do is be slightly above 50% motivated towards service to others.

10. The best way to do this is to learn to see others as yourself.

11. When you see things in others that bother you, recognize that you are seeing the mirror of your own shadow side—the part of you that is still not spiritually integrated, which you probably are not even aware exists.

12. By learning to forgive and accept other people in their entirety, without judging what you perceive as their negativity or weaknesses, you also learn to accept yourself.

13. The more integrated you become, the less you choose to view any people or experiences with negative emotions such as fear, anger, jealousy, and resentment.

14. When you begin seeing the good in other people and honoring that goodness, you are also honoring yourself.

15. Recognize that every day, every moment, you are making a choice—a choice of whether you are serving yourself or serving others. What are you choosing?

16. You can choose to remember that you are the light. You are the love. You, and all others, are the One Infinite Creator. Learn to love your Self. Graduation Day is coming.

If you've come to the point where this all makes sense to you, considering that it might be true, and wondering what to do next, I'd like to make a suggestion. Recommend this book to others. I believe that Ra's words can create cellular resonances with those who read them, and the responses created will uplift the vibrations of the planet as well as the individual. If your sharing of this should create an upliftment in others, the gratitude that is returned will uplift you as well, and bonds of spiritual camaraderie will be created. I have read the channelings in this book out loud many times in the presence of others, and I have always noticed a distinct shift in the energy.

In conclusion, I share the words of David Wilcock from an interview I did with him in the year 2000:

> When you leave your body and move into these higher realms of consciousness, all those earthly things will be meaningless. When you get out of this world without these braces, guess what? Your memory will be your sole companion. And then you will realize that the only thing that ever mattered was how much love you were willing to share while you were incarnated on Earth.[2]

We leave you with the notion that the fruit of the vine can produce the purest wine, or the sourest of vinegar. It is up to you how you will decide to milk your own fruits of the Spirit, so that the lamb may again come and choose to lie in your pasture, radiating peace, serenity, and believability that there is indeed a Oneness.

—Ra/Wilcock, September 4, 1999

Part Three

―――――

Science of Ascension

The Energetic Engine of Evolution

by David Wilcock
(Edited excerpts from *The Divine Cosmos* and *Divine Nature* with
permission of David Wilcock)

Summary/Abstract

Many leading voices of modern spirituality and metaphysics have
spoken of their belief that a change is occurring in human DNA. The
one crucial element that has been missing in these discussions so far
is a scientific framework that can either confirm or deny such speculations. In previous chapters of this book, we have seen that the entire
solar system is undergoing a remarkable and very measurable energetic increase. In this part of the book we will lay out a simple, easy-
to-understand model that connects this interplanetary event with the
evolution of species, both in terms of their biological makeup and
their sophistication of consciousness. Best of all, we will show that
there is an ample historical record of these energetically-triggered evolution events in Earth's own history. Although this section features
less than 5% of the facts contained in the *Convergence* series, it includes
some of the most fascinating things uncovered by the last twenty-
three years of my research (since age seven).

If you find yourself confused on small points as you read along, don't give up.... I recommend that you just keep on going to the end. It's worth it. If you then read the essay a second time more slowly and carefully, by this point familiar with the overall concepts, you are likely to discover a great deal that you originally missed. I am thrilled to present you with such a compact, distilled summary of the vision that has taken me more than two decades of diligent, needle-in-a-haystack research to be able to see for myself. The Internet is the biggest haystack ever created by the human mind, and if you stack up all the 8.5x11 research books that I printed out and bound from various websites on the Internet since 1996, you get a pile more than ten feet tall. This is "the best of the best" from that stack. Enjoy.

Introduction:
Evolution As "Intelligent Design"

For most people, the question of "how we got here" appears to have a rather simple answer—namely that through a slow, ongoing series of "random" mutations, human beings evolved from microscopic single-celled organisms. In this theory, first put forward by Charles Darwin in 1859,[1] only the "fittest" of these new creatures survive by competing with each other, a process known as "natural selection," as the apparent mutations continue. Then, we have a smaller section of the public, usually those with Fundamentalist Christian beliefs, who take a quite literal interpretation of the Bible and believe that "Adam and Eve" were placed on Earth in a completed state by a Supreme Being, possibly as recently as four thousand years ago. This model carries the added caveat of an "original sin," committed by a woman, that all of humanity will now be punished if they do not "accept Christ."

Those in the former category of thinkers are often called "Evolutionists," and the latter are known as "Creationists." The media lead us to believe that we must simply choose one of these two per-spectives, and then file that knowledge away without ever needing to review it again. And the "authorities" also tell us that since the Cre-ationist view is based on a naïve interpretation of ancient texts, whereas the theory of Evolution is based on scientific fact, the deci-sion should be a rather simple one. Case closed. Anyone who ques-tions the theory of Evolution is automatically labeled as a deluded Fundamentalist religious zealot, not able to think rationally. No room is given in the media for the possibility that a third group could exist, which is neither Evolutionist nor Creationist in nature. However, this group is very much alive and well, albeit with very little media pub-licity, and the movement has taken on the name "Intelligent Design."[2]

Despite this growing new movement, the traditional theory of evolution does seem to satisfy most schools, universities, and media outlets as an accepted fact, and there appears to be no need to search any further or think for oneself—the scientific community has "solved" the puzzle, and nothing more needs to be said. However, there is a clear difference between mass-media newspeak and scien-tific realities. And if one actually begins examining what the scien-tific community knows, the Darwinian theory of evolution cannot stand erect on its own two feet.

With the work of gifted researchers such as Tim Harwood, Bruce Lipton, Glen Rein, Aleskey Dmitriev, and Richard Pasichnyk, we can now present a model that fills in many of the "cracks," so to speak, and provides us with an intelligent, energetic model of evo-lution. And most extraordinarily, this model suggests that human-ity is on the verge of a near-spontaneous metamorphosis into a more highly evolved state of consciousness, which will impart miraculous "psychic" abilities now only dreamed of in science-fiction and fan-tasy movies, and which will also instill a vastly more harmonious civilization than the one we now live in. We only naïvely assume that we represent the pinnacle of evolution in this universe, but sig-nificant facts suggest otherwise. Though this chapter is not intended to "push" any specific religious beliefs, what we are now heading into appears to be the literal fulfillment of Jesus' statement, "As I do these things, so shall ye do them, and greater things, for I go unto my Father."[3]

The Theory of Evolution Is Extinct

The following series of quotes shows that there simply is no scientific evidence for the Darwinian theory of evolution—we believe it out of habit and repetition of a few small conjectures that have since been proven wrong. In order for true Darwinian evolution to occur, there must be ever-gradual changes with creatures that represent each stage of transformation quite well. If a moviemaker wanted to morph a shellfish with a hard, simple outer skeleton into a finned fish with a far more complex inner skeleton, for example, she would need to render digital images of each precise stage in the transition process in order for it to look believable.

However, the "transitional" life forms that we would need to find in order to support Darwin's evolution theory simply do not exist in the fossil record. There are no "morphing" forms that suggest how finned fish came into being, as one of many examples. We see creatures that do not have an internal skeleton (invertebrates), and then suddenly creatures with backbones show up (vertebrates). Hence, the species on Earth make abrupt changes from one configuration to another in short periods of time, according to the fossil record, followed by millions of years without change.

The following quotes are all compiled by the breakthrough researcher Tim Harwood and shared freely with the public on the Internet. Each bulleted quote is from a separate, respected member of the scientific community, usually with the most prestigious university credentials and professorships. For those interested in doing follow-up research or fact-checking, full reference information is given after each quote on Harwood's brilliant website:[4]

- Evolutionism is a fairy tale for grown-ups. This theory has helped nothing in the progress of science. It is useless.

- I myself am convinced that the theory of evolution ... will be one of the great jokes in the history books of the future. [We] will marvel that so very flimsy and dubious an [idea] could be accepted with the incredible credulity that it has.

- Scientists who utterly reject Evolution may be one of our fastest-growing controversial minorities. ... Many of the scientists supporting this position hold impressive credentials in science.

- Today ... the Darwinian theory of evolution stands under attack as never before ... a growing number of respectable scientists are defecting from the evolutionist camp. ... For the most part, these "experts" have abandoned Darwinism, not on the basis of religious faith or biblical persuasions, but on strictly scientific grounds, and in some instances regretfully, as one could say.

- Scientists who go about teaching that evolution is a fact of life are great con-men, and the story they are telling may be the greatest hoax ever. In explaining evolution we do not have one iota of fact.

- Every single concept advanced by the theory of evolution ... is imaginary as it is not supported by the scientifically established facts of microbiology, fossils, and mathematical probability concepts. Darwin was wrong. ... The theory of evolution may be the worst mistake [ever] made in science.

- In fact, evolution became in a sense a scientific religion; almost all scientists accepted it and many are prepared to "bend" their observations to fit in with it.

- Considering its historic significance and the social and moral transformation it caused in Western thought, one might have hoped that Darwinian theory ... a theory of such cardinal importance, a theory that literally changed the world, would have been something more than metaphysics, something more than a myth.

- One is forced to conclude that many scientists and technologists pay lip-service to Darwinian theory only because it supposedly excludes a Creator....

- I think we need to go further than this and admit that the only acceptable explanation is creation. I know this is an anathema to physicists, as indeed it is to me, but we must not reject a theory that we do not like if the experimental evidence supports it.

The next series of quotes from Harwood's website go into specific detail about the lack of evidence in the fossil record for Darwin's beliefs:

- Beginning about six hundred million years ago ... all over the world, at roughly the same time, thick sequences of rocks, barren of any easily detected fossils, are overlain by sediments containing a gorgeous array of shelly invertebrates: trilobites, brachiopods, mollusks.... Creationists have made much of this sudden development of a rich and varied fossil record where, just before, there was none.... [This] does pose a fascinating intellectual challenge.

- The geological record has so far provided no evidence as to the origin of the fishes....

- There are no intermediate forms between finned [fish] and limbed [reptilian] creatures in the fossil collections of the world.

- There is no fossil evidence of the stages through which the remarkable change from reptile to bird was achieved.

- It must be significant that nearly all the evolutionary stories I learned as a student ... have now been "debunked."

And finally, consider these statements regarding the apparent transformation of apes into human beings through Darwinian evolution:

- ... if man evolved from an apelike creature, he did so without leaving a trace of that evolution in the fossil record.

- The entire hominid (a so-called "ape-man" fossil) collection known today would barely cover a billiard table.

- The remarkable fact is that all the physical evidence we have for human evolution can still be placed, with room to spare, inside a single coffin. Modern apes, for instance, seem to have sprung out of nowhere. They have no yesterday, no fossil record. And the true origin of modern humans—of upright, naked, tool-making, big-brained beings—is, to be honest with ourselves, an equally mysterious manner.

- A five-million-year-old piece of bone that was thought to be a collarbone of a humanlike creature is actually part of a dolphin rib.... The problem with a lot of anthropologists is that they want so much to find a hominid that any scrap of bone becomes a hominid bone.

- ... if you were to spend your life picking up bones and finding little fragments of head and little fragments of jaw, there's a very strong desire to exaggerate the importance of those fragments....

- Echoing the criticism made of his father's *Homo habilis* skulls, he [Richard Leakey] added that Lucy's skull was so incomplete that most of it was "imagination, made of plaster of paris," thus making it impossible to draw any firm conclusion about what species she belonged to.

- The above considerations make it overwhelmingly likely that Lucy was no more than a variety of pygmy chimpanzee, and walked the same way (awkwardly upright on occasions, but mostly on all fours). The "evidence" for the alleged transformation from ape to man is extremely unconvincing.

• Neanderthals had short, narrow skulls, large cheekbones and noses and, most distinctive, bunlike bony bumps on the backs of their heads. Many modern Danes and Norwegians have identical features, Brace reported at the annual meeting of the American Anthropological Association in Phoenix.... Indeed, the present-day European skulls resemble Neanderthal skulls more closely than they resemble the skulls of [present-day] American Indians or Australian aborigines, he said. Brace ... measured more than five hundred relatively modern northwestern Europeans' craniums last year....

When we consider that the size of the brain literally doubled between that of humanity's apparent ancestors and ourselves, with no evidence of a smooth transformation whatsoever, once again we see a spontaneous evolution of the creatures on Earth, in this case human beings. The oldest anatomically modern human to be discovered, where DNA could be extracted, analyzed and dated, walked the earth no earlier than 68,000 years ago, and was in Australia, not Africa.[5] Recent discoveries at Blombos Cave in South Africa, first published in November 2001, show that "modern" human behavior, the ornate and symbolic carving of bone and other items, dates back to at least 70,000 years ago. One scientist on the National Geographic website said that these new findings force us to conclude that "behavioral evolution (moves) in step with anatomical development," meaning that the spontaneous evolution is not simply physiological, but consciousness-related as well. When a new bodily form has emerged, consciousness changes appear to occur at just about the same time. The *Law of One* series states that "third density" humans first evolved on Earth roughly 75,000 years ago, so the latest DNA evidence validates this statement quite well.[6]

The Mystery of DNA

How in the world could creatures, including ourselves, be spontaneously evolving? What about the DNA molecule? Can it undergo such spontaneous changes? Do we really understand DNA? This final quote from Harwood's website deals with the impossibility of DNA evolving through random processes:

> Now that the actual physical structure of ... [DNA] has come into view, scientists are finding—frequently to their dismay— that the evolutionist thesis has become more stringently unthinkable than ever before.... On the fundamental level it becomes a rigorously demonstrable fact that ... the so-called "missing links" are indeed non-existent.

The probabilities that DNA could evolve by "random mutation" are so minute as to be utterly laughable—akin to the idea that if you have enough monkeys tapping away on typewriters, one of them will eventually produce a complete Shakespearean play. So, since there are 50 to 70 trillion cells in the human body and each of them contains enough information in its DNA blueprint to reproduce the entire organism, how did this DNA arrive at its current, amazingly complicated configuration if Darwinian evolution is flawed? We will look at this question with a series of surprising facts that completely change the prevailing viewpoints about DNA and evolution.

Dr. Bruce Lipton has provided a strong, credentialed, almost solitary voice in the alternative science community regarding anomalies in the structure of human DNA, and here we will follow up on some of the research links[7] that he often presents. Most scientists still teach that in order for some part of the body to be "built," a corresponding code must exist in the DNA—a code that we call a "gene." Since there

343

are 70,000 to 90,000 different proteins in the human body, it was automatically assumed that human DNA should have at least 100,000 different genes—say, 70,000 for the proteins to build the body and a minimum of 30,000 to help tackle the mystery of human consciousness.

However, when the 3.1 billion "base pairs" of human DNA were actually mapped out (sequenced) on a computer, the initial process completed in 2001, only 30,000 different genes were found. Even stranger, an extremely simple microscopic white worm with only 1,029 different cells had fully 20,000 genes in its DNA—meaning that it has two-thirds the number of genes as a human being. And the mustard weed, which we cultivate to make the zesty yellow spread for our sandwiches, has just about as many genes as we do. Hence, all the extra code that should be there to make us different and special simply does not exist.

Dr. Francis Collins, head of the International Human Genome Project responsible for this DNA sequencing, also revealed that all human beings are literally 99.9% identical at the DNA level.[8] This means that only three million base pairs, each of which is composed of only four simple building blocks labeled A, C, T, or G, differentiate one human being from another at the genetic level. Even further, Collins revealed that "there is no scientific basis for precise racial categories,"[9] meaning that you cannot identify someone's race by studying the three million base pairs of DNA that set us apart: the patterns are too similar.

The naked, ironic truth is that each "base pair" has only four parts, made up of some combination of the four basic proteins, though not all four proteins show up in every base pair—there can be duplicates of one or more proteins. If we were able to create an ultra-simplified digital code for DNA that uses four digits—A, C, T, and G—instead of two (0 or 1) as "bits," then with eight bits in a byte and 1000 bytes in a kilobyte, that means that the entire three million base pairs that make us separate and unique beings would take up only 1.5 megabytes of storage space—just slightly over the amount of space on one floppy disk. One single scan of a color picture at 300 dots per inch into a bitmap file can easily consume this much space. If the reader is wondering what exactly this proves, the answer is quite simple. DNA in and of itself does not appear to contain the codes to build the body. Quite surprisingly, only 3% of human DNA is composed of the 30,000 genes that encode the physical body, and the other 97% was, until recently, considered to be "junk DNA," with basic sequences that repeat over and over again like a broken record—sequences that remain the same for each DNA molecule under study, hence our 99.9% genetic similarities to each other. However, scientists are now aware of the existence of over a million different structures of "jumping DNA" or "transposons" in this remaining 97% of the molecule.[10] Scientists named it "jumping DNA" for a very good reason—these one million different proteins can break loose from one area, move to another area, settle down, and thereby rewrite the DNA code. Hence, as Drs. Hartman[11] and Wintersberger[12] both indicated, "It is well established in the molecular biology community, but unknown to most people, that the primary structure of DNA does actually change."[13]

Undoubtedly, as this knowledge becomes increasingly mainstream, geneticists will try to theorize that the activities of "jumping DNA" are all programmed strictly by the genetic code within the DNA molecule itself, and not by any outside energetic influence such as consciousness. This might seem to be a more "comfortable" viewpoint, since it denies the importance of a higher form of consciousness and/or Ultimate Being, but clear scientific evidence suggests that consciousness does have a direct effect on the jumping DNA.

Dr. Bruce Lipton's research states, point-blank, that cells have the capability to rewrite their own DNA when their surrounding environment prompts them to do so. Such rewriting is typically beneficial, and he believes that it accounts for 95–98% of evolutionary change. One study that Lipton frequently mentions to support this point was published by a Harvard geneticist and biochemist named John Kearns in 1988. Kearns took certain bacteria that could not digest milk sugar (lactose) and placed them into an environment where lactose was the only food they had. Instead of dying off, the bacteria sensed this change in their environment and somehow reprogrammed their own DNA to genetically evolve their digestive parts to be able to eat lactose.[14]

Though this might not seem very important, Dr. Lipton says that "the implications are enormous," as it means that evolution does not occur by random chance, as most evolutionists believe. The bacteria have access to some form of consciousness that senses an environmental change and reprograms (evolves) accordingly.

A 1982 study by Francis Hitching[15] produced a similar result involving the fruit fly, known technically as Drosophila. Since it has a simple genetic structure and breeds very quickly, it is often used in genetics experiments. When Hitching eliminated all information from the DNA of the fruit fly that is used to build its eyes, he obviously got blind fruit flies. However, in about five generations of offspring, the eyes mysteriously return in a perfect form, as if the code had never been lost. Again, this suggests that there is a field of information outside the fruit fly's own DNA which is responsible for arranging the "jumping DNA" inside the molecule to handle the various tasks involved in producing a healthy organism. If the eye information disappears from the DNA completely, then over time, the hidden energy wave simply puts the code back in.

Other scientists have concluded that the human DNA molecule has all the genetic information necessary to rebuild any other creature on Earth—it is the same information in various arrangements. Surprisingly, the Human Genome Project found that we are more genetically similar to dolphins than we are to any apes, monkeys, or chimpanzees. Considering how dissimilar we appear from dolphins visually, this contradicts the idea that our DNA code is a result of random mutations. With only a tiny amount of code separating a human being from a dolphin, and with the entire fossil record capable of being rebuilt by rearranging the material in our own DNA, this suggests that life on Earth is the product of a single "life wave" that can be intelligently directed into various configurations as needed.

Hence, it becomes obvious that when spontaneous evolutions in our past have occurred, the hypothetical DNA life-wave would have made a sudden increase in its complexity. Later in this section is striking evidence that such a wave does exist.

Cyclical Extinction Events

To summarize the information in the quotes on evolution above, what we do see in the fossil record is a situation where the species on the planet essentially remain the same for millions of years at a time, and then there are quite spontaneous changes where the given species suddenly die out and newer, more complex species emerge. The moments of die-off are known as "extinctions," and in every case they are very soon followed by the sudden emergence of many new species all over the Earth, known as "speciations."

Many people erroneously believe that there was only one major extinction event, which erased almost all dinosaur species from the Earth some 65 million years ago. This is by far the most well-known event, referred to as the *Cretaceous-Tertiary boundary* or "K/T boundary." However, we now know that mass extinction/speciation events occur every 26 million years in our Earth's history, just like clockwork.[16] This concept was first formulated by Alfred Fischer and Michael Arthur, and was given solid scientific evidence by University of Chicago paleontologists David Raup and John Sepkoski. They arrived at this finding from studying the most exhaustive fossil record ever compiled on Earth—a collection of more than 36,000 different genera of marine organisms. The more they studied and added to the collection, the clearer the pattern became. Make sure that you didn't miss this point, as it is very important: **all species on Earth have been spontaneously evolving every 26 million years.** This strongly suggests an outside energetic influence that operates in a regular, cyclic fashion.

347

In *The Divine Cosmos* and my in-progress book *Divine Nature,* I suggest that these mass evolution events are caused by our solar system passing through evenly-spaced zones of energy in our galaxy that are not visible to the naked eye, similar to how we cannot see the energetic fields surrounding a magnet. One period of 26 million years represents how long it took our solar system to pass through one zone of this energy. It is important to point out here that we are not at the end of another 26-million-year cycle—we are actually at the *exact halfway point* of the cycle right now, with 13 million years since the last event. The evidence that we will present later in this chapter from Dr. Aleskey Dmitriev and others makes a very strong case for the idea that we are again moving into a more highly charged energetic zone in the galaxy. Though it is too complicated to explain in this book, the geometry of the energy fields involved does suggest that the cycles could cleanly divide in half like this as the galaxy evolves.

However, our simple statements about "zones of energy" do not yet account for all the mysteries that this question raises: "If energy increases are responsible for these DNA changes, then how does this work?" More specifically, there is an abundance of evidence, mostly from Russian scientists, which shows us that energy is consciousness and consciousness is energy. So, when we pass into a zone of more highly charged energy in the galaxy, we are also passing into a zone of higher consciousness. This is the energetic engine of evolution.

Making the Case

What we have already set forth in these last few pages suggests a radically different view of DNA evolution than what the vast majority of our civilization is aware of. However, in order for this new model to be acceptable, several different areas of proof need to be satisfied. The *Convergence* series attempts to provide clear scientific evidence to satisfy every question that such a grandiose idea would bring up. The following sections touch upon some of the most significant questions—the connection between consciousness and energy, the evidence for structured, regular energy zones in the galaxy, the effect of our position in the galaxy on matter and energy, the effect of our position in the galaxy on consciousness, and the effect of consciousness on the DNA molecule—giving proof that DNA can be altered by a strictly energetic/consciousness-related source. You may want to read through this chapter more than once to absorb all the information and how it connects, as some of these points require several pages for even a cursory explanation.

The Consciousness/Energy Connection

The first and most obvious need would be to establish a clear connection between consciousness and energy. In the field of parapsychology, which is solidly empirical (scientific) and has struggled in vain for mainstream academic acceptance for many years, we have prestigious institutions such as Princeton Engineering Anomalies Research or PEAR[17] that have absolutely proven that human consciousness can affect the outcome of seemingly "random" procedures involving physical matter. This can include effects where the participant is able to demonstrate the following statistically significant results:

- affecting random-number generators inside a computer system;

- changing the speed of radiation emissions as they are measured by a Geiger counter;

- and even affecting the random movement of ping-pong balls as they drop through a matrix of pins, causing them to selectively land more often in one out of, say, ten different slots along the bottom.

It is also important to remember that the subjects for these sorts of experiments are not heavy-duty psychics but ordinary people; so we are not talking about something that is only available to certain "elite" humans in our society. These experiments clearly reveal that the human being possesses untapped potential that has not yet gained mainstream scientific acceptance. Furthermore, many Russian and Chinese studies came up with results so dazzling that most Western skeptics would dismiss the findings without a second glance.

The Science of Torsion Fields

It is important to point out that over and over again, frontier researchers across the globe are discovering a new source of energy, different from any known electromagnetic, gravitational or atomic forces, which travels in a spiraling, wavelike pattern. In Russia, the study of these energy waves has been very advanced since at least the 1950s, though it has remained almost totally hidden from Western scientists. Everyone who discovers this energy tends to come up with their own name for it, and New Agers often simply call it "spiritual energy," but the most common scientific term that we will use is "torsion fields" and/or "torsion waves." The word "torsion" essentially has the same meaning as other words like "spiraling" or "twisting," hence the name constantly reminds us of the spiraling nature of these waves. I consider this new science to be so dramatically important that the entire text of *The Divine Cosmos* is densely packed with information about the science of torsion fields. Here, we will only scratch the surface.

To put it bluntly, torsion fields break all the "rules" that most scientists expect to see, which is why they have evaded mainstream detection in the Western world. It is wise to remember that the force of magnetism was not known until someone discovered it when their metal-tipped walking stick got stuck to a lodestone, and the force of gravity was not actually thought of until an apple dropped on Isaac Newton's head. Even air can be taken for granted, since we do not see it. Of course, magnetism and gravity had always existed as a vital part of nature before they were "officially" discovered, but no one bothered to think of them before, because there was no real need to know about them—humanity knew as much as it needed to know for that time in history.

The initial "learning curve" on the science of torsion fields can be rather steep for some people, because it forces them to use their imagination and think in new ways about matter, energy, and consciousness. For example, simply moving an object through space, even if there is no air in that space, will create a torsion field that can be measured some distance away with a mechanical or electromagnetic detector. This has been repeated in the laboratory by scientists such as Dr. Nikolai Kozyrev, and it works just as well in a completely dark room, so visible light is not the key. When you think about an experiment like this and attempt to explain it, you are left with the idea that when you move the object, it creates a disturbance in some form of *energy* that exists in apparently "empty space." Without some energy source that could act as a conductor between the moving object and the detector, the whole model falls apart, since in a truly "empty" space without air, visible light, or energy, there would be no way for the detector to pick up the movement of that object.

Those in the alternative science community have brought back the ancient Greek term "aether" for this hidden, non-physical energy source, and throughout the *Convergence* series one finds strong evidence that it must exist throughout every part of the entire universe. Modern scientists do acknowledge its existence by calling it such things as the "quantum medium" or "dark energy," but they are unaware of how important it really is, or the full nature of its behavior. Suffice it to say that in our new model, all of physical matter is "breathing." In each moment, atoms are inhaling "clean" aetheric energy and exhaling energy that has been temporarily devitalized.

This is what allows atoms to continue to act as "perpetual motion" machines, maintaining their structure despite all their internal activity; they draw off the aether as their source of energy and life. If you could somehow shield a physical object from all aetheric energy, then over time it would disintegrate. (Please understand that we are being very friendly to the lay reader by not bringing in complicated physics discussions to prove these points, though we certainly could.) This information also suggests that atoms behave similarly to what we call living organisms, thus hinting that life is the rule, not the exception, of the laws of the universe.

So again, when we talk about torsion waves, we are simply talking about something that creates "waves" in the aether, similar to the waves on the surface of a lake. Now obviously you can't remove a wave from a lake and have anything left to study—the wave only exists as a movement, a pressure current, in the water. Similarly, torsion waves are simply pressure currents moving through the "sea" of aether energy that is all around us. Eventually, if a whirlpool or vortex is created in the aether with sufficient rotational speed, physical matter will emerge, initially as visible light (electromagnetic energy). This is how the physical universe appears to have been created, and in *The Divine Cosmos* this theory is explained in detail.

We can learn more about this new science by learning how Kozyrev and others have been able to create measurable torsion waves in the laboratory. The following is a list of some simple methods that produced positive results.

- the deforming of a physical object (e.g., stress fields)
- the encounter of an air jet with an obstacle
- the operation of an hourglass filled with sand
- the absorption of light
- friction (again, stress fields)
- burning
- the actions of an observer, such as a movement of the head
- the heating or cooling of an object
- phase transitions in substances (frozen to liquid, liquid to vapor, etc.)
- dissolving and mixing substances
- the fading death of plants

- non-light radiation from astronomical objects

- sudden changes in human consciousness, especially those infused with strong emotion

We will tackle the implications of this list in just a moment. Next we have a list of some non-mechanical methods in which torsion fields can be detected, without constructing a machine that has any moving parts. (There are several mechanical methods as well that are discussed in *The Divine Cosmos*.) All of the following characteristics will change in the presence of torsion fields, such as can be weakly generated by the processes we just listed above; they can also be generated much more strongly via other methods, some "dynamic" (mechanically-driven) and some "passive" ("shape power," such as that harnessed in a pyramid structure, which will be discussed later in this essay).

- the conductiveness of electronic resistors, especially those made from tungsten metal

- the mercury level in thermometers (shielded from normal temperature changes)

- the vibrational frequencies of quartz crystal oscillators

- the electric potentials of thermocouples

- the viscosity (thickness) of water

- the amount of electronic work that can be performed in a photoelectric cell

- the reaction rates of chemical compounds (such as the Belousov-Zhabotinsky effect)

- the growth parameters of bacteria and plants

Most scientists want to jump and run when information like this suddenly takes on a spiritual quality, giving the forbidden suggestion that "God" really does exist. Hence, we will invariably lose some readers when we mention the connection between torsion fields and consciousness. To put it as bluntly as possible, you cannot separate consciousness and torsion waves—they are the same thing. When we use our minds to think, we are creating movements of electrical impulses in the brain, and when any electrical energy moves, torsion waves are also created. Similarly, any torsion wave, even if it is mechanically created, contains some form of information that can be detected by consciousness.

Here is one very simple example of how mechanically-produced torsion fields can be mentally detected to aid our survival. Let's say that you're walking near the edge of a cliff or on the surface of an iced-over lake, and in either case you are consciously unaware that it is about to collapse under your weight if you don't move out of that area. When any physical matter is strained to a point where it is about to break, a distinct form of torsion wave is created by that stress. All organisms have the bio-energetic ability to detect these stress fields, and the more matter is about to break, the stronger the stress fields will be.

Hence, without any audible sound or other clues that something is wrong, a part of us feels the stress fields, and a fight-or-flight response is created in the body, complete with an increase in the heart rate, adrenaline secretions, and an often-noticeable sense of pressure in the head surrounding the ear and forehead area, which can create a strange sense of impending dread. Animals automatically respond to such instincts if they have time, whereas human beings can choose to discount these impressions. Earthquakes are obviously the ultimate example of the creation of "stress fields" in action. In the case of an impending earthquake, the animals in that area can end up going completely wild, because the stress fields are so great that if they were not chained up, they would be running for all they were worth to try to get away from them. This effect has been measured again and again, but until now we did not have a good means of explaining it.

As the reader has probably already realized, a psychic is simply a person who has learned how to receive and interpret torsion-wave signals from their environment, and possibly is able to send them out as well. Any time someone has a thought, it creates a torsion wave, and this wave ripples out in all directions from that person's mind. Russian researchers have proven that if there is a strong emotional energy connected to a particular thought, the torsion waves created are much more powerful. Hence, if a child is suddenly hurt badly, the intense emotional energy of that pain releases strong torsion waves that are vibrationally encoded with the sensory information and psychic impressions related to the accident. Then, the mother may not know exactly what has happened, but she senses that something is wrong with her child. If that strong emotional energy were to be released near a Russian torsion-field detecting machine that uses a sort of compass needle, then the needle will point towards the source of the energy once it is released. Dr. Nikolai Kozyrev was the first to discover this phenomenon.

Some readers might stumble on the idea that a spiraling "torsion wave" could have so much specific sensory and emotional information encoded within it. However, this concept becomes less and less implausible once we realize that we are constantly surrounded by electromagnetic waves that can be decoded to produce television, radio, telephone, and other signals. However, if we do not have the right instrument, the waves are not detectable. Similarly, if you want to be able to detect and decode the torsion fields around you, the mind must be cleared from thoughts as much as possible. This is why meditation is so important.

The information from torsion waves is always a part of your conscious mind on some level, but your own thoughts have a much "louder" signal. If you can control your mind enough to reduce or eliminate most of your thoughts, such as by focusing all your energy on your breathing, then you will begin receiving spontaneous visual images and emotional impressions that do not require any concentration or thinking, i.e., "daydreaming." This information will arrive in a completed form, and disappear just as quickly to be replaced by something else. Most people are unaware that this apparently useless "fantasy" information actually contains real psychic data. The true work of a psychic is in practicing this technique enough to detect these fleeting thoughts, and then slow them down and solidify them enough to explore them in detail. The best way to learn to do this is to keep trying, with a daily meditation practice.

As one example, the science of "psychometry," or reading the stored torsion fields in an object, was taken to an extreme by Edgar Cayce, who could sleep with a book under his pillow and then wake up with a photographic recall of what content appeared on what page. This technique works most effectively if someone has personally handled and read the copy being used. His or her thoughts are stored as torsion fields within the molecular structures of the paper and ink in the book.

To give another example of someone reading the torsion fields that are all around us, the average driver feels some degree of emotional shock when they suddenly realize that they have passed by a hidden police car, especially if they are traveling above the speed limit. For that moment of time, they are not sure whether or not they are about to be pulled over, and there is a surge of panic. The torsion fields that this creates are relatively easy to detect with practice, as they consist of a feeling of sudden fear and panic coupled with the image of the flashing lights. If someone up the road from you has just had this experience and you are driving without any music, radio, or other distraction and have a relatively clear mind, you will feel their pain and see the lights in your mind, thereby taking the hint and slowing down. With time this becomes a rather reliable psychic trick, but you have to learn to always keep your mind clear— and we assume no legal or karmic liabilities here, nor does it work if you are really speeding, since that extra nervous energy creates many "false positives." And if there is no one ahead of you, then there is no psychic instrument to detect a speed trap.

Pyramid Power Is No Joke

The science of torsion fields goes well beyond an explanation of extra-sensory perception. For example, the Earth is always sending and receiving torsion fields, as does any physical object by virtue of its "breathing." However, the fields from the Earth, the Sun, or the center of the galaxy are a lot stronger than from any smaller object, due to the sizes involved. The easiest low-tech way to harness these energy fields is to build a pyramid or other cone-shaped structure. Since all physical matter is absorbing and releasing torsion fields in this new model, you can capture and direct these waves by building the right type of structure. The most effective slope angle for such a pyramid is 70 degrees, and you must not use any metal in its construction, as metal has a tendency to absorb the torsion fields around itself.

Until Dr. John DeSalvo of the Giza Pyramid Research Association published the Russian and Ukranian pyramid research[18] of A. Golod, V. Krasnoholovets and associates, the complete picture of how much progress had been made in these areas was not available online. This research comes from the Institute of Physics in Kiev, Ukraine, a basic institution of the National Academy of Sciences of Ukraine, which was one of the leading scientific centers in the former USSR and the premier military research association. Once the Soviet Union collapsed, many highly intelligent scientists had little or nothing to do, and because of their background in torsion-wave physics, a variety of pyramid experiments were conducted.

Two steep pyramids with 70-degree slope angles were constructed in Russia near Moscow, one at a height of 22 meters and another at a height of 44 meters (144 feet), costing over a million dollars to build. Since the early 1990s, a total of 17 different pyramids have been built altogether. In order for the pyramid effects to emerge, it was found that *no metal* could be used in the construction; thus modular fiberglass plastics were used instead. The pyramids were aligned to the North Star and built away from populated areas. At the base of the

22-meter pyramid the fiberglass wall was 36 centimeters thick, and at the base of the 44-meter pyramid the fiberglass wall was 70 centimeters thick. The 22-meter pyramid weighed a total of 25 tons, and the 44-meter pyramid weighed a total of 55 tons. Several different teams from the Russian Academy of Sciences carried out all sorts of experiments in these pyramids, with surprising results. Following is a summary of the most dramatic findings:

- Prof. S.M. Klimenko and D.N. Nosik, M.D., from the Ivanovskii R&D Institute of Virology within the Russian Academy of Medical Science, conducted a study involving the drug venoglobulin, which is a naturally-occurring virus-fighting compound in human beings. When the drug was diluted into a concentration of 50 micrograms per milliliter and stored in the pyramid for a time, it became approximately *three times more effective at fighting viruses.*

- Prof. A.G. Antonov et al., from the Russian R&D Institute of Pediatrics, Obstetrics and Gynecology, tested the effects of a solution of 40% glucose in distilled water after it had been stored in the pyramid. By administering only one milliliter of the glucose to twenty different prematurely born infant patients with compromised immune systems, their levels of health were seen to rapidly increase up to practically normal values. The researchers furthermore discovered that the same effect could be produced by simply using one milliliter of ordinary water that had been stored in the pyramid.

- Dr. N.B. Egorova at the Mechnikov R&D Institute within the Russian Academy of Medical Science tested living organisms placed directly inside the pyramid. An experimental and a control group of white underbred mice weighing 12 to 14 grams were both tainted with strain 415 of the virus *S. typhimurium* (typhoid fever) in equal amounts over the course of one day. In smaller doses of contamination, the mice stored in the pyramid survived at a rate of 60% whereas only 7% survived in the control group.

In larger doses of contamination, 30% of the mice in the pyramid survived as opposed to only 3% in the control group.

- In other experiments by Egorova et al., mice were exposed to various carcinogens, and an experimental group drank pyramid water whereas the control group drank ordinary water. The mice drinking the pyramid water had significantly fewer tumors develop than the mice drinking the ordinary water.

Along similar lines, Dr. A.A. Golod directed a team from the Scientific Manufacturing Union Gidrometpribor in Russia that came up with a variety of results, including the following:

- Plastic bottles of distilled water were kept in the pyramid during three winter months where the air temperature sank as low as −38° C, or −6° F. Thermometers inside the bottles revealed that the temperature of the water was equal to the air temperature, but *the water remained in a liquid form and would not turn into ice!* However, if the water in any of the bottles was shaken or bumped in any way, it would immediately start crystallizing and quickly turn into a block of ice. Golod and his associates have videotaped these results.

- Chunks of granite and crystal were scattered along the entire floor of the pyramid for longer periods of time. A visible ring, centered perfectly with the edges of the pyramid, would appear evenly throughout the chunks, showing a clear change in the appearance of the stones when under the torsion-wave influence, obviously whitening the quartz inside the granite as it becomes a purer crystal. Between the end of 1997 and the beginning of 1999, this result was duplicated forty different times in the same pyramid, with different rocks each time. Each ring would cover between fifty and three hundred rocks, with a total weight from twenty to two hundred kilograms. Golod et al. have gathered evidence to suggest that when the rings form most visibly, the amount of epidemics in the surrounding area decreases.

- With Golod, the joint-stock company Scientific and Technological Institute of Transcription, Translation and Replication (TTR), in Kharkiv, Ukraine, conducted studies of the air above the pyramid with a Russian instrument similar to radar known as a "military locator." A column of "unknown energy" was detected at a width of 500 meters and a height of 2,000 meters. Further studies confirmed that a larger circle of this energy surrounded the area above the pyramid in a 300-kilometer-wide range. Golod's team calculated that if such an energy column were to be produced electromagnetically, it would require all the energy of the various power plants in Russia combined. Furthermore, they observed that after the pyramid's presence was established, an ozone hole that had existed over that area of Russia was seen to repair itself in only two months' time.

- A series of pyramids was built over one of a number of oil wells. It was discovered that *the viscosity of the oil under the pyramids decreased by 30%, while the production rate accordingly increased by 30%* compared to the surrounding wells. There was a decrease in the amount of unwanted materials in the oil, such as gums, pyrobitumen, and paraffin. These results were confirmed by the Gubkin Moscow Academy of Oil and Gas.

- Agricultural seeds were kept in a pyramid for one to five days before being planted. More than twenty different seed varieties were planted across tens of thousands of hectares. In all cases, the seeds from the pyramid had a *20 to 100% increase in their yield;* the plants did not get sick and were not affected by droughts.

- Poisons and other toxins become less destructive to living systems after even a short term of exposure in the pyramid.

- Radioactive materials held inside a pyramid decay more rapidly than expected.

- Pathogenic viruses and bacteria become significantly less damaging to life after being held in the pyramid.

- Psychotropic drugs (LSD is one example) have less of an effect on people either staying inside a pyramid or within close range of a pyramid.

- Standard solutions such as glucose and iso-osmotic solution become effective for treating alcoholism and drug addiction after being placed in the pyramid. They can be administered either intravenously or outwardly.

Next, I will share the results of Dr. Yuri Bogdanov, who also conducted a whole series of studies on behalf of the joint-stock company Scientific and Technological Institute of Transcription, Translation and Replication (TTR), in Kharkiv, Ukraine.

- A twelve-meter pyramid was used to increase the productivity of wheat by 400% in the Ramenskoe settlement of Moscow.

- The half-life of radioactive carbon was shortened.

- The crystallization patterns of salts changed.

- Concrete became stronger.

- Crystals exhibited different optical behaviors, such as becoming clearer.

- Rabbits and white rats exposed to the pyramid gained 200% more endurance and a higher concentration of white blood cells.

- Water within or underneath a pyramid is purified. A complex of pyramids was built in a town near the Arkhangelsk region of Russia by order of the domestic administration there. In this case, strontium and heavy metals that had contaminated the public's water source were able to be cleared by the effects of the pyramids, which were built over the well. In the town of

Krasnogorskoe near Moscow, a pyramid was constructed to reduce the amount of salt in water.

- Diamonds synthesized within the pyramid turned out harder and purer than they would otherwise. Again, this suggests that the torsion-wave component is of central importance in the forming of chemical bonds to create a crystal.

In our last category, teams from the Russian National Academy of Sciences conducted the following studies:

- By comparing earthquake data from the areas surrounding the pyramids to earlier data from a time before the pyramids were built, they discovered that instead of seeing one large and powerful quake, several hundred tiny earthquakes are registered instead. Hence, the pyramids have the ability to dissipate the energetic buildup and friction that would normally create sudden, violent earthquakes.

- The atmosphere surrounding the pyramid seems to be shielded from severe weather as well, causing an overall decrease in the amount of violent weather patterns, which are deflected around the area where the pyramid is located.

- Pyramid-charged foods can make people more loving. A quantity of salt and pepper was stored inside the pyramid by these teams. This salt and pepper was later removed and fed to about five thousand people in different selected jails in Russia. Amazingly, within a few months there was a dramatic improvement in their behavior, and most criminal behavior almost completely disappeared, whereas the "control" jails showed no signs of behavioral change. Nothing in the jails under study had changed except that this salt and pepper was secretly added to their food.

This last study regarding the prisoners is one of the most important points, as it validates the idea that aetheric energy is "spiritual energy," and that as a person is exposed to higher intensities of it, there is a propensity for greater feelings of love and compassion for others. Hence, if we can make a strong case that we are moving into a more highly charged area of torsion-wave energy, then we can also assume that our civilization will exhibit some very positive changes.

Considering the almost incredible nature of these findings, all by reputable Russian institutions, the true importance of harnessing torsion waves becomes obvious. It can literally heal the Earth. Radiation from various sources could be quickly reduced, the ozone holes repaired, earthquakes and severe weather reduced, buildings made far more structurally sound, water purified, crops enhanced, diseases reversed, and even mental illness cured. It is no wonder that so many ancient cultures erected pyramids around the world. Any culture on any planet will eventually discover the massive benefits of this very simple technology and begin putting it to good use.

More importantly, these studies give extremely convincing evidence that the DNA molecule is directly affected by outside energy sources. If DNA is actually assembled by an unseen source of energy, then when we increase the flow of that energy into the DNA, we can also expect that the health and vitality of the organism will increase. In fact, the results of these Russian experiments are so extraordinary that we are left with the strong suggestion that torsion waves are the single most important factor in an organism's health. Factors such as sunlight, fresh air with negative ions, clean water, natural medicines, and healthy foods are all ways in which we can bring torsion fields into our bodies. Viruses, bacteria, poisonous substances, and radiation are all made far less toxic in the presence of torsion waves, which suggests that they are all relatively "out of harmony" with the wave that forms DNA—a lower form of vibration, if you will.

It is important here to point out that most foods in the "typical American diet" have almost no torsion-wave energy whatsoever. We know from Dr. Kozyrev's research that salt, a neatly organized cubical crystal, enhances the flow of torsion fields whereas sugar, a complex, knotted polysaccharide, absorbs torsion fields. Refined sugar appears to be far worse than natural sugars such as brown rice syrup, honey, and molasses. It is therefore quite interesting that the Zen macrobiotic diet specifies the importance of eating a balance of "yin" (sugary/fruits) and "yang" (salty/vegetables) foods, with a focus on the fact that both are necessary and an over-abundance of either one will make you unhealthy. Most American diets are vastly overabundant in the yin/sugary category, thus the importance of eating fresh organic nuts, seeds, raw fruits, and vegetables, which are abundant sources of torsion fields. Simply increasing how salty your food is will not help you, since salt in and of itself is not a source of torsion fields—it only amplifies what is already there.

Lastly, I am aware that some people will invariably try to capitalize on the information in this chapter and set up a business selling pyramid energy-charged foods or beverages, claiming that they can cure diseases and the like. I do not endorse such businesses and would caution you to be extremely skeptical of any and all such claims. This information has been presented for research purposes only and is not intended to replace or substitute for the guidance of a trained medical professional. Furthermore, Dr. Alexandr Shpilman's research shows that torsion-charged water only holds its energetic charge for three or four days at the most, and nothing can be done to prolong it. This makes distribution of genuinely "charged water" just about impossible. If you would like to further this research for experimental purposes only, it is far better to make a steep 70-degree-angle pyramid out of non-metallic materials and charge your own food and water at home.

Zones of Energy in the Galaxy

Now you know a great deal of surprising new evidence to suggest a connection between consciousness and energy. So, for the next level of proof for our "energetic evolution" model to be satisfied, clear evidence of structured, regular energetic zones in the galaxy must be provided. Most of this information is too complicated to try to explain in this chapter, as it gets into some advanced physics concepts, but it is described fully in *The Divine Cosmos*. Suffice it to say that these higher-energy regions create measurable changes in the electromagnetic vibrations above the level of visible light, such as infrared, ultraviolet, and microwaves. Richard Pasichnyk reports that "zones" of evenly varying microwave intensity have been found between the arms of a single galaxy. Most astronomers use this measurement, known as "redshift," to indicate distance, so they are forced to reject data like this out of hand. Dr. Harold Aspden has done a remarkable job of showing that these microwave vibrations are equal to varying levels of aetheric energy, using equations that do not violate the laws of physics.

Below a whole section is devoted to the very physical, very measurable changes that are occurring throughout our entire solar system as a result of our movement into a more highly energetic region. One brief example of this evidence is that the front end of the Sun's magnetic field, which is large enough to surround all the planets, has a charged, glowing zone of energy that has grown over 1000% brighter and deeper over the second half of the twentieth century. This obvious energetic excitation is a direct result of the solar system passing into a zone with a higher energetic charge.

If such zones of energy do indeed exist, and the newest zone is having a noticeable effect on our solar system right now, then our next task in supporting this energetic model of evolution would be to establish a connection between our galactic position and its effects on physical matter, energy, and consciousness.

Cosmic Influences on Matter, Energy, and Consciousness

Most current scientists believe that the Earth is unaffected by any forces except for the occasional stray asteroid or comet, the force of gravity, and the Sun's emissions of light, heat, and charged particles. Asteroid collisions with the Earth's surface are believed to have caused mass extinctions, even though Pasichnyk and others have shown that the evidence for this is very weak. The Moon's gravity pulls on the oceans, causing the tides to occur, and the Sun's gravity holds our planet in place in the solar system. The Sun's light keeps our planet warm and feeds plant life through photosynthesis, and there may be a connection between the light of the full moon and the number of people experiencing mental disturbances. We can see the visible light of stars, galaxies, nebulae, and the like with the naked eye or in our telescopes. Solar particle emissions can fry our satellites and interrupt radio waves and other forms of communication, and that's about the visible extent of the effects of the cosmic influences.

Despite the long-standing science of astrology, few scientists believe that the movement of the planets or of our solar system through the galaxy has any discernible effect on us; other than gravity and light, we are insulated from the rest of the galaxy. All of this changes when we look at the work of the Russian professor Simon Shnoll, which was brought into view for Western readers through an article in the summer 2000 issue of *21st Century Science and Technology* magazine.[19] After more than thirty years of investigation, Shnoll came to a startling conclusion. All the basic reactions that occur in biology, chemistry, quantum physics, and radioactivity—the processes that keep things moving and/or keep us alive—are directly influenced by celestial movements, including the day, the month, the year, and even our movement through the galaxy. Again, these effects appear to be caused by torsion waves being radiated from the various celestial bodies around us. These waves then affect the vibrations within physical matter and energy.

When we want to study a biological, chemical, atomic, or radioactive reaction in the laboratory, such as by mixing two things together, we expect that the resulting reaction will start slowly, build up to a maximum speed and power, and then gradually taper off to its original starting point again. This pattern is expected to take the same length of time to build up as it does to move back down, forming a smooth, uniform pattern known as a "bell curve." However, Shnoll noticed that when we actually make graphs to chart out biological, chemical, atomic, and radioactive reactions in the laboratory, we do not see strict bell curves at all; the speed of the reactions makes sudden jerks up and down that create unique, spiky patterns in the graphs. Most scientists use special equations to throw out these spikes as "noise" in their data, since they automatically expect to see a bell curve. Shnoll simply decided that he would start studying the jerky patterns and see if they had any deeper meaning.

From this standpoint, Shnoll found that if you measure any biological (B), chemical (C), atomic (A), or radioactive (R) processes at the *same time,* which he called "zero time," the same spiky patterns will show up in the different graphs. This alone is a discovery that should shake the foundations of current science, as it shows that in each and every moment, some outside force is causing living and non-living energy systems to react in *exactly* the same way. However, this alone does not prove that the effects are being caused by anything outside our own planet, such as a random fluctuation in the Earth's magnetic or gravitational field.

The proof of a "cosmic connection" is satisfied by Shnoll's discovery that the same patterns repeat in any of the four systems, B, C, A, or R, in even intervals of time such as 24 hours (one rotation of the Earth on its axis,) 27.28 days (the approximate time for one revolution of the Moon around the Earth, and also close to one rotation of the Sun on its axis), and three time intervals very close to a year: 364.4, 365.2 and 366.6 days. (The Earth revolves around the Sun in 365.2422 days.)

Only recently, Shnoll and his associates realized that the 24-hour period of time was slightly shorter than a true Earth "day." They quickly discovered that this actual length of time was precisely identical to a "sidereal" day, which is the length of time that it takes for the Earth to rotate on its axis in comparison to a fixed point in our galaxy, such as the galactic center. This gives us absolute proof that some part of the galaxy is having a direct energetic effect upon biology, chemistry, quantum physics, and radioactivity. Since the galactic center is the most energetic area of our galaxy, it is natural to assume that it would be the source of these energetic effects, which are transmitted to us as torsion waves.

Galactic Position and Consciousness

If our position in the galaxy affects biology, chemistry, quantum physics, and radioactivity, what, if anything, does it do to our consciousness? One particular study sheds light on this issue. Dr. James Spottiswoode of the Cognitive Sciences Laboratory in Palo Alto, California, conducted rigorous studies to try to pin down any one single factor that could affect how well people access intuitive states of consciousness at any one moment.[20] He was looking for something related to time, which would naturally repeat in a predictable fashion. In order for this study to have credibility, he needed to gather a very large pool of data, so he connected with the institutions responsible for every professional laboratory study of human psychic ability that he could find over a twenty-year period, including remote viewing experiments, ganzfeld, Zener cards, et cetera. Spottiswoode asserts that no ESP study this massive had ever been performed before, and many of these groups had never before shared their data.

Spottiswoode did find exactly what he was looking for, and it was an effect that would repeat once each day. However, it did not repeat at a certain hour or minute of each day—it did not line up with, say, twelve noon. Instead, the effect was related to our position in the galaxy.[21]

Once again, the key was "sidereal" time, which measures how long it takes the Earth to rotate once on its axis relative to the galactic center. Spottiswoode's findings showed that when a certain area of the Earth is aimed directly towards the center of the galaxy, at 12 to 14½ hours "local sidereal time," the average person living in that area will have a whopping **400% increase** in their psychic accuracy. Most of the ESP studies that Spottiswoode compiled were of ordinary people as participants, not trained intuitives. No other time factors could be found that had any similar effect, and this effect consistently shows up throughout twenty years' worth of data from many different laboratories that often did not have access to each other's results before.

Spottiswoode's results suggest that the galactic center is a vitally important source of torsion waves for our planet. Based on the surprising results of the Russian pyramid studies, we can almost expect that when this energy is directed at us, our consciousness will be enhanced. And, if we are moving into an area of the galaxy where this energy is higher, it may indeed restructure the DNA molecule and enhance consciousness at the same time.

What Does It All Mean?

With this much new information being presented in such a short time, some readers will undoubtedly be left scratching their heads, wondering about the point of all this. The point is that our position in the galaxy can be shown to have a direct effect on biology, chemistry, quantum physics, radioactivity, and consciousness. When we are in greatest alignment with the galactic center, our consciousness will function most efficiently in its highest forms. These effects seem to be produced by the "torsion waves" that move throughout the universe. Hence, by moving into a more energetic area of the galaxy, we can expect higher consciousness, greater health, and possibly even changes in the way that matter and energy behave.

Now we must take all of this new information and combine it with our examination of the puzzle of evolution. We have shown that this energy has a direct effect on the DNA molecule, but we have not yet explained exactly how or why this would occur.

The DNA Phantom

Even in apparently total darkness, tiny bursts of light known as "photons" will still appear. These are known as "virtual photons," since they appear to come "from nowhere." This is yet another way in which we can prove that the "aether" really exists. Normally, these virtual photons emerge evenly throughout an entire "dark" area. However, Russian scientists Gariaev and Poponin found that if you place DNA inside a tiny chamber, all the surrounding "virtual" photons of light will be attracted into it like a funnel. Thus DNA acts like a prism or a lens, gathering all the light around itself and drawing it inward, causing it to travel in a spiraling path inside.[22]

Even more surprisingly, **if the DNA is removed from the tube, the light will continue to travel in the same spiraling shape, as if the DNA were still there.** Best of all, this effect can continue for up to thirty days after the DNA molecule itself has been removed from the chamber. This effect has been meticulously researched and documented in the laboratory, and through the efforts of gifted researchers such as the popular metaphysical speaker and ex-geological scientist Gregg Braden of Santa Fe, New Mexico,[23] humanity is becoming increasingly aware of this fact.

If you are reading too quickly, it is easy to miss the stunning importance of this finding. We have already suggested that the galactic center is transmitting energy to us that raises our consciousness. Now we are seeing that there must be an energy field around the DNA, which can continue to remain in one place after the DNA has been removed. Most people tend to think that the DNA created the energy field, and that the energy field is somehow just a "shadow" of the DNA once it has left a certain area. However, I believe that the wave actually exists before the DNA; the wave actually exists throughout the entire galaxy. Over time, I realized that the only logical explanation is that the phantom energy of DNA is actually the *creator* of DNA. This energy exists all throughout the galaxy, and wherever the materials that can create life exist, the subtle, spiraling pressure currents of this energy will arrange the DNA molecule into existence.

Cells Transmit Information Even When Separated

Regarding the idea that a conscious energy field is responsible for forming DNA, Cleve Backster's studies[24] involving human cells are relevant, as documented in Dr. Robert Stone's book *The Secret Life of Your Cells*. In this case, the epithelial (skin) cells of a human being, gathered from inside the cheek with a cotton swab, were stored in a separate room and connected to a lie-detector machine, which measures changes in the amount of electrical energy that can be conducted through living tissue. Backster was able to prove repetitively that the cheek cells demonstrated sudden responses that corresponded *precisely* with the timing of tailor-made emotional shocks that were carefully induced to the participant.

It wasn't necessarily easy to ethically shock a human being, so there was no "standardized" way for Backster to run the experiment. The tailored shocks were administered through such methods as the viewing of violent movie footage that would have a particular emotional impact to that individual, such as a World War II fighter pilot veteran watching a film of an airplane being shot down. In such a case, as the ex-pilot squirmed in his chair, creating electromagnetic frequency changes in his Galvanic Skin Response, his cheek cells squirmed in the next room in the same measurable way. Another example would be to leave a young man in a room with a pornographic magazine, and to then barge into the room after he had started looking at it, creating a rush of embarrassment. His cells showed the same response in the next room.

Perhaps the most amazing aspect of this research was that distance was determined not to be a factor. Cheek cells from a person in the United States could be shipped over to Russia, and the effect was still instantaneously measurable. Therefore, shocks and negative emotions in the mind are instantaneously moving throughout the cells of the body and affecting them, whether those cells are connected to the body or not!

Separated Cells Spontaneously Reunite

Other pieces of evidence cited by independent researcher Tim Harwood[25] show that the same energy that connects the cells of an organism at a distance can be responsible for pulling them back together. At the turn of the twentieth century, a researcher named Henry Williams pressed living sea sponges through a cloth until they were deconstructed into individual cells. However, in a very short period of time the cells would spontaneously reunite and form new sponges. This was also duplicated by T. Humphreys, 1963. And along the same lines, A.A. Moscona in 1959 observed the same behavior with kidney and heart cells. Harwood also points out the little-known fact that once a caterpillar forms a hard outer chrysalis in the process of metamorphosis, it dissolves into a nutrient broth before becoming a butterfly. This broth does not have any visible cells or DNA as we now know it, yet within this liquid the DNA and cells spontaneously emerge, eventually creating the butterfly.

Transmission of DNA between Organisms

The case for a "DNA life wave" is made complete by the Russian physicists Dr. Yu V. Dzang Kangeng and Dr. Peter Gariaev (the DNA Phantom co-discoverer). As written in a recent article by Dr. Gariaev,[26] and in another Russian physics article by Drs. Nachalov and Sokolov,[27] Dr. Kangeng was able to use a high-powered electrostatic energy source to generate torsion waves that transferred the energetic DNA code of a duck into a hen.[28, 29] The duck was placed in a five-sided room about the size of a hat box with a parabolic domed roof, and on each of the five walls in the room, a funnel was placed with the tip pointing away from the center. Then, narrow copper pipes were routed between the open ends of each funnel and on into a second room, which was shaped like a rectangle, and had the hen placed within it. A roughly two-gigahertz electrostatic generator was placed inside the five-sided room. The idea behind this experiment was that the electrostatic energy would generate powerful torsion waves that would strike the duck's DNA, causing the waves to pick up the duck's characteristic patterns. Then, just like a pyramid, each funnel would capture these waves and direct them through the copper pipes into the adjacent box.

After as little as five days of exposure, the rapidly-developing embryos within the pregnant hen would be genetically reprogrammed at the DNA level into duck-hen hybrid creatures that would hatch and live a normal, healthy life. In Gariaev's own words, this is what happened:

[The] hybrid chickens of [the] hens [in this experiment] had typical features of a duck—a flat beak, an elongated neck and larger internal organs (heart, liver, stomach and bowels). The weight of a one-year-old hen-duck hybrid was 70% higher than the weight of hens grown from irradiated eggs. The second generation of the hen-duck hybrids retained all changes which were obtained in the first generation, even without further re-radiation. A wave transfer of peanuts' features to sunflower seeds resulted in the change of form, taste and odor of the hybrid plant, which became similar to those of peanuts. Productivity grew by 1.8-fold; new features are transferred from one generation to another even without further re-radiation. (http://www.emergentmind.org/gariaev12.htm)

Additionally, in Nachalov and Sokolov's paper, we find that the duck-hen hybrids had webbing between their toes, although normal chickens do not.

Just as this book goes to press, my associate Dr. Terry Bugno sent me an email which gives priceless support to Kangeng's discovery. As written in the German-only book *Vernetze Intelligenz* by von Graznya Fosar and Franz Bludorf (www.fosar-bludorf.com; ISBN# 3930243237), Russian biophysicist Peter Gariaev was able to use a "vibrational wave" of "DNA information patterns" to transform hermetically-sealed frog embryos into salamander embryos, "without any of the side effects or disharmonies encountered when cutting out and re-introducing single genes from the DNA."[30] These transformed frog embryos grew into fully healthy adult salamanders, as if nothing abnormal had happened—as if they had been born salamanders, not frogs. The intense, concentrated light of a laser beam was the method used to carry this information from the salamander embryo to the frog embryo, and in *The Divine Cosmos* we discuss how laser light also creates spiraling torsion waves as it travels. Hence, the DNA molecule is like a programmable piece of hardware for the energy of the soul, so that if you change the energy wave that moves through it, the jumping DNA will encode it into a completely different form. It is therefore possible that as we move into increasingly "intelligent" zones of energy in the galaxy, the DNA energy patterns for the creatures on the planet are all upgraded, and the mutations occur so rapidly—well within one lifetime—that no "transitional" fossils exist.

This would also explain why a reincarnating soul will take on similar facial features from one lifetime to another. It also helps to explain why it is often said that "people look like their pets," and why couples end up looking more alike as they continue aging together.

So, we are also being programmed by the galactic center to become more advanced while we are still here in our bodies. We may not look any different on the outside yet, but we are definitely changing inside. This explains the exponential increases in our consciousness, literacy, spiritual, and technological advancement that have been observed just in the last century. Cornell University researchers have discovered that overall IQ scores have tended to rise by 5 to 25 points every 15 to 20 years, requiring the scoring system for IQ tests to be continually readjusted.[31] Taken together, all of these changes will probably lead to a physical transformation at some point as well, similar to the idea of the Ascension of the master Jesus.

Loving Energy Expands the DNA Molecule

The last DNA-related scientific evidence that I will present at this time comes from Dr. Glen Rein.[32] In this case, undifferentiated cells were extracted from a human placenta and placed into tubes. Then these tubes were given to people trained in producing strong, accurate human emotions. If such a person wants to feel anger, for example, then they do not just "pretend" to be angry—they have all the physiological responses that a person in rage normally would. If the person wants to be sad, then they will literally break down crying. If the person wants to feel love and compassion, then it is just as genuine as that which can be felt between a mother and a newborn child.

After these different emotions had been strongly experienced by the test participants, the DNA that they had been holding in the tubes was analyzed. Dr. Rein found that when the people felt anger or other negative emotions, the DNA contracted and knotted up like a braid of hair. However, when the people felt love, gratitude, and compassion, the DNA would unwind.

This experiment is very important for several reasons. First of all, it gives a solid connection between love and torsion waves, showing that love is the primary emotional/energetic quality that forms the DNA and is causing evolution to occur. Secondly, it is only when DNA unwinds that messenger RNA is capable of accessing its codes to provide for the healing of the body. So, when a person feels anger, stress, sadness, boredom, and depression, their DNA remains tightly braided, and the body cannot access the information that is necessary for it to heal itself. When a person feels love, compassion, and gratitude, their body can then heal in a natural fashion. The Edgar Cayce readings always said that health problems began as a spiritual issue long before they became physical issues, and that no physical healing could occur if the spiritual/psychological issues were not addressed at the same time.

The Transformation of the Solar System

Now that we have assembled quite a case for the connection between energy, intelligence, DNA, and evolution, the final myth to be shattered is the idea that "nothing much has changed" in the solar system. Some people acknowledge global warming but state that it is simply the result of human pollution, nothing more. Others recognize that such things as an increase in earthquake and solar activity cannot be caused by humanity in any conventional sense. However, it is still the case that very few people are aware that these changes are going on throughout the entire solar system.

The work of Dr. Aleskey Dmitriev entitled "Planetophysical State of the Earth and Life"[33] gives critical information to validate the concept that the solar system is undergoing a massive energetic change at this time. Dr. Dmitriev is a professor of geology and mineralogy and the chief scientific member of the United Institute of Geology, Geophysics and Mineralogy, within the Siberian department of the Russian Academy of Sciences. His work is published in English on the Millennium Group website, at www.tmgnow.com.

Changes of the Earth

Everyone knows that there are changes occurring on the Earth. A recent United Nations study showed that fully 600,000 plant and animal species have gone extinct since 1950, with as much as two-thirds of all species on Earth threatened with extinction within another hundred years.[34] This is the fastest rate of extinction since the dinosaurs disappeared sixty-five million years ago. Many would like to believe, almost without question, that these changes are entirely caused by the rapid industrial growth of human civilization. However, when we start looking at the facts throughout the Earth and solar system at large, it certainly is not that simple. I believe that energetic causes are at work here, especially if you remember our discussion about the 26-million-year evolutionary cycle at the beginning of this section of the book.

As anyone can see, Earth's weather patterns have become increasingly chaotic, damaging, and unpredictable. We have hurricanes, typhoons, tornadoes, mudslides, floods, droughts, and other catastrophes occurring on an ever-increasing basis. Furthermore, the Intergovernmental Panel on Climate Change has reported that global warming is no longer a myth—"the average surface temperature around the globe has risen by about 1 degree Farenheit since 1880."[35]

One could argue that the unchained force of nature is a far wider threat to Americans than terrorism. Dr. Aleskey Dmitriev's calculations suggest that "The dynamic growth of significant catastrophes shows a major increase in the rate of production since 1973. And in general, the number of catastrophes has grown by 410% between 1963 and 1993." Furthermore, a researcher named Michael Mandeville has clearly shown that worldwide, the number of earthquakes over 2.5 on the Richter scale has increased by as much as 400% since 1973.[36] Volcanic activity has also seen an almost 500% increase between 1875 and 1993.[37]

Now we must keep in mind how *unusual* all of these changes are, from a scientific standpoint. Conventional science has no explanation for these things. And not only do we see things going on within the Earth, but we see changes in the atmosphere as well, which Dmitriev says are *not* being caused by human pollution. As one example, we have seen a significant new growth of hydroperoxyl gas at an altitude of eleven miles, which is completely inexplicable by any known source or mechanism, including ozone depletion or human pollution.

Another curious anomaly is the phenomenon of La Niña or El Niño. On our weather satellite photographs there is clear infrared data that a massive heating of the Earth's oceans is now occurring. These heat increases are occurring well *below the surface of the ocean, so the Sun's rays are by no means strong enough to be causing it. This suggests that the oceans are being heated from within the Earth itself.*[38]

Furthermore, Dr. Dmitriev has shown that the strength of the Earth's magnetic field rises up and down in direct synchronization with these temperature changes in the ocean. This shows that the Earth's magnetic field is mysteriously interlinked with the Earth's temperature, which suggests that all of these processes are related to an outside energy change.

We can also see this increased heat energy with the rapid melting of our polar icecaps. The Ross Ice Shelf of Antarctica, which is as large as the state of Rhode Island, fully broke off and dropped into the ocean in the year 2000,[39] as have several others in the last decade.[40] Many scientists have come forward to admit that the polar icecap melt is far more rapid than they could have ever imagined. A recent United Nations study found that there has been nearly a 40% decrease in the average thickness of Arctic sea ice in just the last thirty years.[41] On October 17, 2003, the *London Guardian* published a study from a team led by Eric Rignot of the Jet Propulsion Laboratory in Pasadena, California, which showed that "glaciers in Argentina and Chile are melting at double the rate of 1975 because of global warming."[42]

Lastly, as this book goes to press, Agence France Presse has announced that the world's largest iceberg B15, the size of Jamaica, has split in half.[43]

Now if you remember that the temperature of the oceans is rising and falling along with the magnetic field, then you might expect that our magnetic field would be changing in other ways as well. And indeed, the Novosibirsk Klyuchi Observatory in Russia has reported that the height of the magnetic field is increasing by up to thirty nanoteslas per year.[44]

The magnetic poles have been rapidly shifting as well, currently estimated at a rate of acceleration that is 150% above normal, which may lead up to what many authorities believe will be a complete flip in their north-south orientation. This shift is occurring so rapidly that airports all over the world are having to redraw their runways to follow the Earth's changing magnetic field, since airplanes use compasses to land.

Dr. Dmitriev and others remind us that as the Earth's magnetic poles continue to drift, they are traveling through a "magnetic pole shift corridor," which is a narrow strip of the Earth's geography that the poles have followed in the past prior to a complete reversal. Such reversals are not unusual throughout history. There is an increasing number of solid data points to suggest that such a shift is coming, as discussed in the *Convergence* series. More and more scientists, including those in the mainstream, are coming to the conclusion that this is going to happen at some point in the relatively near future.

So based on this idea, many researchers have concluded that such a pole shift will cause a tremendous cataclysm that will extinguish human civilization as we know it. It is important for us to state here that most people do not understand the metaphysical implications of this energetic change; it appears that this is definitely not intended to be a disaster, but rather a spontaneous transformation of matter, energy, and consciousness.

Changes of the Sun

We can clearly see that there are changes going on within and around the Earth; so now we will turn our focus towards the Sun, where we find similar anomalies and many clues that its behavior is changing in much the same way that of the Earth is.

A team at the Rutherford Appleton Laboratory near Oxford, England, led by Dr. Mike Lockwood, discovered that in the last century, the overall strength of the Sun's magnetic field more than doubled, becoming *230% stronger than it was in 1901*.[45] And more recently, Dr. Richard Wilson of NASA's Goddard Institute for Space Studies concluded that the Sun's total energetic output has increased by .05% per decade since at least the late 1970s.[46] This might not seem like very much, but it is important to remember that the Sun is so huge—fully 99.86% of all the mass in the solar system—that the planets are mere specks of dust in comparison. So, as Wilson says, "This trend is important because, if sustained over many decades, it could cause significant climate change.... Solar activity has apparently been going upward for a century or more."

Dr. Aleskey Dmitriev is arguably the best source for breakthrough research in this area, known as *heliophysics*. As he reports in his paper "Planetophysical State of the Earth and Life" at www.tmgnow.com, "As a whole, all of the reporting and observation facilities give evidence to a growth in the *velocity, quality, quantity, and energetic power* of our solar system's heliospheric properties." (Emphasis mine.) The heliosphere is the magnetic field that emanates from the Sun, surrounding our solar system and extending beyond it.

Every eleven years the Sun's total activity peaks in a constantly-repeating "solar cycle," and this solar maximum has again peaked in the period of 1999 to 2003, showing no signs of declining yet. The last solar minimum was in 1996, and the appearance of the Sun at such a time is dramatically different than during a maximum—like the difference between the surface of a still lake and one that is being rained on. The study that we just mentioned about the Sun's total increase in energetic output is a result of taking the combined average throughout the entire eleven-year cycle.

During the previous solar maximum in March of 1989, a very powerful X-ray flare on March 5 led to the Sun emitting a stream of high-energy protons, which flowed to the Earth continuously until March 13. This caused the Earth's magnetic poles to deviate by a whopping eight degrees in only a few hours, the most substantial sudden change in Earth's magnetic field since 1952. This event also caused serious disruption of communications systems, created intense aurora borealis phenomena, and completely collapsed the Canadian power grid, with more than a million people losing their electricity for several days.

Furthermore, Dr. Aleskey Dmitriev has correlated intense solar emissions with Earth phenomena, including severe weather such as hurricanes and tornadoes, earthquakes, and volcanic activity. So as the Sun's energy output continues to increase, all other energy processes on the Earth will accelerate as well.

Arguably the ultimate energy release from our Sun comes from what are known as coronal mass ejections. In these cases, the entire Sun releases a super-flash of energy over much of its surface simultaneously, which travels out into space as a halo-like expanding bubble that can contain up to ten billion tons of electrified gas.

In keeping with our theory, Dr. Dmitriev explains that with each passing year, these super-flashes are actually traveling *faster* through space than ever before! This is analogous to why you can swim faster in water than molasses; interplanetary space has become a better conductor.

One example of this is the two coronal mass ejections that occurred April 10, 2001, following a record-breaking solar flare on

April 2. Then, on April 11, a rash of severe tornadoes, some a quarter of a mile wide, ripped through the Midwestern United States, affecting Kansas, Iowa, Oklahoma, Missouri, and Nebraska. Furthermore, a 5.7 earthquake occurred in Indonesia on April 7, a 5.9 earthquake on April 13 in China that destroyed 30,000 homes, and a 6.5 on April 15 off the coast of Japan. All this was within days of the solar activity. Most scientists would not be willing to acknowledge the connection between solar activity and events such as these, but the timing cannot be discounted. Solar emissions spiral into the Earth's energy field and trigger massive changes. All these events clustered around April 10.

In short, this most recent solar maximum cycle has been so unusually energetic that George Withbroe, Science Director for NASA's Sun-Earth Connection Program, issued a statement in 2000 saying, "This is a unique solar maximum in history. The images and data are beyond the wildest expectations of the astronomers of a generation ago."[47] And the gigantic X-38 flare of November 4, 2003, which we mentioned in the "Scientific Blueprint for Ascension" chapter, led Dr. Paal Brekke, deputy project scientist for the Solar Heliospheric Observatory (SOHO) Sun-monitoring satellite, to tell BBC News Online that "I think the last week will go into the history books as one of the most dramatic solar activity periods we have seen in modern times. As far as I know there has been nothing like this before."[48]

Dr. Brekke may not have been aware of another study that was revealed three days earlier in *New Scientist* magazine, from Ilya Usoskin, a geophysicist who worked with colleagues from the University of Oulu in Finland and the Max Planck Institute for Aeronomy in Katlenberg-Lindau, Germany. Usoskin and associates calculated that "there have been more sunspots since the 1940s than for the past 1150 years."[49] This was discovered through analyzing the visual record of sunspots since the seventeenth century and correlating it with the concentration of radioactive beryllium-10 in ice cores from Greenland and Antarctica.

Changes in the Heliosphere

The heliosphere, the teardrop-shaped egg of energy that surrounds our solar system—is created by the Sun's magnetic field. As the heliosphere drifts through the galaxy, it is not drifting through empty space. Rather, it is reacting with the local particles and energy in our area of the galaxy, known as the Local Interstellar Medium or LISM. This energetic interaction forms an observable area of visible light, or plasma, which was measured by the Russians in the late 1960s to be three to four astronomical units deep at the leading front edge of the heliosphere.[50] NASA did not start trying to measure this same area until 1978.[51]

No one expected the size of this plasma cloud in the front to change, but by 1997 it was being registered at forty astronomical units instead of four, fully 1000% deeper within thirty years! And if that weren't enough, the most recent measurements have revealed that it now may be as much as sixty-five to seventy astronomical units in depth. So something big is going on here.

Furthermore, Dmitriev and other Russian scientists have noticed that since the 1960s, our Local Interstellar Medium has distinctly changed. It is now showing significantly higher concentrations of matter and energy, including charged particles of hydrogen, helium, and hydroxyl in addition to other new combinations of elements. And this is what is causing the brightness increase mentioned earlier.

Although the West has always lagged behind the Russians in the scientific arena, they are finally catching up. As of August 2003, an ESA/NASA experiment called DUST, launched with the *Ulysses* satellite in 1990, has discovered that there is 300% more dust from our galaxy entering the solar system now than there was throughout all of the 1990s.[52] More dust and more charged particles means more energy, more *density,* which is exactly the word Ra used to describe this new intergalactic zone.

Many have asked why NASA is not discussing this if in fact it is true. Professor D.E. Shemansky of UCLA is one of the only specialists in the Western world who has suggested that the energy around us in the galaxy is changing. On his website, he says that NASA has shown a "persistent, pernicious bias" against this work, making sure that it never gets published or even mentioned.[53] So far the secret has been kept very well, even from the metaphysical community.

Changes of the Planets

Dr. Dmitriev's research on the planets shows accelerations in the speed of magnetic pole shifts, climate changes, earthquakes, and cyclones on Earth, increased magnetic and plasma energy charges on other planets, and changes in their atmospheric qualities. In addition, some of the planets are actually becoming noticeably brighter.

Below are mentioned some of the highlights of the planetary changes from this new body of data, which I have continued to update and compile after Dr. Dmitriev's initial findings.

In Dmitriev's original paper, the planet Pluto seemed to be the only disappointment, as there wasn't very much data to suggest that anything had changed in its energetic state except a "change in the distribution of light and dark spots." However, as of September 2002, a team of top-notch scientists led by James Eliot, professor of planetary astronomy at MIT, discovered that even though Pluto has been drifting away from the Sun since 1989, there has been a 300% increase in its atmospheric pressure in just the previous fourteen years, causing a noticeable rise in surface temperatures.[54] And yet, these experts say that Pluto's global warming was "likely not connected with that of the Earth" since the "Sun's output is much too steady." The facts we have shared above suggest otherwise.

As the *Voyager* space probe passed Neptune, the magnetic field was nearly 50 degrees offset from the north-south rotational axis, suggesting that a magnetic pole shift may have taken place sometime within the last century.[55] Also, observations by the University of Wisconsin-Madison, headed by Dr. Lawrence Sromovsky, show that in just six years between 1996 and 2002, Neptune has become 40% brighter in the 850- to 1000-nanometer band of light, which is considered the near-infrared range.[56] Certain "cloud bands" at fixed latitudes on Neptune have become fully 100% brighter in the visible range during this same period of time. This effect has become so pronounced that Neptune is now significantly brighter in its visible appearance than the dim sphere of blue that most of us are familiar with from the *Voyager* days. It literally appears as if Neptune got "turned on" like a lampshade that is suddenly throwing off light. Although they cannot explain these changes with their model, saying that Neptune "seems to run on almost no energy," Sromovsky et al. attribute this to a "seasonal" change, meaning that it will continue increasing for another twenty years before again moving into a decline. Yet, such a "seasonal" change is obviously affecting Pluto as well.

Voyager also saw that the magnetic field of Uranus was nearly 60 degrees out of balance with the rotational axis, again suggesting that a magnetic pole shift has taken place within the last century. Furthermore, Dmitriev's research indicates that the magnetic field of Uranus has shown an "abrupt, large-scale growth" in its intensity.

Brightly colored auroras were observed on Saturn in the late 1990s, clearly indicating energetic charge. These brightness changes have been directly correlated with solar activity. Most auroras cluster near the poles, and we can see the dramatic energy increases there in the infrared spectrum.

Jupiter has shown a 200% increase in the intensity of its magnetic field since 1992, and its total brightness has also increased. The charge has since become so high that a tube of glowing plasma energy has formed between the planet and its moon Io, at an unbelievable electromagnetic strength of one million amperes. This is a visible phenomenon, which appears as a gigantic white circle that emerges from the north and south pole of Jupiter, stretching over to intersect with the north and south pole of Io, as if both planets were connected like beads on a bracelet. This tube is so powerful that it actually stretches the clouds at the north and south pole of Jupiter in the direction of Io, wherever it is in its orbital pattern.

The atmosphere of Mars has shown definite signs of growth, as reported by Dr. Dmitriev, including an apparent 200% increase in the density of its atmosphere as of 1997, an increase in the amount of ozone, and the appearance of more clouds than ever seen before. Even NASA is saying, "Mars may be in the midst of a profound climate change."[57] In December of 2001 NASA released photographic images showing a dramatic increase in the speed with which the Martian polar icecaps are melting, with features having eroded away by up to 50% just since 1999.[58] Of course, there is not even one word in the article about any connection between this and the global warming on Earth.

We have already covered the changes of the Earth in detail, including massive increases in earthquakes and volcanoes, with a 410% overall increase in catastrophes from 1963 to 1993, as well as anomalous changes in the chemical composition of the atmosphere. Furthermore, there is a new outer layer of what is being called "interstellar matter" in the Van Allen Belts, with qualities that are normally seen only in stars. The most recent diagrams of Earth's magnetic field give these layers a yellow-orange color and label them the "New Belt."[59]

The moon has a new atmosphere of sodium and potassium ions seen in ground-based observations in 1988, which were not detected at the time of the *Apollo* missions in the late 1960s.[60]

The planet Venus has shown a sharp decrease in the amount of sulfur-containing gases, a reversal in the areas of light and dark spots, and a significant increase in its overall brightness.[61]

The 26,000-Year Cycle and the Mayan Calendar

As we have now seen, there is a wide variety of events occurring all throughout our solar system. These effects appear to be caused by our movement through organized layers of energy in the galaxy, which can be measured by a master time cycle.

The evidence suggests that the master time cycle that we are now working with can be measured by a slow counter-rotating wobble in the Earth's axis that takes about 26,000 years to complete, or Plato's "ideal" number of 25,920 years. (As explained in the *Convergence* series, Plato's number was based on his research into the connection between numbers, harmony, and vibration—the more ways a number can be divided, the more it "vibrates.") This 26,000-year Earth cycle is known as the precession of the equinoxes, or "precession" for short. This causes the visible positions of the stars in the night sky to move by one degree every 72 years. Controversial evidence uncovered by Zecharia Sitchin, Graham Hancock, and others suggests that this cycle was known throughout many ancient cultures, including the Egyptians, Hindus, Sumerians, and Maya, and may well be traced back some 12,500 years into the past or more.

In the book *Shift of the Ages* on my website ascension2000.com, I have reprinted data from Maurice Cotterell in his book *The Mayan Prophecies,* which leads us to solid evidence that this same 26,000-year cycle shows up in the Sun. I theorize that this is a demonstration of the fact that both the Sun and the Earth are being directly influenced by strips or zones of energy that we regularly pass through in the galaxy. It is also interesting to note that a 26,000-year cycle is a thousand times smaller than a 26-million-year cycle (the length of time between mass extinctions/evolutionary events in the Earth's fossil record), suggesting that the two are harmonically interrelated.

The Mayan Calendar has pinpointed the end of this cycle as occurring on December 22, 2012, which fits nicely with official estimates regarding the end point for the Earth's precession. Mayan scholar John Major Jenkins,[62] the author of *Maya Cosmogenesis 2012* and several other books, has proven that surrounding this time of the Winter Solstice, the Earth's axis will be in a perfect alignment with the center of the galaxy. This only happens once in the entire 26,000-year period of time. Ancient cultures such as the Maya touted this galactic conjunction as the beginning of a new world. Other evidence discussed in *The Divine Cosmos* suggests that we will finally "cross the line" from one energy level to another, like crossing a line that has formed between oil and water, as of December 22, 2012. This may or may not produce immediate results, but the evidence is certainly compelling.

As Above, So Below

To conclude, another interesting "factoid" concerns the relationship between the human being and the cosmos itself. In Richard Pasichnyk's *The Vital Vastness, Volume Two,* he reveals that when you average together the dimensions of the planets in the Solar System, you get the exact geometric average between the size of the universe and the size of an atom.[63] The mass of a human being is the geometric average between the mass of a planet and the mass of a proton. This is actually just one small part of the case that we make in *The Divine Cosmos* which suggests that the universe behaves similarly on every level of energy. Whether we study an atom, a fruit, a human being, a tree, a planet, a solar system, a galaxy, a supercluster, or the visible universe, the same laws always apply. Hence, "as above, so below." We can also state that like a hologram or a fractal, every minute part of our Universe contains the image of the One Creator, including ourselves. In the deepest sense, We Are One.[64]

Summary

In this chapter, we have covered the following topics:

- the complete lack of evidence for transitional fossils as needed in the Darwinian model
- the 26-million-year cycles of species evolution
- the connection between consciousness and torsion-field energy
- the evidence for structured, regular torsion-field energy zones in the galaxy
- the effect of our position in the galaxy on matter and energy
- the miracles of pyramid power, showing a connection between energy, DNA, and the Earth's health

- the effect of our position in the galaxy on consciousness
- the effect of consciousness on the DNA molecule
- the current solar-system-wide energetic transformation now taking place.

The energy of our DNA is all around us—living information written into the very fabric of space and time. The idea of an "Ascension" taking place on Earth, and dramatically affecting the evolution of the human species, is not a one-time-only, scientifically unfounded event. We have an ample historical record of mass evolution events that have repeated in even cycles of time—and like all life that has come before us, we should assume that we *also* can and will evolve. In Kangeng's experiment, a great source of energy from an electromagnetic generator was required to send the DNA energy waves of the duck into the embryos of the hen, which then hatched into healthy duck-hen hybrid creatures that could sexually reproduce with each other and produce more "duckhens." In Gariaev's experiment, a great source of energy from a concentrated beam of electromagnetic energy (a laser) was used to completely transform frog embryos into salamander embryos, which grew into healthy adult salamanders without any of the complications of gene-splicing. For the Ascension process now underway, a "great source of energy" has indeed been identified. It is actively transforming our entire solar system, considerably raising the average IQ of a human being and producing a global awakening of consciousness. The most important defining characteristic of this "great source of energy" is Love, the very energy that lengthens and untangles our DNA in Dr. Glen Rein's experiments, allowing healing to occur. If Love is the primary motivation behind our thoughts and actions towards others, then we are more than adequately prepared for the changes still ahead. No matter what experiences come our way, all we have to do is ask, "Where is the love in this moment?" I wish you well on your path and remind you that you are loved more than you could ever possibly imagine.

Appendix

A Poem by Wynn Free

The poem below was written before I met David Wilcock. It was written from my own intuitive sensibilities prior to being exposed to Wilcock's message of planetary shift, but on some level I must have sensed it.

Urgent
I feel the urgency in the air
To complete the things in my life I've left hanging.
I feel the urgency to reach out to everyone I can touch,
And make whatever difference I can.
I feel the urgency to reach into the depth of my soul
To find the words that would have meaning to you.
I understand the fragility of life,
And how fast life can pass.
The world is moving at breakneck speed,
Like a runaway train with consequences unknown,
And we're all aboard for the ride of our lives.
The clock is ticking.
It's getting frantic.
Urgency is in the air.
Reach into your heart and find peace.
Reach for your fellow man and find empathy.
Reach for God and find your soul.
It's urgent.
Do it now.

Resources

There is a wealth of free information on the website of David Wilcock at www.ascension2000.com, including the complete texts of most of the readings and discussions in this book. Consult David's website for more information about music, DVD and published book availability.

In addition, you can find various items for sale, along with notice of future books and events, at www.reincarnationofedgar.com/resources, including:

From Eternity to Here by Wynn Free—a collection of original poems

Musical CD by Wynn Free—a collection of Wynn's songs

Lastly, at the website http://www.llresearch.org, you can order various products associated with the *Law of One* series, including audio-tape recordings, T-shirts, Carla Rueckert's revered latest book *Wanderer's Handbook,* and, of course, all five books of the *Law of One* series.

Glossary

A.R.E.—The Association for Research and Enlightenment, founded by the children of Edgar Cayce to perpetuate his readings. Located in Virginia Beach, Virginia.

Ascension—The process whereby an entity "graduates" from one dimension to the next.

Astrological Chart—A circular graph that shows the positions of the astrological signs, the planets, and the houses at the time of one's birth. Can be used to indicate predispositions, habits, and personality.

Atlantis—According to the Edgar Cayce readings, Atlantis was a continent containing a civilization of advanced technology which was destroyed by an inundation around 10,500 B.C. Edgar Cayce in his life as Ra-Ta helped save a small group of Turks by giving forewarning of the impending cataclysm and providing a safe haven in Egypt.

Catalyst—As given by Ra in the *Law of One* series from L/L Research, a catalyst is a stimulus for growth, something that presents a challenge and an opportunity to learn a lesson.

Channel—An individual who channels.

Channeling—The process whereby an entity or group of entities in another density (dimension) communicates with/through an individual in this dimension.

Confederation of Planets—An interdimensional organization of representatives of different planetary systems whose purpose is to regulate life in our solar system. Similar to the intent of the United Nations.

Crop Circles—Geometric forms and pictures that are often created in agricultural fields using the foliage as the creative medium. Their manner of creation is not known, and many attribute crop circles to interdimensional sources or ETs trying to signal us about their existence. Wilcock believes that the geometric forms are representative of the existence of other dimensions.

Density—Density of consciousness, or density of vibration (*Law of One* series, Book Four, p. 28). Frequently used by Ra as an analog to what are currently thought of as "dimensions" in the universe. The densities are organized into an eight-fold "octave" system, analogous to the musical octave:

FIRST DENSITY: The cycle of awareness
SECOND DENSITY: Growth
THIRD DENSITY: Self-awareness
FOURTH DENSITY: Love or understanding
FIFTH DENSITY: Light or wisdom
SIXTH DENSITY: Light/love, love/light, or unity
(also frequently referred to as *compassionate wisdom*)
SEVENTH DENSITY: The gateway cycle (also frequently referred to as that density where one perceives the *sacramental nature of all things*)

Dimension—Same as density.

Dimensional Shift—A period where a planet changes its density from one level to another. According to Wilcock and Ra, Earth is in the midst of a dimensional shift from third density to fourth density.

Distortion—Anything that may erroneously be seen as a separate or individual unit (since all is One,) including all philosophical ideas, teachings, and concepts related to Oneness, as well as such things as the nature of light in the different densities, since there is only One Light that has "distorted" itself into an Octave. The frequent use of the word "distortion" has been a stumbling block for many readers of Ra, as it can apply to almost anything and is usually not considered to be a negative term. At times Ra refers to their *own* teachings being distortions, as they themselves have not fully penetrated the Octave and returned to Oneness.

DNA—The basic building block of all life. The coding within DNA determines the growth pattern of a life form. According to Wilcock and Ra, the dimensional shift is causing the DNA on Earth to change its codes to accommodate higher-dimensional energies.

Dream Voice—The name that Wilcock gave to the voice that provides him with messages when he awakes from sleep or goes into a light trance. He later found out that this voice was Ra.

Group Soul—Same as "social memory complex."

Harvest—The process whereby a soul and/or planet "graduates" from one density to the next. Occurs naturally as a planetary system traverses different areas of energy density in the galaxy, thus creating dimensional shifts in precise, measurable cycles of time. Wilcock believes Earth is in the process of such a shift.

Higher Self—The Higher Self is an extended part of oneself living in a higher dimension. It is the part of one's multidimensionality that inspires dreams and intuitions. It could be looked at as a harbinger of what we will evolve to and exist as in the future. The Higher Self is the liaison between our conscious self and God, a.k.a. the One Infinite Creator, as well as whatever group souls are in the pathway.

Instrument—Another term for a channel.

Interdimensional—Relates to crossing or communicating from one dimension to another, as in channeling.

Isis—Another name for Isris.

Isris—The dancer who seduced Ra-Ta in Edgar Cayce's past life in Egypt.

John Bainbridge—The previous lifetime of Edgar Cayce in the 1800s in America. Bainbridge was a gambler and womanizer.

Law of Free Will—For those wishing to evolve spiritually in the service-to-others path, there shall be no infringement on the free will of others, and service shall be rendered only when requested.

Law of One—According to Ra: "You are every thing, every being, every emotion, every situation. You are unity. You are infinity. You are love/light, light/love. You are. This is the Law of One."

Level One—A light trance akin to hypnosis.

Level Two—Wilcock's description of Level Two channeling: "In Level Two, entire sentences would appear in my mind all at once, or at least sentence fragments. I would have to pull myself out far enough so that I could record what I got, and then go back in to get more of it."

Level Three—Wilcock's description of Level Three channeling:

"Level Three is where you could go into the Akashic Records of the area around you and get information. For example, you could diagnose someone's knee problem or read the vibes of what happened in a room previously."

Level Four—Wilcock's description of Level Four channeling: "In Level Four, I was unaware of anything past a maximum of about three words at a time, and they were words that would be within an ongoing sentence. I would say whatever group of words I got between one and three as one unit, and keep on going like that to form sentences. So in Level Four the material got a lot more coherent, and I started to realize that with that level of consciousness, it was starting to get to a point that people might actually be interested in reading it for some sort of spiritual benefit."

Level Five—A deeper trance state than Level Four, where the mind is almost completely disengaged from any awareness of the content of the words coming through.

Light—The generic metaphysical term for Ra's "spiraling lines of light" or Wilcock's "torsion wave energy."

Logos—Creator God of the universe. The nature of the logos is love.

Maldek—According to Ra, in the distant past there was a population of third-density beings upon a former planet called Maldek within the solar system. They had a civilization similar to Atlantis (*Law of One* series, Book One, p. 109). After destroying their planet, they came to Earth. It was the only planet in the solar system that was livable and capable of offering the lessons necessary to decrease their distortions with respect to the Law of One. Many of Earth's present population are of Maldekian descent. When the planet exploded, the Asteroid Belt was created.

Mayan Calendar—This is a calendar that according to some theories was given to the Mayans by interdimensional sources. The end date of the calendar is the year 2012. The Edgar Cayce readings said that the Mayans had been visited by extraterrestrials.

One Infinite Creator—The original source of all creation.

Oversoul—The name of an individualized segment of a group soul which is taking the position as someone's Higher Self or inner guide.

Ra—The name of the "social memory complex" or "group soul" that is the source of David Wilcock's channelings and the hypothe-sized Source of Edgar Cayce. Also the name of the Egyptian Sun God, which was an early life of Edgar Cayce in Egypt.

Ra-Ta—The name that Edgar Cayce used to refer to his early life-time in Egypt, circa 10,500 B.C.

Reincarnation—The process by which a soul re-embodies over many lifetimes as the lessons of different densities are learned.

Service to Others—The path of evolution where the Law of Free Will is invoked, and others are seen and loved as the self.

Service to Self—The path of evolution that involves controlling and manipulating others. Those following the "service to self" path use fear, subservience, and the establishment of hierarchies as methods of control. The service-to-self path cannot sustain its vibration past the very beginning of sixth density, and must either integrate the pos-itive or dissolve from existence. At this point the Law of One becomes more fully operative, and others are experienced as a part of oneself, thus leading to a natural desire to love and serve them rather than manipulate them.

Social Memory Complex—A large group of completely integrated souls—a "group soul" for short.

Solar Cycles—The longer-period cycles that an entire solar system passes through. Edgar Cayce referred to "solar cycles" in his future prophecies but they were not acknowledged by science during his life. In our solar system, a solar cycle is 25,000 years and 75,000 years. According to Wilcock and Ra, we are at the end of a 75,000-year cycle, which is causing the Earth to enter a dimensional shift.

Spiraling Lines of Light—The term used by Ra in the L/L Research channelings for what Wilcock describes as torsion wave radiation. This energy pervades all space, originates from the "galactic center," and is the way the "One Infinite Creator" expands into the universe. "The spiraling energy, which is the characteristic of what you call 'light,' moves in a straight-line spiral thus giving spirals an inevitable vector upwards to a more comprehensive beingness with regard to intelligent infinity."—Ra/the *Law of One* series

Torsion Radiation—The current scientific term used by Russian scientists who have learned how to measure the invisible streaming energy called "spiraling light energy" by Ra.

Transposons—A term used by microbiologists to describe what is known as "jumping DNA," which are small segments of the DNA molecule that can detach from one area and re-attach to another, thus rewriting the code. From this, we can then see that our DNA is somewhat like a computer chip, with different sections that can either be "on" or "off." According to Wilcock, "torsion wave radiation" can reprogram these transposons, causing evolutionary changes. Human DNA is in the process of being reprogrammed by the increased energy resulting from the dimensional shift.

Veil of Forgetting—A necessary consequence of having a life in the third dimension. Because of the veil of forgetting, entities cannot remember their past lifetimes or experience their connection with other dimensions directly. According to Ra via L/L Research: "This is the only place of forgetting. It is necessary for the third-density entity to forget what it really is so that the mechanisms of confusion or free will may operate upon the newly individuated consciousness complex."

Wanderer—A higher-density soul that has volunteered to incarnate as human, with a contractual agreement to forget its true soul nature throughout its human life unless it consciously desires to seek the information.

Bibliography

Note: This is a general bibliography for Wynn Free's portion of this book. For references related to the science of Ascension (David Wilcock's writings), please see the detailed endnotes for Part Three.

Association for Research and Enlightenment, under the Editorship of Hugh Lynn Cayce. *The Edgar Cayce Reader.* New York: Warner Books, 1974.

Braden, Gregg. *Awakening to Zero Point: The Collective Initiation.* Bellevue, WA: Radio Bookstore Press, 1997.

Bro, Harmon Hartzell. *A Seer Out of Season: The Life of Edgar Cayce.* New York: a Signet Book, 1990.

Buhlman, William. *Adventures beyond the Body: How to Experience Out-of-Body Travel.* New York: HarperCollins Publishers, 1996.

Cayce, Edgar. Edgar Cayce Foundation, *The Complete Edgar Cayce Readings on CD-ROM,* 1995.

Church, W.H. *Many Happy Returns: The Lives of Edgar Cayce.* San Francisco: Harper & Row, 1984.

Johnson, K. Paul. *Edgar Cayce in Context: The Readings: Truth and Fiction.* New York: State University of New York, 1998.

Fast, Julius. *Body Language.* New York: Pocket Books, 1988.

Kirkpatrick, Sidney D. *Edgar Cayce, An American Prophet.* New York: Riverhead Books, 2000.

L/L Research, The Ra Material/*Law of One* series, Volumes 1 through 5. Atglen, PA: Schiffer Publishing, 1984.

LaBerge, Dr. Stephen. *Lucid Dreaming.* New York: Random House, 1990.

LaBerge, Dr. Stephen. *Exploring the World of Lucid Dreaming.* New York: Ballantine Books, 1997.

Mandelker, Scott. *From Elsewhere, Being E.T. in America.* New York: Carol Publishing Group, 1995.

Milanovich, Dr. Norma J., Betty Rice, and Cynthia Ploski. *We, The Arcturians.* Albuquerque, NM: Athena Publishing, 1990.

Montgomery, Ruth. *Aliens Among Us.* New York: Putnam Publishing Group, 1985.

Percival, H.W. *Thinking and Destiny.* New York: Word Foundation, 1995.

Recio, Belinda, and London, Eileen. *The Art of Dream Interpretation.* New York: A Bulfinch Book, Little Brown & Co., 2001.

Rueckert, Carla Lisbeth. *A Channeling Handbook.* Louisville, KY: L/L Research, 1987.

Rueckert, Carla Lisbeth. *A Wanderer's Handbook: An Owner's Manual for ETs and Other Spiritual Outsiders.* Louisville, KY: L/L Research, 2001.

Semkiw, Walter. *Return of the Revolutionaries.* Charlottesville, VA: Hampton Roads Publishing Company, Inc., 2002.

Sherman, Harold. *How to Make ESP Work for You.* New York: Fawcett-Crest, 1966.

Sitchin, Zecharia. *The Stairway to Heaven, Book II of the Earth Chronicles.* New York: Avon Books, 1980.

Smith, Robert A. *Edgar Cayce, My Life as a Seer: The Lost Memoirs.* New York: St. Martin's Paperbacks, 1997.

Stearn, Jess. *Edgar Cayce: The Sleeping Prophet.* New York: Bantam Books, 1967.

Stearn, Jess. *Intimates through Time, Edgar Cayce's Mysteries of Reincarnation.* New York: A Signet Book, 1993.

Sugrue, Thomas. *There is a River: The Story of Edgar Cayce.* New York: Holt, Reinhart and Winston, 1942.

Stevens, Jose, and Stevens, Lena S. *The Secrets of Shamanism: Tapping the Spirit Power within You.* New York: Avon Books, 1988.

Wilcock, David. *Convergence,* Volume 1: *The Shift of the Ages.*

http://ascension2000.com/Shift-of-the-Ages/index.htm. May 2000 (active as of November 2003).

Wilcock, David. *Convergence,* Volume 2: *The Science of Oneness.* http://ascension2000.com/ConvergenceIII/April 2001 (active as of November 2003).

Wilcock, David. *Convergence,* Volume 3: *Divine Cosmos.* http://ascension2000.com/DivineCosmos/. June 2002 (active as of November 2003).

Wilcock, David. *Convergence,* Volume 4: *Divine Nature* (still in progress as of this writing).

Wilcock, David. *Convergence,* Volume 5: *Divine Being* (still in progress as of this writing).

Wilcock, David. *Wanderer Awakening.* http://ascension2000.com/wanderer.htm. May 1999 (active as of November 2003).

Wilcock, Donald E. *Damn Right, I've Got the Blues: Buddy Guy and the Blues Roots of Rock-and-Roll.* San Francisco: Woodford Publishing, 1993.

Websites Referenced

Reincarnationofedgar.com—the website dedicated to this book

Ascension2000.com—the original website of David Wilcock

Divinecosmos.com—a newer website of David Wilcock

Llresearch.org—the website of Carla Rueckert and her husband Jim McCarty

Wynnfree.com—the poetry/music/writing website of the author of this book

Uri-geller.com—the website of Uri Geller

Spiritofmaat.com—the Web magazine founded by Drunvalo Melchizedek (where Wynn's interview with David Wilcock, excerpted and updated in this book, first appeared)

Are-cayce.com—the official site of the A.R.E. operated by the Cayce family, which represents the Cayce readings and ancillary products.

Edgarcayce.com—the location to buy books about Edgar Cayce

http://all-ez.com/cayce.htm—an unofficial site with many pages of outtakes from the Cayce readings

www.greatdreams.com—the website of Joe and Dee Mason, where people who have prophetic dreams post them.

Notes

Preface

[1]Website of David Wilcock: http://www.ascension2000.com/intro.html, "Introductory Essay on the Wilcock/Cayce/Ra Connection and the 'Mission'."

[2]Website of Uri Geller: http://www.uri-geller.com/official2.htm.

Chapter 1

[1]Global Consciousness Project: http://www.noosphere.princeton.edu.

[2]L/L Research, The Ra Material/*Law of One* series (Atglen, PA: Schiffer Publishing, 1984); www.llresearch.org.

Chapter 2

[1]http://reincarnation2002.com/_reincarnation/00000075.htm.

[2]Scott Mandelker, *From Elsewhere, Being E.T. in America* (New York: Carol Publishing Group, 1995).

[3]L/L Research, The Ra Material/*Law of One* series (Atglen, PA: Schiffer Publishing, 1984); www.llresearch.org.

[4]Mandelker, *From Elsewhere, Being E.T. in America,* pp. 233–234.

[5]William Buhlman, *Adventures Beyond the Body* (San Francisco: Harper, 1996).

[6]Edgar Cayce Foundation, 1995, *The Complete Edgar Cayce Readings on CD-ROM,* File 2012–001.

[7]Website of David Wilcock, http://www.ascension2000.com, *Convergence* Series.

Chapter 3

[1]Harmon Hartzell Bro, *A Seer Out of Season: The Life of Edgar Cayce* (New York: A Signet Book, 1990), pp. 397–398.

[2]Edgar Cayce Foundation, 1995, *The Complete Edgar Cayce Readings on CD-ROM,* File 5755–001.

[3]Ibid., File 5755–001.

[4]Harmon Hartzell Bro, *A Seer Out of Season,* p. 252.

[5]Ibid., p. 259.

[6]Ibid., pp. 182–183.

[7]Ibid., p. 170.

[8]Jess Stearn, *Intimates Through Time, Edgar Cayce's Mysteries of Reincarnation* (New York: A Signet Book, 1993), p. 42.

[9]Robert A. Smith, *Edgar Cayce, My Life as a Seer: The Lost Memoirs* (New York: St. Martin's Paperbacks, 1997).

[10]Harmon Hartzell Bro, *A Seer Out of Season,* p. 37.

[11]Website of David Wilcock: http://www.ascension2000.com/intro.html.

[12]Harmon Hartzell Bro, *A Seer Out of Season,* p. 16.

[13]Ibid., p. 223.

Chapter 4

[1]The Association for Research and Enlightenment, under the Editorship of Hugh Lynn Cayce, *The Edgar Cayce Reader* (New York: Warner Books, 1967), p. 7.

[2]Paul K. Johnson, *Edgar Cayce in Context* (New York: State University of New York, 1998).

[3]Thomas Sugrue, *There is a River: The Story of Edgar Cayce* (New York: Holt, Reinhart and Winston, 1942, 1945).

[4]Website of David Wilcock: http://www.ascension2000.com/reinc-sup.htm.

[5]Harmon Hartzell Bro, *A Seer Out of Season: The Life of Edgar Cayce* (New York: A Signet Book, 1990), p. 86.

[6]Website of David Wilcock. Rick Martin interview, *Spectrum Magazine,* http://www.ascension2000.com/Wilcock-Martin.htm.

[7]Ibid.

Chapter 5

[1]L/L Research, The Ra Material/*Law of One* series (Atglen, PA: Schiffer Publishing, 1984); www.llresearch.org. Book One, p. 55.

[2]Ibid., Book One, p. 153.

[3]Edgar Cayce Foundation, 1995, *The Complete Edgar Cayce Readings on CD-ROM,* File 5755–2.

[4]Ibid., File 5757–001.

[5]The Bible, King James Version, Genesis 1:27.

[6]Wynn Free, article entitled "A Scientific Blueprint for Ascension," *The Spirit of Ma'at* webzine, January 2002. URL: http://www.spiritofmaat.com.

[7]Yu V. Nachalov, A.N. Sokolov, http://www.amasci.com/freenrg/tors/doc17.html.

[8] Peter Gariaev and V.P. Poponin, www.rialian.com/rnboyd/fabrics-of-consciousness-rev3.rtf.

[9]Dr. Wilhelm Reich, www.orgone.org/IOOeng/historie.htm.

[10]Website of Joseph Myers: http://www.reincarnation2002.com.

[11]Website of Walter Semkiw: http://www.Johnadams.net. Dr. Semkiw has released a book on this subject entitled *Return of the Revolutionaries* (Charlottesville, VA: Hampton Roads Publishing Company, Inc., 2002).

[12]Professor Francis Crick, www.heartmath.org/research papers/dna phantom/dna phantom.html.

[13]http://lrc.geo.umn.edu/people/teed/papers/macroev.html.

[14]L/L Research, The Ra Material/*Law of One* series, Book One, pp. 92–93.

[15]Ibid., Book One, p. 97.

[16]Ibid., Book One, p. 138.

[17]Ibid., Book One, pp. 91, 106.

[18]Ibid., Book One, p. 66.

[19]Ibid., Book One, p. 110.

[20]Hoagland's website http://www.enterprisemission.com. See also Robert Hoagland, *The Monuments of Mars: A City on the Edge of Forever* (Berkeley, CA: North Atlantic Books, 2001).

[21]L/L Research, The Ra Material/*Law of One* series, Book One, p. 107.

[22]Ibid., Book One, p. 135.

[23]Ibid., Book One, p. 90.

[24]Ibid., Book One, p. 66.

[25]Ibid., Book One, p. 77.

[26]Ibid., Book Three, p. 49.

[27]Edgar Cayce Foundation, 1995, *The Complete Edgar Cayce Readings on CD-ROM,* File 5748–006.

Chapter 6

[1]Jess Stearn, *Intimates Through Time, Edgar Cayce's Mysteries of Reincarnation* (New York: A Signet Book, 1993), pp. 76–89.

[2]http://www.sacred-texts.com/egy/ebod/ebod07.htm.

[3]Ibid.

[4]Ibid.

[5]Edgar Cayce Foundation, 1995, *The Complete Edgar Cayce Readings on CD-ROM,* File 294–148.

[6]Ibid., File 820–1.

[7]Ibid., File 294–152.

[8]Ibid., File 5755–1.

[9]Jess Stearn, *Intimates Through Time,* p. 84.

[10]Ibid., pp. 84–85.

[11]Ibid.

[12]Edgar Cayce Foundation, 1995, *The Complete Edgar Cayce Readings on CD-ROM,* File 294–153.

[13]W.H. Church, *Many Happy Returns: The Lives of Edgar Cayce* (New York: Harper & Row, 1984), p. 60; see also Edgar Cayce Foundation, 1995, *The Complete Edgar Cayce Readings on CD-ROM,* File 294–147, 294–151.

[14]L/L Research, The Ra Material/*Law of One* series (Atglen, PA: Schiffer Publishing, 1984); www.llresearch.org. Book One, p. 90.

[15]Jess Stearn, *Intimates Through Time,* pp. 76–89.

[16]Harmon Hartzell Bro, *A Seer Out of Season: The Life of Edgar Cayce* (New York: A Signet Book, 1990), p. 247.

[17]L/L Research, The Ra Material/*Law of One* series, Book One, pp. 70–71.

[18]Website of David Wilcock: http://www.ascension2000.com/Readings/r25.htm.

[19]L/L Research, The Ra Material/*Law of One* series, Book One, p. 127.

Chapter 7

[1]L/L Research, The Ra Material/*Law of One* series (Atglen, PA: Schiffer Publishing, 1984); www.llresearch.org. Book One, p. 77.

[2]BBC Internet - http://news.bbc.co.uk/1/hi/sci/tech/1413326.stm.

[3]http://www.newagetravel.com/info/egypt.htm.

[4]Zecharia Sitchin, *The Stairway to Heaven, Book II of the Earth Chronicles* (New York: Avon Books, 1980), pp. 275–282.

[5]Fadel Gad, *Fox News,* March 2, 1999; http://www.interchange.ubc.ca/quarterm/mudede.htm.

[6]http://ourworld.compuserve.com/homepages/dp5/pyramid.htm.

[7]Pyramid references: http://members.boardhost.com/Bauval/msg/162.html; http://www.geocities.com/Hollywood/Lot/5125/pyramidmath.html.

[8]www.khemet.net/newkhemet/nkgiza.htm.

[9]John Zajac: talk on *The Art Bell Show,* Spring of Living Water, tape library catalog; http://www.geocities.com/Athens/9306/xv17.html.

[10]Ibid.

[11]carlos.emory.edu/ODYSSEY/EGYPT/sekhmet.html.

[12]www.atlantisrising.com/issue3/ar3stargate.html.

Chapter 8

[1] W.H. Church, *Many Happy Returns: The Lives of Edgar Cayce* (New York: Harper & Row, 1984), p. 226.

[2] Harold Sherman, *How to Make ESP Work for You* (New York: Fawcett-Crest, 1966).

[3] Don Wilcock, *Damn Right, I've Got the Blues* (San Francisco: Woodford Publishing, 1993).

[4] W.H. Church, *Many Happy Returns*, p. 201.

[5] Julius Fast, *Body Language* (New York: Pocket Books, reissue edition, 1988).

[6] Dr. Stephen LaBerge, *Lucid Dreaming* (New York: Random House, reissue edition, 1990).

[7] Dr. Stephen LaBerge, *Exploring the World of Lucid Dreaming* (New York: Ballantine Books, 1997).

[8] Jose Stevens and Lena S. Stevens, *The Secrets of Shamanism* (New York: Avon, reissue edition, 1988).

[9] Ruth Montgomery, *Aliens Among Us* (New York: Putnam Pub Group, 1985).

[10] Dr. Norma Milanovich, *We The Arcturians* (Albuquerque, NM: Athena, 1990).

[11] Scott Mandelker, *From Elsewhere: Being E.T. in America* (New York: Carol Publishing Group, 1995), pp. 2–3, 17–18.

[12] Website of David Wilcock, comparison photo, http://www.ascension2000.com/intro.htm.

[13] Website of David Wilcock: http://www.ascension2000.com/Readings/r25.htm.

[14] Ibid., pictures of associates, http://www.ascension2000.com.

[15] Edgar Cayce Foundation, 1995, *The Complete Edgar Cayce Readings on CD-ROM*, File 294–151.

[16] W.H. Church, *Many Happy Returns*, p. 110.

[17] Harmon Hartzell Bro, *A Seer Out of Season: The Life of Edgar Cayce* (New York: A Signet Book, 1990), p. 180.

Chapter 9

[1] Website of David Wilcock: http://www.ascension2000.com/d-c-astro.htm.

[2] Website of Uri Geller: www.uri-geller.com/official2.htm.

[3] Plato quote taken from the website of Joseph Myers: http://reincarnation2002.com/_reincarnation/00000075.htm. See also http://aquarianctr.org/lv/plato.html.

[4]H.W. Percival, *Thinking and Destiny* (New York: Word Foundation, reprint edition, 1995).

[5]Edgar Cayce, *A Search for God* (Virginia Beach, VA: Association for Research & Enlightenment, 1992).

[6]Walter Semkiw, *Return of the Revolutionaries* (Charlottesville, VA: Hampton Roads Publishing Company, Inc., 2002).

[7]Website of Michael Mandeville, http://www.michaelmandeville.com/phoenix/trilogy/bookone/rp1chapter8.htm. *The Chrysalis of Virginia Beach* is a self-published book by Mike Mandeville. The quote referred to can be found where he has posted this particular chapter online (URL above).

[8]Ibid.

[9]Harmon Hartzell Bro, *A Seer Out of Season: The Life of Edgar Cayce* (New York: A Signet Book, 1990), p. 81.

[10]Ibid., p. 203.

[11]Website of David Wilcock: http://www.ascension2000.com/06.21.00-r.htm.

[12]A. Robert Smith, *Edgar Cayce, My Life as a Seer: The Lost Memoirs* (New York: St. Martin's Paperbacks, 1997), pp. 5–6.

[13]Edgar Cayce Foundation, 1995, *The Complete Edgar Cayce Readings on CD-ROM,* Files 262–075 and 262–074.

[14]Harmon Hartzell Bro, *A Seer Out of Season,* p. 402.

[15]Ibid., p. 190.

[16]Sidney D. Kirkpatrick, *Edgar Cayce: An American Prophet* (New York: Riverhead Books, 2000), p. 10.

[17]http://www.phenomenews.com/archives/mch02/kirkpatrick4.html, 1998.

[18]L/L Research, The Ra Material/*Law of One* series (Atglen, PA: Schiffer Publishing, 1984); www.llresearch.org. Book One, p. 127.

[19]Gregg Braden, *Awakening to Zero Point: The Collective Initiation* (Radio Bookstore Press, 1997); http://www.greggbraden.net.

Chapter 10

[1]Website of David Wilcock: http://www.ascension2000.com/07.03.02.htm.

PART TWO

Chapter 11

[1]Joseph E. Mason, *Humanity on the Pollen Path, Part One: Symbols of the Chakras and the Midpoint.* Great Dreams website, April 24, 1999. URL:

http://www.greatdreams.com/plpath1.htm (active as of 12/03).

[2]Information on dreams is derived from *The Art of Dream Interpretation* by Belinda Recio and Eileen London (New York: A Bulfinch Book, Little Brown & Co., 2001).

[3]Carla L. Rueckert, *The Channeling Handbook* (Louisville, KY: L/L Research, 1987).

[4]Law of Free Will: For those who are wishing to evolve spiritually in the service-to-others path, there shall be no infringement on the free will of others, and service shall be rendered only when requested.

Chapter 12
[1]Website of David Wilcock, http://www.ascension2000.com/Readings/readings01.html.

Chapter 13
[1]Website of David Wilcock, http://www.ascension2000.com/Readings/readings07.html; http://www.ascension2000.com/8.24.99.htm; http://www.ascension2000.com/10.24.99.htm.

Chapter 14
[1]Website of David Wilcock, http://www.ascension2000.com/06.21.00-r.htm.

Chapter 15
[1]Website of David Wilcock, http://www.ascension2000.com/Readings/readings07.html.

Chapter 16
[1]Website of David Wilcock, http://www.ascension2000.com/01.05.00.htm.

Chapter 17
[1]Website of David Wilcock, http://www.ascension2000.com/11.09.01.htm.

Chapter 18
[1]Website of David Wilcock, http://www.ascension2000.com/12.22Xmas.html.

Chapter 19
[1]M. Lockwood, R. Stamper, and M.N. Wild, "A doubling of the Sun's

coronal magnetic field during the past 100 years." *Nature,* 3 June 1999, vol. 399, pp. 437NN439. URL: http://helio.estec.esa.nl/ulysses/whatsnew.html# 19990616.

2David Whitehouse, "Sun produces monster solar flare." BBC News Online, 5 November 2003. URL: http://news.bbc.co.uk/1/hi/sci/tech/3242353.stm.

3NASA, "Watching the Angry Sun." Science @ NASA website, December 22, 2000. URL: http://news.bbc.co.uk/1/hi/sci/tech/3242353.stm.

4Aleskey Dmitriev, *Planetophysical State of the Earth and Life* (1997). URL: http://www.tmgnow.com/repository/global/planetophysical.html.

5Ibid.

6Ibid.

7Ibid.

8Sromovsky, Lawrence A. *Neptune's Increased Brightness Provides Evidence of Seasons.* University of Madison-Wisconsin Space Sciences Engineering Center. URL: http://www.ssec.wisc.edu/media/Neptune2003.htm.

9Halber, Deborah. *Pluto is Undergoing Global Warming, Researchers Find.* MIT News, October 9, 2002. URL: http://web.mit.edu/newsoffice/nr/2002/pluto.html.

10Aleskey Dmitriev, *Planetophysical State of the Earth.*

11Clark, Stuart. *Galactic Dust Storm Enters Solar System.* New Scientist; August 5, 2003. URL: http://www.newscientist.com/news/news.jsp?id=ns99994021.

Chapter 20

1Barbara Lamb, Crop Circles Revisited, http://www.blambms.com/index-8.html.

2Steve Alexander and Karen Douglas [temporarytemples@ntlworld.com].

3David Wilcock, "Incredible New Crop Circle Shows 3-D Hyperdimensional Geometry as Described in Convergence," 2000. URL:http://ascension2000.com/octacrop.html.

Chapter 21

1L/L Research, The Ra Material/*Law of One* series (Atglen, PA: Schiffer Publishing, 1984); www.llresearch.org. Book One, p. 156.

2Wynn Free, article entitled "A Scientific Blueprint for Ascension," *The Spirit of Ma'at* webzine, January 2002. URL: http://www.spiritofmaat.com.

PART THREE

Chapter 22

[1]Charles Darwin, M.A., *On the Origin of Species by Means of Natural Selection, or the Preservation of Favoured Races in the Struggle for Life*. November 24, 1859. URL: http://www.literature.org/authors/darwin-charles/the-origin-of-species (accessed 12/03).

[2]Center for Science and Culture, Discovery Institute. URL: http://www.discovery.org/csc/ (accessed 12/03).

[3]Holy Bible, Book of John, Chapter 14, Verse 12.

[4]Tim Harwood, *Quotations on Evolution as a Theory*, November 26, 2001. URL: http://web.archive.org/web/20011126101316/http://www.geocities.com/Area51/Rampart/4871/images/quotes.html (accessed 12/03).

[5]*The Japan Times*, "DNA analysis of skeleton suggests Adam and Eve were Australians," January 10, 2001. URL: http://www.trussel.com/prehist/news235.htm.

[6]Of course, if we consider Richard Thompson and Michael Cremo's 1993 book *Forbidden Archeology*, Earth has had humanoid visitors who occasionally left footprints as far back as ten million years ago. This fits in quite well with the Law of One teachings when we consider how many extraterrestrial groups are said to be operating around our solar system. However, since the vast majority of them do not die here, there are very few corpses that can be recovered.

[7]Bruce Lipton, Ph.D., "The Human Genome Project: A Cosmic Joke that has the Scientists Rolling in the Aisle," 2001. URL: http://spiritcrossing.com/lipton/genome.shtm.

[8]David Berman, *The Inside is Out*, PBS Newshour Extra, February 12, 2001. URL: http://www.pbs.org/newshour/extra/features/jan-june00/genome.html.

[9]Harvard Medical School, *Genome Project Chief Evaluates First Draft*, Focus: News from Harvard Medical, Dental and Public Health Schools. March 9, 2001. URL: http://www.med.harvard.edu/publications/Focus/2001/Mar9_2001/genome_research.html.

[10]Colm A. Kelleher, Ph.D., "Retrotransposons as Engines of Human Bodily Transformation," National Institute for Discovery Science, Las Vegas, NV, first published in the *Journal of Scientific Exploration*, Vol. 13, No. 1, Spring 1999, pp. 9–24. URL: http://www.nidsci.org/articles/kelleher_retrotransposons.html.

[11]H. Hartman, "Speculations on the evolution of the genetic code," *Origins of Life 6* (1974): 423–427.

[12]U. Wintersberger, "On the origins of genetic variants," *FEBS 285* (1991): 160–164.

[13]Robert V. Gerard, Ph.D., "The Hidden Secrets Within Your DNA," 2001. URL: http://www.oughtenhouse.com/_oughtenhouse/ view_article.php? art_ID=2.

[14]Anonymous. *The Science of Innate Intelligence: Videotape Summary.* URL: http://www.angelfire.com/hi/TheSeer/Lipton.html.

[15]Lawrence Keleman, *Permission to Believe: Four Rational Approaches to God's Existence* (Southfield, MI: Targum Press, 1990), pp. 57–58. URL: http:// www.geocities.com/mtgriffith1/facts.htm.

[16]Ron Mwangaguhunga, *Thinking Differently About the Universe.* URL: http:// www.macdirectory.com/ntrvu/Universe/Index.html.

[17]Princeton Engineering Anomalies Research: Scientific Study of Consciousness-Related Physical Phenomena. URL: http://www.princeton.edu/ ~pear/.

[18]International Partnership for Pyramid Research, Great Pyramid of Giza Research Association. URL: http://www.gizapyramid.com/russian/pyramids.htm.

[19]Jonathan Tennenbaum, "Russian Discovery Challenges Existence of 'Absolute Time'," *21st Century Science and Technology Magazine,* Summer 2000. URL: http://www.21stcenturysciencetech.com/articles/time.html.

[20]James P. Spottiswoode, "Apparent Association Between Effect Size in Free Response Anomalous Cognition Experiments and Local Sidereal Time," *Journal of Scientific Exploration,* Vol. 11, No. 2, Article 1. URL: http://www.scientificexploration.org/jse/abstracts/v11n2a1.html.

[21]Paul LaViolette, Ph.D., *Does the Galactic Center Affect ESP Ability?* URL: http://www.etheric.com/GalacticCenter/Galactic5.html.

[22]Peter Gariaev and Vladimir Poponin, *The DNA PHANTOM EFFECT: Direct Measurement of A New Field in the Vacuum Substructure.* URL: http://twm.co.nz/DNAPhantom.htm. For additional information on Gariaev's work, search the alternate spelling "Garjajev."

[23]URL: http://www.greggbraden.net.

[24]URL: http://www.pureinsight.org/pi/articles/2003/3/3/1496p.html. Also, Robert B. Stone, Ph.D., *The Secret Life of Your Cells* (Atglen, PA: Whitford Press, 1989), URL: http://www.geocities.com/misaha93923/issue11.html. See also William C. Gough, "The Cellular Communication Process and Alternative Modes of Healing," published by the Foundation for Mind-Being Research in *Subtle Energies and Energy Medicine: An Interdisciplinary Journal of Energetic & Informational Interactions,* Vol. 8, No. 2 (July 20, 1999). URL: http://www.fmbr.org/abstracts/cell_comm.htm.

[25]Tim Harwood, URL: http://web.archive.org/web/*/http://www.geo-

cities.com/Area51/Rampart/4871/alt-evolu.html.

26Peter P. Gariaev et al., "The Wave, Probabilistic and Linguistic Representations of Cancer and HIV," *Journal of Non-Locality and Remote Mental Interactions*, Vol. I, No. 2. URL: http://www.emergentmind.org/gariaevI2.htm.

27Yu V. Nachalov and A.N. Sokolov, *Experimental Investigation of New Long-Range Actions*. URL: http://www.amasci.com/freenrg/tors/doc17.html.

28Yu V. Dzang Kangeng, *Bioelectromagnetic fields as a material carrier of biogenetic information*. Aura-Z., 1993, N3, pp. 42–54.

29Yu V. Dzang Kangeng, Patent N1828665. *A method of changing a biological object's hereditary signs and a device for biological information directed transfer*. Application N3434801, invention priority as of 30.12.1981, registered 13.10.1992 (Russia).

30Baerbel, *DNA* (Summary of the book *Vernetzte Intelligenz* by von Grazyna Fosar and Franz Bludorf, ISBN 3930243237.) URL: http://home.planet.nl/~holtjo19/GB/DNA.html.

31Stephen J. Ceci et al., "The year in which an IQ test is given can make the difference between life or death, Cornell researchers find," *American Psychologist*, Vol. 58, No. 10, pp. 778–790. URL: http://www.news.cornell.edu/releases/Dec03/IQ.retardation.ssl.html.

32Glen Rein, Ph.D., "Effect of Conscious Intention on Human DNA," Proc.Internat.Forum on New Science, Denver, Colorado (October 1996). URL: http://www.item-bioenergy.com/infocenter/ConsciousIntentiononDNA.pdf.

33Aleskey Dmitriev, *Planetophysical State of the Earth and Life* (1997). URL: http://www.tmgnow.com/repository/global/planetophysical.html.

34Don Hinrichsen, *Hopkins Report: Time Running Out for the Environment*. Johns Hopkins Bloomberg School of Public Health, Information and Knowledge for Optimal Health (INFO) Project, January 5, 2001. URL: http://www.infoforhealth.org/pr/press/010501.shtml.

35Earth Crash, Earth Spirit. *Global Warming: North America*. URL: http://eces.org/archive/ec/globalwarming/northamerica.shtml.

36Michael Mandeville, *Eight Charts Which Prove That Chandler's Wobble Causes Earthquakes, Volcanism, El Niño, and Global Warming*. URL: http://www.michaelmandeville.com/polarmotion/spinaxis/vortex_correlations2.htm.

37Michael Mandeville. *Return of the Phoenix, Book Three, Chapter 40: The Torches of the Annunaki*. URL: http://www.michaelmandeville.com/phoenix/trilogy/bookthree/rp3chapter40.htm.

38Michael Bara and Richard Hoagland, *Global Warming on Mars? The Hyperdimensional Connection* (2001). URL: http://www.enterprisemission.com/warming.htm.

[39]European Space Agency News, "1.4.6: Breakup of the Ross Ice Shelf, Autumn 2000." URL: http://envisat.esa.int/dataproducts/aatsr/CNTR1-4-6.htm.

[40]European Space Agency News, "Giants Joust in the Cold," ESA Portal, October 21, 2002. URL: http://www.esa.int/export/esaCP/ESAAQT-THN6D_index_o.html.

[41]Intergovernmental Panel on Climate Change, *Climate Change 2001: Working Group I: The Scientific Basis: Executive Summary.* URL: http://www.grida.no/climate/ipcc_tar/wg1/049.htm.

[42]London Guardian Press Association, "Warming doubles glacier melt," *London Guardian, Guardian Unlimited,* October 17, 2003. URL: http://www.guardian.co.uk/climatechange/story/0,12374,1064991,00.html.

[43]Agence France Presse correspondents in Auckland, New Zealand, "Largest Iceberg Splits in Two." URL: http://www.news.com.au/common/story_page/0,4057,7764875%255E1702,00.html.

[44]Aleskey Dmitriev, *Planetophysical State of the Earth and Life* (1997). URL: http://www.tmgnow.com/repository/global/planetophysical.html.

[45]Curt Suplee, "Sun Studies May Shed Light on Global Warming," *Washington Post,* October 9, 2000; Page A13. URL: http://www.washingtonpost.com/wp-dyn/articles/A35885-2000Oct8.html.

[46]Goddard Space Flight Center, "NASA Study Finds Increasing Solar Trend That Can Change Climate," March 20, 2003. URL: http://www.gsfc.nasa.gov/topstory/2003/0313irradiance.html.

[47]Science @ NASA, "Watching the Angry Sun," December 22, 2000. URL: http://science.nasa.gov/headlines/y2000/ast22dec_1.htm.

[48]David Whitehouse, Ph.D., "What is Happening to the Sun?" November 4, 2003. URL: http://news.bbc.co.uk/2/hi/science/nature/3238961.stm.

[49]Jenny Hogan, "Sun More Active Than For A Millennium," *New Scientist,* November 2, 2003. URL: http://www.newscientist.com/news/news.jsp?id=ns99994321.

[50]Aleskey Dmitriev, *Planetophysical State of the Earth and Life* (1997). URL: http://www.tmgnow.com/repository/global/planetophysical.html.

[51]D.E. Shemansky, Ph.D., Curriculum Vitae. URL: http://ame-www.usc.edu/bio/dons/ds_biosk.html.

[52]Stuart Clark, "Galactic Dust Storm Enters Solar System," *New Scientist,* August 5, 2003. URL: http://www.newscientist.com/news/news.jsp?id=ns99994021.

[53]D.E. Shemansky, Ph.D., Curriculum Vitae. URL: http://ame-www.usc.edu/bio/dons/ds_biosk.html.

[54]Deborah Halber, "Pluto is Undergoing Global Warming, Researchers Find," *MIT News,* October 9, 2002. URL: http://web.mit.edu/newsoffice/nr/2002/pluto.html.

[55]Aleskey Dmitriev, *Planetophysical State of the Earth and Life.* (1997) URL: http://www.tmgnow.com/repository/global/planetophysical.html.

[56]Lawrence A. Sromovsky, *Neptune's Increased Brightness Provides Evidence of Seasons,* University of Madison-Wisconsin Space Sciences Engineering Center. URL: http://www.ssec.wisc.edu/media/Neptune2003.htm. That link from Wisconsin-Madison U gives full technical information for specialists, including the exact percentages of the brightness increases, but there are numerous links that come up if you search this on Google. These links include the far-easier-to-read but less informative general public release featured at the same university website. The study was published in the May 2003 issue (Vol. 163, No. 1) of Cornell University's science journal *Icarus, International Journal of Solar System Studies,* at http://icarus.cornell.edu.

[57]Robert Roy Britt, "Mars Ski Report: Snow is Hard, Dense and Disappearing," SPACE.com, December 6, 2001. URL: http://www.space.com/scienceastronomy/solarsystem/mars_snow_011206-1.html.

[58]Ibid., Part 2, December 6, 2001. URL: http://www.space.com/scienceastronomy/solarsystem/mars_snow_011206-2.html.

[59]NASA Goddard Space Flight Center. *Explorers: Searching The Universe Forty Years Later.* NASA Facts On Line. URL: http://www.gsfc.nasa.gov/gsfc/service/gallery/ fact_sheets/spacesci/explorers.htm.

[60]Aleskey Dmitriev, *Planetophysical State of the Earth and Life* (1997). URL: http://www.tmgnow.com/repository/global/planetophysical.html.

[61]Ibid.

[62]John Major Jenkins. *Alignment 2012 Website.* URL: http://www.alignment2012.com.

[63]Richard Pasichnyk, *The Vital Vastness, Volume Two: The Living Cosmos* (2002), Writer's Showcase/Iuniverse, Inc., p. 106. URL: http://www.living-cosmos.com.

[64]The One Infinite Creator.

Wynn Free, currently residing in the Flagstaff, Arizona area, expresses himself as a songwriter, poet, and freelance writer. He writes a monthly column for *The Messenger* newspaper in Southern California and is a staff writer for *The Spirit of Ma'at,* the web-magazine of Drunvalo Melchizedek, for which he has interviewed notable luminaries in the metaphysical/spiritual world. He maintains a website, www.wynnfree.com, where he posts many of his written and creative works.

David Wilcock is a professional intuitive consultant who, since 1993, has intensively researched UFOlogy, ancient civilizations, consciousness science, and new paradigms of matter and energy. With the help of "those on the other side," he has assembled an ongoing series of critically acclaimed, breakthrough scientific research works under the master title *Convergence,* published on his website, www.ascension2000.com, and soon to be published in book form. Wilcock has been a guest on numerous radio programs and has lectured throughout the United States and Japan. He is also an accomplished musician and composer of jazz-fusion, New Age/meditative, and world music pieces.